William Woodruff was ███████ ████████ ██ cotton workers. Leavin██ ██████ ██████ ████ boy in a grocer's shop███ ██ ██████ ██ ████ north of England, he ████ ██████ ██ ██████ bestseller, *The Road to* ███ ███████ ██████ in Lancashire. *Beyond Nab End* continues his story.
William Woodruff died in 2008.

Praise for *The Road to Nab End*

'A masterpiece' *Independent*

'A combination of an almost photographic memory, a wonderful writing gift and a keen eye for personal dramas, which even Ibsen would have admired' *Spectator*

'Extraordinarily well written and vividly told, his book is rich in characters, facts, atmosphere and indomitable spirit. It is absolutely fascinating as a social as well as a family history' Eric Hobsbawm, *Guardian*

'Once started, it is impossible to put this book down. The author is a born writer with an eye for character and a natural way of writing. He has the historian's gift for bringing to life a particular society at a particular time' Alan Bullock, *Times Literary Supplement*

'Memories pour forth with photographic clarity to make this remarkable book' *Express*

Also by William Woodruff

BEYOND NAB END

William Woodruff

ABACUS

First published in Great Britain as a paperback original
by Abacus in 2003
Reprinted 2003 (seven times), 2004, 2008, 2009, 2011, 2012

A CIP catalogue record for this book
is available from the British Library.

ISBN 978-0-349-11622-8

Typeset in Sabon by Palimpsest Book Production Limited,
Polmont, Stirlingshire
Printed and bound in Great Britain by
Clays Ltd, St Ives plc

Papers used by Abacus are from well-managed forests
and other responsible sources.

MIX
Paper from
responsible sources
FSC
www.fsc.org   FSC® C104740

Abacus
An imprint of
Little, Brown Book Group
100 Victoria Embankment
London EC4Y 0DY

An Hachette UK Company
www.hachette.co.uk

www.littlebrown.co.uk

www.williamwoodruff.com

To the memory of Leo O'Hea and
Alexander B. Rodger to whom I owe so much

Contents

Contents

Chapter I

To London

'Tha's started to shave, I 'ope,' Mr Bundle shouted, as the lorry ground its way up the hill that led from Lancashire to Cheshire. I think he'd begun to worry about me. I nodded and offered him a cigarette. His smoking added to the fog. 'Not right that tha should go to Lundun on thi own.' He sneezed. 'How old art tha?'

'Sixteen.' It was the summer of 1933.

'Tha too young to be goin' off like that. Can't think what's got into thi 'ead. Can't think . . .' Drugged by fumes and weariness, I fell asleep.

Several hours later I woke to the rattle of the engine. I was cooked at the front and frozen at the side. It was still dark. Our headlights danced on the road.

'Where are we?'

'Midlands!' Mr Bundle drew his gloved hand across the glass.

All I could see was the shadow of wayside trees, the veiled lights of towns in the distance, and approaching cars, which burst out of the darkness in a glittering stream – a bright flash, a muffled thump and they were gone. Now and again the moon broke through. I'd never been so far from home; it made me catch my breath. There was no going back now; I'd gone and done it.

The cold air blew through the torn canvas at my side. I pulled my cap down hard, tightened my muffler, and rolled myself into a ball.

I woke with a start when Mr Bundle crashed to a lower gear and pulled off the road. The truck shuddered to a halt before a wayside café.

We scrambled down, stamped our cramped legs, and made our way across the parking lot. Some drivers were cranking up, ready to leave. Moths jittered around the swaying bulb above the door.

The smell of sausages and mash hit us as we entered. A row of dim lights hung over oilcloth-covered tables. There was a rumble of talk. Through a cloud of tobacco smoke, dim figures shuffled across the worn linoleum. Pictures of boxers stared from the whitewashed walls. In a corner a blanket-covered driver lay snoring. I took off my coat.

At the counter a fellow in a brown apron slopped out tea from a dented urn. Rock buns and 'doorstep' ham sandwiches were stacked on glass trays. Mr Bundle put a bun on my plate. I offered a penny to pay for his tea. 'Nay, tha'll need that when tha gets to Lundun.' He pushed the coin back with a grubby finger.

Spilling tea from our mugs, we joined several others hunched over a food-splattered table. They had tired faces; some still wore caps and mufflers.

"'Ello, 'ow do, Ernie? Fancy seein' thee.'

I thought it exciting to join a group of night-riders shovelling bangers and onions with HP sauce at two o'clock in the morning.

'Who's young'un, Ernie?'

'Dick Whittington.' Mr Bundle opened his coat and pushed his cap to the back of his head. 'Goin' to Lundun to make his pile, 'e is.'

'Where's t' cat? Dick Whittington 'ad a cat.'
'In t' lorry. Worn out, cat is.'
They burst out laughing.
'Just as well t' lad's using 'is wings afore 'e gets a ball and chain.'
They scraped their forks and slurped their tea.
'Watch out, young'un, London's full of thieves, cheats, tricksters and tarts.'

> Beware of the damsel modest and meek
> She eats thirteen faggots and nine pig's feet.

They thumped the table, shoved each other, and rattled the cups and plates.

Half an hour later, Mr Bundle and I stubbed out our cigarettes, said 'Goodnight' and made for the door, buttoning up our jackets as we went.
'Don't forget to send us a bob or two, nipper, when yer becomes Lord Mayor of Lundun,' one of the men shouted after me.
'Oh, no.'
'Not bad sods.' Mr Bundle sneezed. 'All they need is a good night's sleep. 'Ope weather 'olds up.'
As we crunched across the stones, spots of rain began to fall. While Mr Bundle fought with the starting handle, I climbed into the cab and slammed the door. I was almost asleep by the time he got in.
When I came to, it was daylight. Heavy clouds filled the sky. We were part of an endless column of cars and lorries heaped with cargo going south. I sat up, hardly able to believe that I was part of it all.
'Watford Junction,' Mr Bundle mumbled. 'No rain.'
Watford meant nothing to me. We rattled on.
By the time we'd reached a place called Hendon, the people

of London were up and doing. They hurried along the pavements or stood in long queues at bus stops. I was astonished at the way they pushed past each other as if they were running a race. Instead of clogs and shawls, the women wore frocks; the men wore suits, and polished shoes – even ties. Many carried an umbrella. I'd always wondered what southerners looked like. Well, here they were all around me.

'Wot dost ta think?' Mr Bundle shouted, gesturing at the people and the tall buildings.

'Champion!' I felt a glow of excitement.

'I suppose that's what tha's cum for.'

'Aye.'

He stubbed out his cigarette.

———— ◆ ————

Later that morning we pulled in close to a bus stop in a crowded street. 'Tha'll get thi bus to Bow from 'ere,' Mr Bundle said. As I got down, I studied the road. They'd said in the North, 'The streets are paved with gold.' It looked like ordinary tarmac to me. I wondered what my family would think had they been able to see me in the middle of that busy London street with the crowd rushing by. Shafts of sunlight burst through the clouds.

I knew that having got to London, everything would change for the better. *The Wonderland of Knowledge* – which I had in my bag – assured me that those who ventured forth would win. Where would I have been without that book, which I had read and reread since I was six? The fate of England did not yet hang on my words, but it was only a matter of time before it would.

'Good luck, young'un,' Mr Bundle said. Kindness filled his eyes. With the engine still running, he scrawled an address on a bit of paper. 'Tha must cum 'ere if tha gets lost like. It's all t' same if tha broke. I'll get thi 'ome agin.' He handed me a florin. I protested. 'Tha goin' t' need it,' he persisted. 'Anyroad, ah'll sleep better if tha keeps the two bob.'

'I'm not goin' to fall flat on mi face,' I bridled.

'Tha might.' He got down and fished out my suitcase from under the tarpaulin.

He wrung my hand, squeezed my shoulders, sneezed into my face and was gone.

As the lorry disappeared, I suddenly felt lost. What was I to do now?

After a few minutes, a red double-decker bus approached. I tightened my grip on my suitcase.

'Bus for Bow and Stratford?' I asked the man in the queue before me.

'You betcher, come olong wi' me.' We found a seat together. He guessed that I was a northerner. I told him that I was going to an important job at the Bow Bridge Iron Foundry, that I was well on in Labour politics, and that I eventually intended to become a Member of Parliament. The excitement of the long journey and the fluster of getting to London had loosened my tongue.

Judging me by my cardboard case rather than by my boasting, the stranger smiled. 'Tahr's over there.'

'Fancy seeing that,' I answered. Everybody in England knew about the Tower. Dreadful things had happened there. Henry VIII's wife, Anne Boleyn, had lost her head in t' Bloody Tower.

When we reached Bow he pointed to a modest house. 'George Lansbury's,' he said. I knew that Lansbury was the leader of the British Labour Party. 'Saint 'e is, 's a fact. Trouble with George is 'e lets 'is bleedin' 'eart lead 'is blinkin' 'ead.'

We drove past a long brick building. 'Bow Bridge Iron Foundry,' he said. With its black roof and closed iron gates it looked as forbidding as a Blackburn cotton mill. Its three stacks stood smokeless.

'Yer gits orf 'ere,' called the conductor, his finger on the bell. I collected my belongings, said goodbye to my friend, and went to the end of the bus.

'I'll watch out for yer in t' piper,' he called after me.

'Tha kind.'

The bus pulled in against the kerb. I stepped down into a

milling crowd. 'Friday street market,' the conductor shouted. 'Mind yer don't git yerself killed.'

No sooner had I put my foot on the pavement than I was swept along by a human tide. Holding my suitcase before me as a shield, I was pushed along past stalls piled high with old shoes and hats, eggs, chickens, oranges, cabbages and meats. Everyone yelled their wares at me as if they had been awaiting my arrival.

While I was looking around, a young ragamuffin plucked at my sleeve. He had a mop of black hair. His coat was split from top to bottom on both sides. He took a white pup out of his pocket and held it under my nose. It didn't look like any pup I'd seen before. 'A bob,' the urchin said, 'come on, let's see if you're a gint – a bob.'

With one hand on my case and the other on my money ('Dick Whittington, you'll be robbed the moment you arrive, you will,' the lorry drivers had warned), I fled the dog and the boy. 'Wot's a bob?' the lad bawled after me, 'Gimme a tanner.' I dodged behind a bicycle pushed by an old gentleman in a tall hat, and ran through the traffic across the street. The ragamuffin and another urchin chased after me.

<hr />

It must have been fate that led me to cross the street, for at the other side, in front of the Talbot pub, I ran into a little barrel of a woman with a pot of beer under her shawl. She almost knocked me over.

"'Ere, look whe' yer gowin' young un. Yer nearly lorst me bleedin' wallop. Wot you bleeders want?' she demanded of the two urchins.

'Nuffink, lidy,' they said, pocketing the pup and turning tail.

The woman wore a man's velvet trilby pulled down over her eyes and ears. It was decorated with a large wax flower and a stiletto hatpin. Battered and limp-crowned, it had a defiant look. From neck to knee she was wrapped in a black woollen shawl. Her dark, rough skirt reached down to a ridiculously large pair of men's shoes. They were cracked and looked as if they had never seen a brush.

Fat-faced, with little black sharp eyes, glistening jowls, and a button of a nose, the woman studied my case. 'You lorst?' Her eyes ran over me.

'Not lost. Just looking for a bed. Know one?'

There was a thoughtful silence.

''Ow's 'alf a kip?' She shifted her pot of beer.

'Better than none.'

'Fast bird you are. Come on and I'll show you what you've won.'

I followed the heavy figure round the pub corner into a dim, narrow street marked 'The Cut'. At the other end, shutting out the sky, was a grey gasometer. ''Ome sweet 'ome,' she said as she lifted the latch of the first cottage.

Stepping across the threshold, I entered a low-ceilinged corridor, which led to an ill-lit living room. There were several chairs, a cluttered table and a rocker. Bald patches marked the plaster walls. In a corner, hanging over a low window was a canary in a cage. 'That's Dick,' she said. 'Give us a song, Dick.' Washing hung before a low fire; cracked oilcloth covered the floor. There was a rotting smell.

She put her beer on the table, ignoring the cockroach that scurried away, and proceeded to show me around. The cottage was a two-up, two-down affair, such as I had known in Lancashire. Beyond the living room was a poky kitchen with a sagging ceiling. It had a small table, a coal-cooking range, a gas ring, a cracked mirror, a pile of unwashed dishes, and a bucket filled with dirty laundry. A smell of burned food hung in the air.

Beyond the kitchen was the toilet. The narrow backyard was crammed with a mountain of machine parts, rusty engines, metal bars, gratings, tubes, and nuts and bolts. There was hardly room to get by. The pile looked as though it might collapse. 'All fall dahn,' the woman croaked, as she gave a flick of her fingers across her throat.

A miry alleyway lay farther on; colonies of beetles lived

in the cindery mud. The whole area reeked of toilets and dust-bins. We heard snatches of laughter from the boozer next door. Beyond the pub was the angry rumble of the road.

When we reached the front room, the woman fell silent. Her shrewd eyes watched me. I took in the room at a glance. There was a single bed, a chair and a pisspot. On a high wooden stand in the corner stood an aspidistra. The cracked walls were held together by layers of bulging wallpaper. Aged oilcloth covered the slanting floor. A bare bulb hung from the ceiling. A radio could be heard through the wall.

'No extra charge for the music,' she grinned.

A lace curtain covered the lower half of the dirt-streaked window through which came a feeble light.

What held my attention was the bed. It was a single iron bedstead covered with threadbare blankets. The half-bed she had promised had shrunk to a quarter. She read my thoughts. 'Ben at the top, you at the bottom. A good kip.'

I felt the bed. The mattress was as hard as rock, the pillow was lumpy.

'Fifteen bob a week with grub,' she said, as if the question of my tenancy was settled. 'Five bob dahn, a week's notice to quit on either side. If yer keeps the window shut, yer'll find it stuffy. If yer opens it, yer'll get the gasworks. Ben 'as it shut.' She didn't mention that to the smell of gas should be added the smell of stale beer, as well as the smell of perfume from Yardley's factory in the next street.

'Looks all right,' I lied, as I peered through the window at the abandoned Church of the Nazarene opposite. Hesitantly, I fished out five bob and put them in her eager hand. I'd stay until I could find something better.

'Must be yer lucky day,' she said, tucking the money into her clothing. 'I've always said it, some people is born lucky.' We shook on it. Her hand felt sticky. 'Wot's yer nime? Mine's Tinker.'

The five shillings must have gone to Mrs Tinker's head, for she hustled me back to the kitchen and made me some bread and jam and a cup of tea. She put hot water on the dead tea leaves and swished the pot around. It tasted stale. The sandwich was gritty, but I was hungry.

Between gulps of beer, Mrs Tinker told me about her family: her husband Bert, her daughters Sarah and Maisy, and her son Ben. Parents and daughters slept in the two rooms upstairs. 'My "pot and pan" works on the river. 'Eavy work, Bert 'as, enough to kill 'im.' She took another gulp, wiping her mouth with the back of her hand. 'Sarah's twenty and Maisy's eighteen, them works at Bryant and May's match factory in Bow. Workers loses their jaws doin' that. They calls it "phossy-jaw", 'orrible 't is. Ben's twenty-two, 'e works for a wrecker in Stratford.'

I wondered how so many people could have so many jobs and so little to show for it.

Settling down, my landlady drew a small leather bag from deep inside her skirt. She untied the string and shook a heap of little polished stones on to the newspaper covering the table. She rubbed them with the corner of a dirty dishcloth. 'Well?' Her bright eyes quizzed me. 'More 'en you can count. Wot are them? Guess.' She took another swig of beer.

I rubbed one of the stones between thumb and finger, then another. I didn't know what they were. 'Stones?'

'Stones . . . of course them's stones. Wot else? Wot I arsks yer is wot kind o' stones?'

A heavy silence hung between us.

'I don't know.'

'Gallstones, you dummy! Mine! A record!'

I just stared.

''Struth,' she exploded, gathering up her treasures. 'Wasting my time you is. You're the kind of bloke wot gets no 'appy in anyfink.' Swearing loudly, she tucked the bag inside her skirt again.

––––––––<o>––––––––

When the rest of the family came in that evening they took my presence in their stride. Evidently I was not the first lodger to rent part of Ben's bed. Yet I was the first to come from so far away. Maisy exploded in laughter at my accent, "Ark at 'im; off 'is chump 'e is.' It was the first time anyone had laughed at me like that and it hurt. The two girls were small, though what they lacked in build they made up for with quick wit and deft talk. Their nails and faces were painted.

Later we had supper together. Although I was hungry, I managed to control my appetite lest Mrs Tinker should take alarm and raise her price. Fifteen shillings was all I could afford, and that depended on my getting a job.

As we ate, I studied my landlord. He was a tall, muscular man with a long sliding jaw, protruding cheekbones, grizzled hair and a clipped moustache. He surveyed me cautiously with one eye. The other was covered with a black shield. 'The war,' he said. He wore an old navy suit with a faded anchor on the breast pocket, a blue roll-neck pullover, and – even at table – black rubber galoshes up to his knees.

The pile of scrap metal in the backyard was his pride and joy. 'Come in 'andy one day. There's gotta be a war.'

'Die in our bleedin' beds, we will,' his wife grumped.

The moment Ben came in my heart sank. He was a hulking gorilla of a fellow with tousled hair, work-begrimed arms and a tattooed chest. He had the oddest pointed ears, but no neck. He spoke with an unmanly voice. I worried how the two of us could possibly fit into his narrow bed.

After supper, I followed Ben to his room. I sat on the chair, while he stuffed a rolled blanket between the bed and the wall to give us another inch or two. He'd obviously done it before.

'The thing yer've got ter watch is if yer jumps out the bleedin' bed on to t' floor yer'll go right through it; the floorboards are rotten. Look behind t' aspidistra. That's where Mum 'ides 'er beer. Knock it dahn and you'll go straight through t' bleedin' window. The old man is sumfink shockin', 'e is, about beer in t' 'ouse. She'll get 'er 'ead punched in if 'e finds it.' It explained why the room smelled like a brewery.

We climbed into bed, he was at the top, I was at the bottom. 'Can't beat it 'ere,' he kept saying, tucking the blanket under his chin. Using my coat as a pillow, I tried to keep my feet off his face. Before falling asleep, I asked him about his job.

'I smash stones . . . wiv a sledge 'ammer.'

I wondered whether the stones he broke hadn't broken him.

I got up that first Saturday morning without waking Ben. After a hurried breakfast of an egg, bread, tea and tinned milk, I put on my cap and went in search of the Bow Bridge Iron Foundry I'd seen from the bus. The chimneys were still idle; the iron-barred windows were thick with dirt; stunted patches of sooty grass grew against the high walls. The tall gates were chained and locked. My pulse quickened as I tried one gate after another.

'Shut Sat'day! Short time,' a passerby called.

That was all I needed to cheer me up. Factories on short time are not looking for workers. The foundry began to take on a hostile look.

With nowhere else to go and nothing else to do, I went in search of the Thames. Every northerner who comes to London wants to see the Thames.

For an hour or more, I walked down warren-like streets, past squalid alleyways and dank courtyards festooned with lines of washing. The gloomy dwellings seemed to go on and on for ever. Ragged children stopped their dancing to turn and gape at me. Some people peered from basements, others sat at open windows in their shirtsleeves. Knots of men idled at street corners. I saw a Chinaman and a Negro, and some swarthy people wearing red turbans. I'd never seen so many different faces. In one street I came upon a Temperance speaker who pointed an accusing finger at me. 'Drink is the devil's brew,' she cried. I moved on quickly. Only in a church-yard did I see grass and trees. When I got lost the Cockneys put me straight, though they did so in an offhand manner.

Eventually, I made my way round a high wall and came to a causeway overlooking the largest river I'd ever seen. The tide was rippling across the mudflats; slimy stakes stuck out of the water; rusting cranes stood against the grey sky. Excited, I made my way to the edge of the water, where I sat on some stone steps to eat my sandwich. Fort-like docks stretched as far as I could see.

Moored barges linked together with rope creaked and groaned at the rising tide. Screaming gulls fought over swill on the oily surface. An old straw mattress floated by, surrounded by pieces of driftwood. Farther out, steamers and tugs boomed, piped and whistled; a graceful sailing barge went by loaded with bricks. It had one tall mast with a patched sail and a tiny mast at the stern. There were so many ships that I wondered where they all came from and where they were going.

Much later, I left the Thames and began to make my way back to Stratford. As I walked, I knew I'd done the right thing in leaving Lancashire. Unlike the North, which had suffered a stroke and was dying, London was vibrantly alive. In Blackburn it had been pointless to look for a job. London offered hope. What I saw wasn't the London Harold Watkins and I had listened to on the radio – Saturday-night bands forever going *boom-ta-da-da-boom*, tinkling glasses, and happy voices calling across crowded dance floors – but it was the most exciting place I'd ever seen and I intended to hang on to it.

It was early evening when I arrived back at The Cut. Ben Tinker was shambling off down the street in ill-fitting clothes. 'Do yer want some beer and jellied eels?' he asked. I declined.

That night, I luxuriated in his bed. He woke me up in the early hours of the next morning smelling to the moon. In minutes he was sleeping like a log. With my head at the bottom, I kept the odour of Ben's beer and eels at bay; but there was still the smell of his feet.

---<o>---

'Well I'm blessed,' Mr Tinker said the next morning, when I told him that I was about to take a bus to the City. The way he looked at me suggested that to go to the City simply for pleasure was unforgivable.

Ben, who was still in bed, took his dad's view. 'Never bin, an' hain't goin' now,' he said, pulling the blanket over his head. ''S fact.'

I caught a red double-decker bus at the corner. My face pressed against an upstairs window; I stared through the smoking chimney pots into the bright sky. My head and heart were full of expectations.

Westminster Bridge was humming with life when I got there. Cars, buses and trams were rushing by. There was an endless stream of people – all dressed up and many of them talking in languages I had never heard before. Boats hooted on the river below. The buildings were so high that I had to crane my neck to see the top. *Boom, boom, boom* went Big Ben, a stone's throw away, tolling out ten o'clock to the City and the world. I'd heard it on the radio, but that couldn't match the real thing. The sound hung in the air even after the booming was done.

With a map the bus conductor had given me, I walked round the outside of the Houses of Parliament and Westminster Abbey. I knew that the Houses of Parliament were the heart of England and the British Empire – nay, of the world.

In Downing Street I missed seeing Ramsay MacDonald, the Prime Minister, by five minutes. That was something worth writing home about. Buckingham Palace had a flag on top, but you could hardly get near it because of the crowd. Soldiers on horseback, complete with trumpets, swords, tall black fur hats and shining breastplates, had difficulty getting by. After the Palace, I visited Nelson's Column in Trafalgar Square, where a cloud of pigeons flew around me. I made my way to St Paul's Cathedral, and then to the Old Bailey. One look at the scales of justice hanging above its entrance was enough. How many times had I read in *Thompson's Weekly* about judges doffing black caps and sentencing poor people to death there. That was something else I'd have to write home about.

All that day I rushed from one thing to the next, almost forgetting to eat the bread and jam sandwich Mrs Tinker had given me. The more I saw, the more I wanted to see. It was late by the time I reached Piccadilly Circus. Coloured lights, shiny cars and double-decker buses filled the street. Shop windows displayed every luxury. I saw people in real evening dress getting in and out of taxis. How different from Blackburn it was!

Tired out, I finally returned to Stratford. Sarah had saved me some supper. The Tinkers didn't say much. When I began to tell them about the wonderful things I had seen, they gave each other queer looks, which made me feel uncomfortable. I thought Ben might have been more sympathetic, but by the time I got to bed he was snoring.

———◇———

At seven-thirty the next morning, with washed face and clean overalls, and with my straw-like hair sticking out from under my cap, I climbed the stairs to the office of the Bow Bridge Iron Foundry. The three chimneys were belching thick black smoke. The bright sun made the building look friendly. All the gates were open; people and lorries were coming and going. In my hand was the crumpled letter of introduction from Mr Dimbleby at the brick works in Darwen, Lancashire, to Mr Dent. As I knocked on Mr Dent's glass-panelled door, I became hot around the collar. The longer I stood there, the more worked up I got. The banging and thumping in the foundry below shook the windows.

Eventually a plumpish, middle-aged woman answered my knocking.

"Oojah want?'

'Mr Dent.'

'Won't be 'ere for 'alf an 'our. What's your business, anyway?'

'Private,' I said, pushing the letter back inside my overalls. I hadn't come all this way to be put off by a secretary. 'I'll be back at eight,' I called as I made for the stairs. I was so nervous and moved so fast that you might have thought the building was on fire.

'Better few minutes before,' she shouted after me. Her tone was friendly. There's one thing I thought, as I went down the steps two at a time, there is a Mr Dent; he's not dead or gone to Australia.

I spent the next half-hour pacing up and down the street carrying on an imagined conversation with Mr Dent. The people who passed me must have thought I was crazy. 'Yes Mr Dent, no Mr Dent,' I practised. I knew that the upcoming interview was vital to both Harold Watkins and me. 'Billy,' Harold had said when I was leaving the North, 'Billy, when you meet that London chap, you've got to nail him. For God's sake, don't let him get away. He's our only hope.'

Just before eight, with office workers pushing past me, I knocked on Mr Dent's door again. The plumpish woman greeted me. 'Wait and I'll try to fit you in, dearie.' Encouraged by the 'dearie' bit, I walked up and down the corridor until a small, bent figure carrying a briefcase and umbrella, whom I presumed to be Mr Dent, brushed past me. He entered his office and shouted for the secretary. Everybody in the building shouted because of the din. Doors banged, people came and went. I wondered if I would ever see either of them again. You could tell it was Monday.

Thirty minutes later I was still waiting. It didn't bother me; I'd been brought up to wait. I watched the tea urn being pushed from room to room, hoping that someone would offer me a cup. They smiled, but there was no tea forthcoming. I was just about to sit cross-legged on the floor when the 'dearie' woman popped her head round the door and asked me to come in.

She sat me opposite her boss, who didn't even look up. He was a grey-haired man, with a strong face. He wore a striped shirt with rolled-up sleeves and braces. His great unkempt moustache contrasted with his stiff, celluloid collar and glittering tiepin. Steel-rimmed spectacles sat on the end of his nose; a cloud of cigarette smoke hung above his head. He wasn't anything like the photograph that Mr Dimbleby had shown me.

Against the door stood a hatstand with a trilby, a jacket, and an umbrella. There was dust everywhere. The desk, the windows and the pictures of foundries on the walls were covered with it; so was the carpet and the black cat asleep on a chair. There was a strong smell of burning.

Clutching my letter and my cap, I watched Mr Dent as he shuffled his papers. Every now and again he would talk to himself or use the telephone. His tone was always brisk and aggressive – and loud, because of the *thump*, *thump*, *thump* of the drop hammers below.

Just when I'd begun to wonder whether I was going to have to sit on the edge of that chair for the rest of my life, Mr Dent looked up and fixed me with a stare. 'Yes?' he demanded brusquely, as if I'd just arrived. I handed him Mr Dimbleby's letter. He opened it with a knife and read it slowly. I watched him closely. Instead of questions such as 'And how is Mr Dimbleby?' or 'When did you arrive?' (the answers to which I'd rehearsed in the street), he shouted, 'Christ!' and put the letter down as if it had burned his fingers. 'Get Charlie,' he called to the secretary through the open door. My heart sank. His voice sounded cross. As I waited, Harold Watkins' anxious face passed before my eyes. ('Billy, for God's sake, nail him!')

It was a relief when Charlie Bobbit the foreman arrived to end the painful silence. I liked Charlie Bobbit from the start. He was as round as a ball. A brown dustcoat covered him

18

from top to toe. He had twinkling eyes and wore a crushed bowler above his soot-smudged face. A short-stemmed pipe stuck out of the side of his mouth. He nodded affably to me, picked up the teapot and poured the last drop of tea into Mr Dent's empty cup. Only when he had drunk the dregs did he speak up.

'What's doin', 'Arry?'

Mr Dent nodded at me. 'That silly bugger Arthur Dimbleby has gone and sent this lad on spec.' He handed Charlie the letter. Draping himself over a chair, Charlie read it and then looked at me. I felt hot under his gaze.

'No warnin', 'Arry?'

'Months ago I heard from him . . . didn't reply because there were no jobs. Standing our own people down, we were.'

'Lost a lot of good sods.'

'Dimbleby could at least have rung. I'll give him what for on the blower later. He's a bloody fool to put a youngster out on a limb like this.'

Charlie turned to me. 'When did you get here, son?'

'Friday.'

'Could you go back?'

'I've nothing to go back to.'

'Any friends in London?'

'No.'

'Where are you living?'

'I found half a bed in The Cut near the canal in Stratford.' Our conversation was interrupted by the phone ringing. 'What can I do about it?' Mr Dent shouted into the phone. 'What do you mean? . . . No I won't shoot myself.' He slammed the phone down. 'What do your folks do?' he asked me, as if the phone had never rung.

'Cotton workers, with no jobs.'

'The trouble with you northerners is that you think that jobs in London are two-a-penny,' Mr Dent said, speaking to the wall.

The secretary entered with some letters to sign. Unnoticed by the others she caught my eye, placed her finger under her chin and raised her head. I got the message: keep your chin up. She'd been listening through the open door.

'Ever worked in a foundry?' Charlie asked.

'No, but I'm a quick learner,' I answered, a note of desperation in my voice. I could feel Harold Watkins prodding me.

There was a long silence while Charlie removed his bowler and wiped his brow.

'Well?'

'Well,' answered Charlie, 'you can either send this little bugger back to where 'e's come from, or . . .' here he paused, 'for Arthur's sake, you can 'elp 'im out for a couple o' weeks while 'e tries to find a better 'ole. We've drunk a lot of beer with Arthur Dimbleby, we 'ave.'

'What are they going to say in the shop? And what about the Union? We're on short time. And what would the chairman say?'

'Nobody's goin' to know nothin', unless you shout it from t' bleedin' roof.'

For a few moments Mr Dent nursed his pen. He then turned to me. 'Count your blessings, young man, that Mr Bobbit didn't die coming up the stairs. He'll put us all in the workhouse, he will, before he's done.'

'Worrygut!' Charlie grinned.

And so it was settled. They'd let me hang on for a week or two while I searched for something else. I'd get one pound a week for which I thanked them. Cap in hand, I followed Charlie down the stairs. Mr Dent looked unhappy, but the secretary smiled as I left.

———◦———

When I reached the foundry floor, I wondered why I'd tried so hard to get there. The air was stifling; everything breathed fire. 'A soddin' place occupied by lunatics,' shouted Mr Bobbit. Welders' torches sizzled and flared; black leather belts hummed up and down; stamping machines and drop hammers shook the building; clouds of steam and smoke rose from bubbling pits of red molten ore; half-clad, black-grimed shadowy figures flitted about. 'Sand rats,' said Bobbit. In the rafters, sparrows flew. As I looked on, my eyes watered; dust clogged my nose and throat. I feared I was about to choke.

—◇—

By the end of the day, I was trembling with fatigue. My face was plastered with mud, the armpits of my shirt were black with sweat; my trousers were wet from the steam. To save the bus fare, I walked to Stratford. I needed the fresh air.

I reached the Tinkers on the point of collapse. Stripping to the waist, I cleaned up at the kitchen sink. It was the only place to wash. Having struggled to stay awake through supper, I fell on Ben's bed. He had to sleep at the bottom that night.

The next week was a test of endurance gauged by the foundry hooter. From seven-thirty until five, with an hour off at midday, I worked harder than I'd ever done. Shovelling sand and fighting trolleys with lives of their own left me so exhausted that I didn't know which day of the week it was. When I wasn't shovelling sand, or pushing a trolley, or carrying ladles, forceps, tongs and hammers, I was cleaning up after somebody else. Clay, water and sand became second nature to me – so too did burns and blisters.

Every day was a battle to get up, work and sleep. I learned to breathe while being roasted. I also learned to take a cursing when I did the wrong thing. Praise was unknown. Flopping down on Ben's bed at night was the only escape from the battles of the day. The screaming of injured metal drove everything else out of my head. Going to the tap for a drink, or to the toilet for a smoke were the only ways to relieve the pressure. I remembered the look of exhaustion I'd seen on my brother's face when he was a foundry worker years before. It had never occurred to me that I would find myself in the same boat. Time became a blur. I was engaged in a struggle in which I dared not fail.

21

I'd have been out of a job had I not won the friendship of Charlie Bobbit. Every now and again he let me off for an hour to chase other jobs that were being offered locally. My efforts were a waste of time and bus fares. For every job there were a dozen applicants. When I told Bobbit that I hadn't got the job, he'd remove his pipe, shrug and say, 'She'll be right tomorrow.' But tomorrow came and I still hadn't landed anything. I suppose Bobbit delayed throwing me out because I was working my hide off.

At the end of the first week I didn't need anyone to explain to me the need for the Sabbath – a day of rest. I wrote post-cards to my sister Brenda, my friend Harold Watkins, and Mr Dimbleby at the Darwen Brick Works. I knew that Brenda would share my card with the family.

Chapter II

A Different World

Once I'd adjusted to the pace at the foundry, I woke each morning with a new feeling of adventure and excitement. Life began to have meaning again. Had Ben not warned me about the rotten floor, I'd have jumped out of bed.

Mr Tinker's shout, 'It's four bells,' made me hurry to breakfast. After that I joined the endless flow of vehicles and people going westwards towards the City. There were no pedestrian crossings on Bow Road. Sometimes I dashed across; other times the traffic was so dense that I had to wait. I loved the excitement and the danger of it all. I accepted the turmoil of city life as I accepted the cloud of sulphur on the foundry floor – without thinking. To stay in London, I was prepared to put up with anything.

After each gruelling day at the foundry, I'd tramp back to Stratford. It was a blessing to reach The Cut, clean up at the sink and sit down with the family for some food. Of the Tinkers, Sarah soon became my favourite. She was the giving type. She was decent and never did me a wrong. She had a suitor with the improbable name of Widge, of whom she was very fond. 'It's as if sumfink nice 'ad 'appened every time 'e cums in,' she would say. Widge was an ordinary fellow with a low forehead and heavily lidded eyes, who carried on a conversation by jerking his head. Yet his heart was in the right place; his eyes said so. He used to come every Friday night to court Sarah against the wall in the dingy area between the front door and the living room. There was nowhere else. They used to push and scramble so hard against the wall behind which I was trying to sleep that it was a relief when the lovemaking reached its climax and the wall stopped bulging against my bed. Without fail, the affair would be repeated the next night.

Sarah was the only Tinker with ideals. With Widge, she was determined to escape from The Cut. Her ambition was to start all over again in the countryside where she could bring up a family 'in t' fresh air'. She wanted a garden where her children could play – even if they had to live in a caravan. Anything was better than spending the rest of her life making matches. I did so want her dream to come true. With tears in her eyes, she used to say that she wasn't asking for anything to which she wasn't entitled; whereas I knew she was asking for the moon. Widge and Sarah were really good people. The trouble was that they were poorer than the proverbial church mouse.

Sarah's sister Maisy was all for herself. She wore a thick layer of mascara and used so much powder on her face that it used to flake off and fall in her food. Her idea of heaven was to go to the Troxy on Commercial Road on Saturday nights with some bloke who was prepared to stuff her with chocolate, ice cream and oranges. For those few hours she lived the life of the screen. When she came home she'd dance about the living room taking off the stars she'd seen. The Troxy was where we all went to dream. It relieved us of the drabness of our surroundings. In other people's hopes, loves and hates, we saw ourselves.

Reality was to return to The Cut and get involved in a Tinker fight. One night Mr Tinker threw a dreadful tantrum. Once the "Arf a mo, shut that, missus' phase had begun, the battle was on. The girls ran upstairs; Ben and I took refuge on our bed. After several minutes of bloodthirsty howls, Mrs Tinker gave such a scream that her daughters came running. Ben remained completely unmoved, except for having a good scratch.

I didn't like Maisy. Her darting eyes were always watching me. Once when I came home she was the only one there. She offered to wash the dirt off my back at the sink. I was surprised at her sudden helpfulness; I was even more surprised when she tried to wash my thighs. I felt her hands against my skin; they were hot and clammy. Repelled by her, I grabbed my towel and made for the door. She never forgave me. After that, I avoided being in the house with her alone. I would wash my back and below the waist on a Sunday morning when everybody else was asleep. Sarah feared that her sister was out to devour me; she watched us like an old hen.

I not only became daggers drawn with Maisy, I also had to watch my step with her mother. When Mrs Tinker wasn't nagging her husband, she was nagging me about the dirt I brought home. I was using too much soap and hot water. I would gladly have walked out on her had I been able to. But what was on offer for fifteen shillings was as miserable as the Tinkers. I put up with the awful conditions because I had to.

Food was the greatest trial. Mrs Tinker might claim that she'd bought "arf a shoulder o' mutton and pertaters', but the meal didn't even faintly resemble mutton or potatoes. It was a gala occasion when she took to her bed and Sarah cooked. Whenever I had pennies to spare, I bought food on the street. The parcels of buns and shortbread that my sisters sent helped me to get by.

Mrs Tinker's idea of housekeeping was not very ambitious. The kitchen sink was always covered with grime. The bugs, which dropped down the walls with the noise of grains of sand, were worse, though in fairness, she would have had to burn down the house to defeat them. She had no sense of smell. I would come back from the foundry at the end of the day to find Ben's window shut and the stench of the unemptied pisspot under the bed unbearable. Yet I hated her emptying the pisspots in the morning. She'd stick her thumb in all of them, and then make breakfast.

One of the reasons why Mrs Tinker could not smell urine was that there were so many other smells in the house. The smell of beer was awful. I never knew any woman drink such quantities; I think it was where my fifteen shillings went. She always had a jugful hidden behind the aspidistra in Ben's room. There was also a sour, earthy smell, which was worse after rain. The house was always damp and cold.

The Cut was a cul-de-sac. At dawn, while scrambling to get dressed, I watched my neighbours pass my window on their way to work. Like myself, they went off to poorly paid jobs. They were hardened by poverty and misfortune. 'Got to tike wot yer finds,' they'd say. Some laboured at the gasworks, others on the docks as stevedores, riggers, ballast-heavers, or winchmen. There was also a chimney sweep, who cycled past wearing a tall hat, carrying his brushes. One little woman never passed without having to run back – I suspected a pot left on the stove. Sometimes I'd watch children skip and jump. They were small for their age and intense. 'Punch and Judies [school inspectors] catches 'em and makes 'em go to school,' said Ben. If I had the light on, the odd gawking face would peer in. Stark naked, I would gawk back at the two eyes frozen to the glass. I would see our neighbours again when they returned at night, flitting by like bats. On Saturday nights they would spruce up and head for the pub. Though the majority were steady, sober people, there were always one or two who returned drunk.

In time I became part of the street. I knew who was sick, who was not speaking to whom, who had illegitimate babies, and who was queer in the head. I knew who had died. You stood in your doorway when the cortège went past.

28

I got to know our next-door neighbour, hollow-cheeked, watery-eyed Mrs Wheeler, a little better than most. Her radio against my wall was always turned up to get maximum effect. She was a drinking companion of Mrs Tinker's. Unrestrained by my presence, she would go into all the seedy gossip of the street. She had a passion for making a story larger than life – 'filling in the corners' she called it. She never imparted a spicy titbit without prefacing her comments with, 'Wot I'm abaht to tell yer must stiy within these four walls.'

Sustained by 'the spot of tiddly', Mrs Wheeler was convinced that she would 'larst a loiftoim' – which was more than could be said for her family. Her husband and son had worked as wreckers. They'd lived a cat-like existence demolishing buildings all over London. She told me how her menfolk had stood and talked on top of a chimney before taking it down brick by brick. A high wind never bothered them. Other times they'd used dynamite. That's where the Wheeler skill came in.

Having avoided accidents for a long time, their luck eventually ran out. Peter tumbled off a wall and finished up in a wheelchair; his father fell off a factory chimney. The street duly gave him a funeral full of dignity and respect. In this the Cockneys were like the poor of the North: they loved to squander on a funeral. Death was something special.

The Nicholls farther down the street worked on the wrong side of the law. The old man and two of his older sons had done time for what Ben called 'dippin'' or 'shoot-flyin''. The younger members picked the pockets of ladies; the more experienced picked the pockets of gentlemen. They looked perfectly respectable. Mr Nicholls boasted a gold watch chain and a sovereign across his waistcoat, but those presumably were not his. I'm sure they thought their thieving was honest work. 'Too many wicked people abaht,' Mr Nicholls used to say. Whenever a 'grasshopper' (a policeman) went past my window, the odds were he was on his way to the Nicholls.

'Good neighbours, that's what the Nicholls is,' old man Tinker used to say. 'They keeps a large family goin' without

askin' no one for nuffink. Keeps 'is family out of the insti-
tooshun, 'e do. And gentle they is. Tikes yer watch or yer
wallet without ye knowin' it. Down on gamblin' and drink
they is too.'

I'd never run into people like the Nicholls and I didn't
know what to make of them. I'd come from a community
that condemned stealing, regardless of the circumstances.
Later, when I learned about the wild, homicidal bullies who
terrorised London's underworld, I came to think of the
Nicholls as relatively harmless.

The richest woman in The Cut was Pearly Lilly, an attractive blonde, who by plying her profession as a 'bride' among
the nobs of the West End, earned more in a night than any of
us earned in a week. 'Oh my word, rich she is,' said Mrs
Tinker enviously. 'Would like to see the inside of 'er purse, I
would.' Pearly Lilly was not ostracised as she would have been
in the street where I was born. In The Cut people talked to
her like they would to anybody else. She was the only one
who could afford to come home in the early hours like a queen
in a cab all to herself. Now that for us was living it up:

> See her riding in a carriage,
> In the park and all so gay;
> All the nibs and nobby persons
> Come to pass the time of day.

I used to contrast Lilly's attractiveness with the grimy face
of her slovenly old mother.

Pearly Lilly was preferable to Mrs Bindy, who had a large
number of children, but no husband. Where the husband had
gone to, not even Mrs Wheeler knew. The woman was a profes-
sional beggar. The children could take off a blind or crippled
child, as mute and pious as could be. I gave an involuntary
shudder every time I saw her setting out with her brood.

I was shocked at the waywardness of some of my neighbours. I'd been brought up with a strict code of ethics; revival Methodism had drummed into us the difference between right and wrong. In Blackburn the Sabbath was a day of prayer – the trains did not run, and shops and cinemas were closed; even whistling was frowned upon. I had an awful sense of guilt the first time I went to see a film on a Sunday; it spoiled the show.

In Stratford, Sunday was deafening: children screamed, newspaper boys shouted 'piper!', radios blasted, and the Salvation Army band blared at the pub corner, accompanied by the crash of tambourines:

> Here we suffer grief and pain
> Here we meet to part again
> In Heaven we part no more
> Oh, that will be joyful.

I don't wonder that some churchmen preferred to make their conversions in Africa or in the West Indies. Only the tough ones remained in the East End trying to guide and guard their flock.

Sunday was the day I went exploring. I'd never seen so many colourful little shops – they were strung across the district like beads on a string. Everything was available to those with money. You couldn't walk down a street without somebody trying to sell you something: "Ere y' are! Tyke yer chyce!' Street vendors offered fish and chips (wrapped in greasy newspaper), roasted chestnuts, 'taters – all 'ot!', black puddings, pies, sausages and muffins, ice cream and soft drinks. Raw oysters were eaten on the spot with vinegar and pepper. With or without money, people swarmed. They were like floodwater, filling every space. I used to wonder where they all came from and where they went at night.

What the Cockneys lacked in physical strength – they seemed to be small and narrow-chested – they made up for with nimble wits. Whereas Lancashire men might go to pieces because they were on the dole, unemployed Cockneys laughed it off. They didn't moralise about being without a job. Another one would be sure to turn up, or family and friends would provide. A man could hire a 'cock sparrow' and push a barrow selling fruit and vegetables, or play a mouth-organ or a concertina, or buy a box of chalks and become a 'screever'. I never went out without seeing someone on his hands and knees 'makin' skitches'. Portraits of the King were mixed with those of the dapper Prince of Wales and favourite racehorses.

'Griddling' at street corners was open to anyone with a good voice. There was a fellow in The Cut who swore that 'Sins are wot piys. If yer tells 'em 'ow wicked yer've bin and 'ow yer fell dahn, and 'ow yer now tikes up yer Cross dily – and sings 'ymns about redemption – they'll fill yer 'at.'

In spite of the excitement of urban life, I never lost my love of the countryside. Victoria Park in Bow was the only large piece of open ground easily accessible to me. The avenues planted with trees, the green turf, the rustic bridges, and the swans and boats on the lake – all these things were wonderful. One could even find a songbird there among the swarms of sparrows. The drawback was the crowds – especially at weekends. If the weather was fair, bodies lay thick on the grass and covered the benches. One couldn't move for them. Yet nobody grumbled. People were only too happy to sit or lie in the open air, while the children ran wild. They didn't seem to notice the traffic rushing by outside the railings. On my first visit I was surprised to see people swimming in such a dirty lake.

I not only missed the countryside, I missed the people I'd left behind. As the weeks passed, I became homesick. Loneliness took as much out of me as the heavy work I was doing. At the foundry I couldn't talk because there was so much noise; at the Tinkers' I'd only Sarah to talk to. Conversation with Ben consisted of a few well-meant grunts. I never discovered what went on in his head. He had no idea about the world in which he lived; his expectation of life was the next meal. I cannot believe that no one had mentioned Jesus Christ to him. 'Caw!' he said. 'I've never 'eard of 'im.' Even when he opened up with me, I had difficulty following him, his mind went off at all angles. ''S fact,' he kept saying, staring at some point above my head. I became convinced that he didn't know what he was saying. The family treated him as a kind of cuckoo clock that sounded off at regular intervals, but did not need an answer. They thought him a bit 'loopy'.

I don't know what I'd have done without the letters from home. They affected me like water splashing on a parched plant. Harold Watkins' letters were marvels of hope. 'We'll go a long way in politics,' he wrote. 'Don't forget that when I'm Prime Minister, you'll be my Foreign Secretary.' That's what he'd promised, and Harold kept his promises. I didn't breathe a word of this to anyone.

My parents never wrote. My mother couldn't write, my father didn't think it necessary; nor did my brother Dan. I dropped everything to read letters from my sisters. Jenny wrote about her son and that her husband Gordon had got a job painting again. It saddened me for days to learn from Brenda that my dog Bess had run away the day after I left Lancashire. I knew that she was trying to find me. I felt terrible about it; we'd been inseparable. I knew at the time that in leaving her I was doing wrong. To my sorrow, I never heard of her again.

To ease my loneliness I started to look for Betty Weatherby, my north-of-England sweetheart, who'd been sent to school in London after her family discovered our romance. My love for her was still strong; often at work I'd catch myself daydreaming about her. I went to Stratford Public Library and asked a librarian to help me find her. She looked at me queerly: 'There are dozens of women's colleges in London,' she shrugged. Heartaches and loneliness weren't her business.

———◇———

To my delight, Harold wrote one October day to say that he had left the ACDO soap company in Blackburn and was about to join me in London. A cousin of his in west London, who had migrated from Lancashire some months before, had offered him shelter until he could get on his feet.

I met Harold at Euston Station two weeks later on a cold, blustery Saturday afternoon. I'd never been in a big London railway station before and I found it gloomy and bewildering. I had to fight my way through crowds going to Wales, Scotland, Ireland and perhaps America. I wondered where they'd got the money.

I could hardly contain myself when I saw Harold coming down the platform with our bikes and a load of luggage. He would have brought Bess if he could have found her. Except for a luxuriant moustache, he was just as I'd left him. We couldn't help giving each other a hug. We even had a cup of tea and a bun at the station restaurant to celebrate. While we drank, I listened to his news from the North. He spoke of our families, the Rovers football team, and the depression that still gripped the town. He thought us lucky to have got away.

Sharing the luggage, we then cycled to Harold's cousin in Southall, fifteen miles away. There had been a light snowfall earlier and there was black slush about. Like a couple of country bumpkins we were oblivious of the cars and lorries hooting their horns while trying to pass us; those who cursed us, we cursed back. It never occurred to us that it would have been better for everybody had we taken a train. That would have cost money; to pedal a bike cost nothing but time and energy and we had plenty of both.

It took us a long time to reach Southall, and almost as long to find Harold's cousin, Jack Connor. We found him in the middle of a new, treeless, muddy housing estate where every house looked exactly like every other. They were so small, so raw, so thin that the locals called them 'hen huts'. The estate was full of migrants from northern Britain, Wales and Ireland. A corner had become the preserve of a small coloured group. No one knew whether they had come from India or the Caribbean, or both.

Mr Connor's 'hen hut' was packed with Lancashire migrants, most of them young men like ourselves who had come to London to make their fortune. Some had been so desperate that they'd cycled all the way. There were so many bodies that it was almost impossible to move from one room to another. People slept on collapsible cots or on the floor; planks of wood on bricks served as tables. At least these people weren't strangers to each other, as was the bewildering crowd of faces in the streets. 'If you put on a new suit here, nobody would notice,' one of them said. Some of them would have gone back to the North, had they had a job to go to.

Harold's roguish-looking cousin met his mortgage payments by everybody pitching in. Not that Mr Connor stayed awake at night worrying about it. A natural gambler, he seemed quite happy to have signed away his future earnings. He slapped his head and roared with laughter at the idea of a crippling thirty-year mortgage. 'We'll go to prison? Will we heck!' He was probably as poor as he had ever been, but now for the first time in his life he had electric light, hot and cold water, a bath, a gas stove, a flush toilet, a new galvanised dustbin, and an unconscionable debt he could never hope to repay.

Mr Connor survived by working as a dishwasher in a high-class restaurant on the outskirts of Southall. He brought home the leftovers and shared them with the others. Sometimes his boss gave him the used flowers, which brightened up the house.

I spent only one night in the 'hen hut'. As it was the weekend and pointless to go looking for work, we talked and sang and laughed together until late. Harold and I slept in a corner covered with an old curtain.

On Sunday afternoon I cycled back to Stratford. Before leaving, we agreed that as soon as Harold could find a job, we'd meet in the City for a night on the town. I got home late in the evening, half dead. Against Mrs Tinker's protests, I put my bike in Ben's room next to the aspidistra. Unless I was to leave it in the street and have it pinched, there was nowhere else I could put it – the backyard was full. I couldn't afford to lose anything as precious as my bike.

About a month later I had a letter from Harold. 'I've landed a job as a weaver in a fly-by-night place in west London. If you're willing, I'll fit you in alongside me. We could live at Connor's place until something better turns up.' As I was still hanging on to my job at the foundry through Bobbit's kindness, and other jobs were not to be had, I agreed at once. I knew that Mrs Tinker would be happy to see me go. Harold also said that now that he had a shilling or two, the time had come for me to show him the sights of London. We agreed to meet on a Saturday morning in two weeks' time at the Marble Arch. He would tell me about the weaving job then. He also said that he had news from Blackburn about Betty Weatherby. My heart skipped.

As agreed, we met at the Marble Arch a fortnight later. We were both dressed up in suit, shirt and tie. The weather was cold but sunny.

The first thing I asked him about was Betty Weatherby. 'She's at St Anne's, a girls' college near Berkhamsted. I've looked it up. We could cycle there from Southall and give her a surprise.'

It didn't occur to us to pick up a telephone and call: I'd never used one, neither had Harold.

We spent the whole day seeing the sights. Food we got from street vendors. When Harold saw the Houses of

Parliament, and Big Ben, and Buckingham Palace, and No. 10 Downing Street, and all the other things I tried to squeeze in, he was just as excited as I had been. 'By gum!' he kept saying. The more we saw, the farther we went, the greater our mutual sense of accomplishment. We went on hour after hour, never tiring. We were not awkward rustics any more; we were two special young northerners who were seeing the largest city on earth.

As soapbox orators, we were eager to visit Speaker's Corner in Hyde Park. We found a dozen speakers. The first fellow was able to communicate with the dead. The next one wanted to get rid of the British in India. Alongside him was a wild character quoting great chunks from the Bible, who said that our end was near. He was drowned out by hecklers. The last fellow in the row was a chap with a bowler hat, who offered us an emaciated brown-yellow cat. 'Now I arsk yer, gints, 'ave yer ever seen an animal treated as badly as this? Wot is England cumin' to?

With the coming of evening, we made our way to the Lyons Corner House at the Marble Arch. We wanted to listen to Harry Roy's famous band. What we'd listened to in Lancashire on the radio – the blare of the band, the rattling of cups, the scraping of chairs and the tinkling of glasses – we'd now see for ourselves. Despite the cold, we joined the queue; we weren't going to walk away from the high point of our night out. We felt privileged to be able to queue up outside a restaurant that claimed 'We never close!' What would Blackburn think of that?

While we were waiting, Harold talked about his weaving job. It was in a sweatshop managed by a Hungarian who spoke no English. The pay and working conditions were poor, but it was a job. I could join him in a couple of weeks if I'd take the risk. I said I'd come as soon as he gave me the signal.

37

After standing for ages, we made it inside and were overwhelmed by the lights and the glitter. Feeling that everybody was staring at us, we followed a waitress to a table with gold chairs. The table was so small that our knees touched. Hair shining, Mr Roy turned and smiled at us as we sat down – we might have been royalty. We were so close to him that we could have shaken his hand.

On the table were white napkins, silver cutlery, a bowl of flowers and a starched tablecloth that almost touched the floor – there were even free matches. A chandelier hung above our heads. We waved to the mirror at our side. After all the walking we'd done that day, we couldn't wait to eat.

Our high spirits lasted until we saw the prices on the menu. I nudged Harold's leg. 'We're going to have to wash dishes,' I whispered.

'Oh hell, Woody, this is not the people's palace, it's a toffs' restaurant.'

I looked around at the other diners who were happily stuffing themselves. The prices hadn't put them off – they were so busy eating that they had no time to applaud the band, as Harold and I did.

We eventually ordered a cup of tea and a bun. It was either that or walk out, and we had queued and queued. Of course it was ridiculous to eat a bun under a chandelier with our movements reflected in a mirror in the presence of the famous Harry Roy, but that is all we could afford.

We ate the bun crumb by crumb. 'Non so fast,' Harold kept saying. We sipped our tea as if it was boiling hot. The waitress looked hostile, her frantic hand signals to someone at the entrance made us think she was calling the police. Only Harold's ordering another round stopped her whisking the dishes away. We had taken a lot of trouble to get here, and we refused to take flight.

We ate our second bun as we had eaten our first: crumb by crumb, while enjoying the band. We were so close to a gypsy with a violin that he seemed to be playing just for us.

Only when we had had our fill of entertainment did we

leave a modest tip and flee. We were less nervous in getting
out. We knew we would not be coming back for a long time.

At least we'd seen the real thing. As we left we heard Harry
singing:

> Somebody stole my gal,
> Somebody stole my pal,
> Somebody came and took her away,
> She didn't even say she was leavin'. . .

A week later – in search of Betty Weatherby – Harold and I
cycled to Berkhamsted in Hertfordshire. Harold had worked
out the best route, and had drawn up a map. We brought
capes against rain and, as it was November, pullovers, scarves,
mittens, and woollen caps. We also carried sandwiches and
a flask of tea. Harold had bike tools, spare tyres and tubes.
We planned to reach St Anne's before noon. By our reckon-
ing, having spent an hour with Betty, we'd turn around and
get back to Southall shortly after dark. I would spend the
night there, leaving at four on Monday morning to get to
Bow in time for work. A wild scheme, but then I was in love
and had just turned seventeen.

The day broke cold and clear; the wind had died down.
Once away from London we travelled through a lovely hilly
countryside with fields and woods stretching into the
distance. There were no factory chimneys or coal pitheads to
spoil the view. We kept to the back roads, where the wintry
fields lay bare.

Stopping only to eat and drink, we cycled through
wooded, park-like valleys. After the flatness of east London
it was exciting to struggle up the chalky hills and go helter-
skelter down the other side. Our curiosity was aroused by
a weathered stone cross in the centre of a ploughed field; we
felt for it the reverence due to age. In past times, the plod-
ding peasant would have said a prayer there. In one village
we stopped to look at an impressive Elizabethan mansion

through a hole in a thick yew hedge. Mostly we hurried on.

Sometime during the morning we fell in with a cyclist near St Albans who was out for a day's ride. He was a pleasant fellow who led us through picturesque lanes and byways that we could never have found for ourselves. Sometimes he would point out an important estate or country view. Being a Hertfordshire man, he was aghast at our ignorance of Hertfordshire's vital role in the making of England. To hear him tell it, this was the most important county in the entire realm. Before leaving us at Hemel Hempstead, he gave us directions to Berkhamsted: 'On the Roman road to Wendover, by Tring and Lilley Hoo.' At Berkhamsted we cycled past a castle, low stone houses crouched outside its gate. Beyond the town were stands of beech trees with smooth grey bark and widely branching roots. Through a break in the trees we caught sight of manicured fields alongside an extensive gorse common. A golfer was playing in the distance.

Our final directions came from a man who was watering two white horses. 'Take the first left at the end of the forest,' he said. 'The college is a mile farther on, standing on a hill. Can't miss it.' Both of us breathed a sigh of relief. Our legs were beginning to give out.

We came upon St Anne's at the edge of a great expanse of trees. It was a long sandstone building standing in a quiet park, with a bell tower above the main entrance. Ivy climbed the embattled walls and wound about the leaded windows. Crows were settling in the trees, their cawing echoing through the woods. As we approached, a bell began to toll. One . . . two . . . three. We were shocked how late it was. We parked our bikes and climbed the steps to the front door where several well-dressed young women stood talking.

We were greeted inside by a middle-aged woman who must have seen us arrive. 'Can I help you?' she asked.

'Yes, I would like to speak with one of your students, Betty Weatherby.'

There was a long moment of silence.

'Please come this way and I'll see what I can do.' She led

us into a panelled waiting room, which despite the season was full of the scent of flowers. Excusing herself, she went in search of the Mother Superior.

Turning my cap in my hands, I watched her go down the corridor. Mysterious candles flickered in the distance, there was a statue of a kneeling monk saying endless prayers in stone.

'We've made it, Woody,' Harold whispered a little nervously.

'Yes,' I answered, more nervous than he.

Before I could stop him, Harold got up and made for the door. 'I'll wait outside.' Wondering what I would say to Betty, I continued to fumble with my cap.

A few moments later I heard steps. The middle-aged woman was returning, accompanied by a black-robed nun in her late sixties. Her penetrating glance intimidated me.

'This is Mother Superior, she will speak to you about Miss Weatherby.'

The nun took a seat and pointed to another chair. A small ivory cross dangled from her wrist. She seemed in no hurry to speak. I thought it better to tell her who I was. 'I know,' she said. I wondered who had written to her about me.

For several moments we sat together, silent and impassive.

'I am afraid I must tell you that Miss Weatherby is no longer here.'

I caught my breath. 'Not here?'

'No, she left for France two weeks ago.' The voice was gentle and warm.

'France?' I stammered.

'Yes.'

'Is she coming back?'

'No. That is all I can tell you.'

Without realising it, I suddenly found tears coursing down my face. I stared at the floor too embarrassed to speak. I found it hard to suppress my tears and a disgrace to shed them.

The nun leaned toward me. 'You need to learn patience, my child, you are very young.'

I shook my head, hurt.

'Don't shake your head like a goat. God knows what He's doing, you'll see.'

Brushing my face with my hands, I got to my feet and slowly made for the door. It seemed pointless to stay any longer.

'How did you get here?'

'We cycled from Southall.'

'Do you intend to return to Southall today?'

'Yes.'

The nun joined me at the door. 'You cannot possibly cycle so far today. It's half past three and the weather is threatening. You'll have an accident.'

'We are using the back roads.'

'Then you'll get lost.'

'Didn't get lost coming.'

'No, that's because you rode in the light.'

'We have no choice. We have to go to work tomorrow.'

There was a silence between us. I made a gesture for her to pass through the door.

'If you insist on cycling through the night you must have some hot food before you go.'

'You're very kind.' I was more upset than hungry.

She accompanied Harold and me to the kitchen and gave orders to serve us a meal.

'God keep you,' she said as she left.

When I told Harold what had happened, he was as bewildered as I. 'Sorry we came on a fool's errand, Woody. Better make tracks home. It's almost four.' We ate in silence. I felt crushed.

We came out of St Anne's to be greeted by a cold, strangely leaden sky. There was a foreboding murmur in the wind. Dead leaves swirled against the college wall and the odd flake of snow was falling. A robin sang his plaintive tune.

We put on our capes. By the time we'd reached the golf links they were blanketed with snow and the wind was quickening. In the forest the trunks of the trees were turning white; the puddles were beginning to freeze over. Smoking snow spun around us; starlings flew low seeking shelter. Save for the raucous cries of crows, the forest was hushed. The falling snow made it seem later than it was; house lights appeared in the gathering gloom. The air grew colder.

Eyes half shut, we cycled against the wind keeping our worries to ourselves. The main thing was to get back to Southall.

An hour later the ground and roofs of the houses were covered with snow; there was a whistle in the wind. As night fell, the shrouded world around us disappeared. The small round patches of light from our lamps preceded us. Even the petrol stations were shut. I had the sensation of marking time – of cycling on the spot in a white, empty world.

With our hoods pulled down over our foreheads and our mufflers wrapped tightly around our faces, we pushed on. Our wet capes swished, our tyres crackled and crunched. Now and again the wind blew the capes over our heads; our mittens froze to the handlebars. Wreaths from a nearby cemetery flew by. Gradually the truth struck home: we were alone in the middle of a blizzard, adrift in a frozen sea.

With every mile the snow became heavier and colder, the wind stronger – it lashed our faces and our legs. Desperately we continued to struggle forwards, one behind the other, taking turns to lead, never once going straight. Our shouting was lost in the wind. There were times when there was no trace of the road and the snow was too thick to cycle, we found ourselves slipping and sliding all over the place. We lugged our bicycles from one snowdrift to another with great clods of frozen snow sticking to our boots. We were too busy fighting the elements to fight each other, though tempers flared.

Too exhausted to go on, bent before the wind, we took shelter behind the trunk of a giant elm. Huddling close for warmth, we ate what scraps of food we had left and drank the flask of hot coffee the nuns had given us. Our breath frosted our mufflers.

'Ah'm tellin' thee,' panted Harold, as he gulped down the hot coffee, 'we maun be gormless to be out here.' Icicles hung from his moustache and his eyebrows.

The coffee saved us from collapse. Even with it we had to get back on to our frozen saddles quickly, for our bodies were losing heat. 'Whatever else, we must keep going, we maun't fall asleep,' Harold warned. We went on, hardly conscious of our direction, averting our heads at each blast, closing our eyes against the needles of snow, gasping for breath. It hurt to breathe. I thought the howling wind vindictive: it pounded me as if I'd done it some wrong. It was all I could do to retain a grip on the handlebars. One moment my hands seemed frozen, the next moment they felt on fire. My body ached to stop and rest; my mind told me that we must go on.

Much later we realised that we'd been riding in a circle. We were too exhausted to cry. By then we had reached the end of our tether and were living in a disconnected world. We should of course have gone and knocked on somebody's door and got somebody up – provided that we could find a door, which we couldn't. Had we known where to find a police station we would have gone there, but there was no one to ask. We hoped that a police car might find us stranded in the blizzard. None did. Several cars, covered with a thick crust of snow, glided past us during the night, but they evidently had more important things to do than rescue two lunatics stumbling about in the storm. The truth is we were too stubborn to seek help: having got ourselves into a pickle we'd somehow get ourselves out. Heads down, we pushed on, fighting against the bitter elements.

Hours later, we emerged from the storm to see the outlines of buildings slowly taking shape. In the distance the lights of London were reflected against the clouds. The more we struggled toward the lights, the more they seemed to recede. The last hour seemed like a lifetime.

It was after midnight when we reached the outskirts of Southall – seven hours later than we had planned. We were chilled to the bone and hardly able to move. We needed all the will we could muster to keep going. When eventually we reached the Connors' house and got off our bikes, great lumps of ice and snow fell from our clothing. Once indoors, we undressed mechanically. Muscles I never knew I had ached all over me. 'Next time tha goes courtin',' said Harold, standing in his shirtsleeves and watching me with frosted eyes, 'tha goes on thi own.' But he said it in jest. It took a gallon of scalding tea and a hard rubbing-down to put back a semblance of life into us. Tired to the point of being drugged, I fell asleep feeling that I had just run a great race.

After only three hours of sleep from which I had to be shaken, I staggered about getting dressed and left Southall for Stratford at about four. Groggily at first, with screwed-up eyes, I pushed on through the frozen stillness and the dark. The saddle of my bike was cold and hard, the chain was stiff. After what seemed like another endless journey, I reached the foundry by seven-thirty – glad for once to get back into the furnace-like heat. That day the papers were full of the blizzard – the worst in decades, they said. They never mentioned us.

———◦———

About a month after returning from St Anne's, Harold and I celebrated our first Christmas away from home. I gave him some cigarettes, he gave me five small cigars. I'd been in London five months, Harold had been there three, and neither of us had much to show for it. To cap it all, Harold had lost his weaving job on Christmas Eve. The weaving shed in which we were both to find a living had shut its doors for good. The Hungarian had vanished. That put a damper on our spirits that not even the convivial Mr Connor could dispel.

Yet neither of us doubted that eventually things would take a turn for the better. We were too young to know what we ought to have been worrying about. Regardless of the obstacles we faced, we looked upon London as the place to be.

Harold and I saw in the New Year of 1934 together. We were full of faith in a boundless future.

Chapter III

Hard Labour

Instead of staying at the Bow Bridge Iron Foundry for a couple of weeks, I stayed there for more than two years. I obeyed the siren when it commanded me to work and I obeyed the siren when it commanded me to stop. The thump, thump, thump of the machinery and the rattle of the overhead cranes numbed my senses. Bobbit continued to pay me one pound a week and to use me as a dog's body: 'The sods have to have somebody to kick,' he said. He knew I didn't intend to stay. He was right. I didn't want to work there for the next five years, with the risk of being thrown out when I became entitled to a man's wage. So many people yelled at me that I'd no need to think for myself.

What a relief it was to be sent out occasionally with a crew to install the foundry's metal work. I could watch the sky, see the trees, hear the birds, and feel free. All I had to do was to give a hand, brew tea and run errands. Alas, such occasions were few. When the job was done, we'd all trail back to the dirt and the din on the foundry floor.

At the outset, the foundry had seemed chaotic. It took some time for me to learn that there was order behind the chaos: ovens, cranes, furnaces and coke bins, as well as the piles of sand and loam, pig iron and charcoal had their proper place. It all made sense once you knew how the foundry worked.

The nerve centre was Bobbit's office, whose dirty bay window projected a few feet into the shop. He used his office chiefly to go over blueprints with Mr Simpson, the draughtsman. Bobbit was the first to arrive in the morning, the last to leave at night. I cannot imagine how the business would have functioned without him. Sometimes I'd catch a glimpse of Mr Dent taking important people round the floor. I never knew who owned the place or for whom I worked. Bobbit ruled my world.

The next most important man to Bobbit was Mr Simpson. He was the fellow who turned ideas into blueprints. He was always dressed in a suit and tie; his hair glistened with oil. His office was next to Bobbit's and was also protected by glass. He worked with slide rules, drawings and tiny blocks of steel to measure things. On the few occasions when I entered his office, he was always pleasant. Yet to my astonishment, I saw him pick up his telephone one day and smash it to bits. He hit an iron pillar with it until there was nothing left. I never saw such a mad act. Then he stood there scratching his head looking puzzled. I thought it was the nature of the job that made him do it, but Bobbit said it was his wife. Eventually, Mrs Simpson was asked to stop calling – the phone smashings were costing the foundry a mint of money. The problem was that he was a chronic womaniser. I once heard him trying to catch a woman on the telephone, it was like a fellow fishing for trout.

Mr Harding the storeman, a gaunt, tall man with a shock of white hair, also had his strange ways. He was forever moaning; every time I visited the stores there was something wrong. 'How are you Mr Harding?' I'd ask in an attempt to cheer him up. 'It's worse, much worse,' he'd mutter throwing his hair back. 'I've got to leave this bleedin' place before it's too late.' What 'it' was I never found out. I told one of the moulders what Harding had said. 'Silly bugger 'as been like that for twenty years. Tryin' it on, 'e is. We ought to drop a crane on 'im.' Bobbit always prefaced his remarks to Harding with, 'I know you're dying, Tom, but . . .' As far as I know, Mr Harding remained as fit as a fiddle until he retired.

At the noon break we'd sit around on the foundry floor and tell stories, laughing as we ate – some of the fellows wolfing the food down in great gobbets. In summer we'd squat outside against the foundry wall among the heavy traffic to get a breath of fresh air. Having eaten, we played cards or tossed coins on to a line drawn in the dirt. We always talked horses; we knew which horse had won the moment the news arrived on the phone – the winner was shouted from the office door. It's just as well I didn't have money to gamble.

Sometimes the laughing and joking would give way to blows. Woe betide anybody who strayed into another moulder's space. Tempers would flare. 'Turn it up! Pack it in!' Bobbit would bawl as he ran to intervene. As a last resort he'd call upon two workers with massive shoulders and gnarled hands, who together had the strength to settle any argument.

Some fights were renewed behind the foundry wall at night. I only went to one and that was enough for me. It was between Standing and White. Both were in their mid-thirties. I knew Standing because he lived close to The Cut. He was a nice sort of bloke. White was taller than Standing, but Standing was heavier. Bared to the waist, they seemed well matched. I don't know what the argument was about, but the two men were determined to settle it with blows.

The ring was a flattened cinder pad, lit by the lamps on the outside walls. The spectators – a fight always raised a crowd – stood in a larger ring, some of them in deep shadow. There was no referee; a fight went on until one of the men was knocked out or surrendered. Kicking with heavy boots was forbidden; that could lead to death. Bets were placed. In the background was the roar of traffic. Cigarette smoke hung above the crowd.

The fight began calmly enough, with each man looking for an opening. They held themselves like professionals and knew how to shift their position to gain a tactical advantage. Sparring and feinting, they concentrated on breaking down the other's defence. Now and again there was a thud to the body or a crack to the jaw, followed by cheering from the crowd.

Standing was the more aggressive and nimbler on his feet. He did the driving. In comparison, White was slow. Yet he was skilful in evading the other's fists, although not for long. Soon, Standing landed a terrific uppercut. The blow, followed up by a quick left to the body, sent White careening into the crowd. Shouting encouragement, his workmates pushed him back into the fight.

White didn't need pushing. Face bleeding and in a flaming temper, he hurled himself at his rival. Before Standing could fall back, White had delivered several blows to the body and a right to the mouth. For a moment, Standing staggered and fell to his knees. When he got up he was bleeding from the mouth. With a crushing blow to the head, White felled him again. 'Give it 'im 'Arry!' the crowd howled.

By now both men had puffed-up faces, bloody chests and red knuckles. White's lightning attack had made Standing wary. For some time he was content to trade blows, hitting and getting out of the way before White could react. The thud of ringing punches, the harsh gasping for breath and the shuffling of feet went on. It was drowned only by the cheering.

Suddenly, Standing hit White on the side of the head. Before White could recover, he hit him again across the eyes. Hands to his head, White reeled to one side and fell. Standing stood over him ready to punch him into submission. There was a tremendous commotion among the crowd. White's supporters yelled at him to get up.

It would have been better for everybody if White had stayed

where he was, but he didn't. Like a drunk, he staggered to his feet, only to be knocked down again. Fighting with a cold anger, Standing hit him when and how he pleased. No sooner did White get up than he was battered to his knees again. His eyes were swollen and his nose bled. He no longer knew what he was doing. Staggering about like an idiot, he fell across Standing in an effort to protect himself. I wanted to run in and stop the fight, but I knew better than to try; the crowd wouldn't have stood for it.

With appalling monotony, White staggered to his feet, tangled with his opponent, only to be knocked down again. Had the crowd not intervened eventually, Standing would have had to kill White to stop him getting up. I thought this bare-fisted way of punching somebody to a jelly was horrible, and I never went to a fight again.

Some months later, I came across Standing having a row with a coal-cart driver who had been beating his horse. 'Yer should be 'ung fer such savagery,' Standing yelled at the driver. I came away thinking about what he'd done to White.

Fortunately, fights usually ended with a few bruises and goodwill between the contestants. Like the metal they poured, moulders' tempers flared up, burned out and died.

<hr/>

After a year, I got a rise of five shillings and was given a steady job as a 'helper' to a moulder. Whether I liked it or not, I was now a 'sand rat'. I was assigned to George Edwards, a good man and a good moulder with years of experience behind him. Edwards was a tall, well-built fellow with a furrowed face, grey hair, shrewd brown eyes and freckled hands. Under his overalls he always wore a plaid shirt. I began to learn about moulds and the priestly cast of moulders. I watched him as he constructed gates and rises to feed the moulds and keep the metal flowing. He taught me about the chemistry of metal – 'mysteries of the craft' he called it. I learned about carbon, silicon, phosphorus, sulphur and manganese. In time I could talk about cheeks, joints, copes, combs, pigs, sows and drags with the rest of them. Edwards taught me not to take short cuts. 'Don't be 'asty; bide yer time,' he'd say. 'Let 'er go steady loike.' I once told him about my political ambitions. 'Aha, um,' he said. I'm sure he looked upon my talk of socialism as blasphemy.

I became one of a four-man team: George Edwards, Reg Leary and Syd Bates, the other helper who was about my own age. Mr Leary was younger, and slim compared with Mr Edwards. He had fair hair, delicate features and unusually blue eyes. He had a habit of staring at you for ages without blinking. He was the only one among us with tufts of hair on his cheekbones. Unlike Edwards, who rarely spoke his mind, Leary was bluff to the point of aggression. 'What the hell are you standing there for? Put the bloody rods down and bugger off.' I learned not to inflame his hot temper.

Syd Bates was a bully who liked to brag about his sexual conquests. Every Monday morning he'd narrate the lascivious details of his weekend exploits. I couldn't help but doubt that this slack-mouthed fellow with a bad complexion could have been such a Romeo.

One day when we were alone his bullying became too much. 'You can go to hell,' I said. He took a swipe at me. Fending him off, I tripped and landed my fist in his face; I felt the crunch of bone. With his nose bleeding, he staggered and fell. For a moment or two he lay there motionless, his eyes rolling grotesquely. Anxiously, I helped him to his feet. Mr Leary returned at that moment. 'Caw, you don't 'arf look seedy, Syd,' he said. He then took the two of us by our hair, banged our heads together and left us. After that Bates and I got on well.

As helpers, Syd and I started our day by removing the previous day's castings. Sometimes it was forty-eight hours before the castings cooled. We then shovelled and riddled the sand for the next pattern. With long-handled spades we spread the sand and broke it up to give it a fluffy texture. It was the moulder who pressed the pattern into the wet sand, rammed the sand around it and withdrew it prior to pouring. He worked with a shiny trowel and a tool called a rammer. His fingers told him when the sand was firm enough. Too dry, it would crumble; too wet, it would cause the metal in the mould to bubble. Only the moulder could judge its consistency; he did so by taking a handful of wet sand and squeezing it. The way Edwards pulled his face and pursed his lips while making the decision reminded me of a tea taster. Sand, I discovered, could be the queerest thing.

The molten metal – spluttering and blazing – was then poured into the mould. Once you started pouring you couldn't stop until the job was done; you couldn't pour according to whim; nor could you take your mind off the process – not even to admire the rainbow colours produced by the fiery metal. Casting was an exact art demanding split-second timing and control – especially when pouring with the help of an overhead crane. It was the moulder who decided when the glowing cascade – too dazzling to look at – would be poured, and when to stop. We helpers handed him the vent rods, but it was he who decided where the gases would escape when the metal was poured.

I learned that everything in moulding must be done right the first time. Even jarring a mould or causing a draught could ruin it – as could steam, air or pockets of impurities. Every mould had a life of its own. 'Hain't it a beaut?' Mr Edwards would say. A 'beaut' had a sound, clean, smooth surface. Workers would admire a particularly good casting as if something new had appeared in the world – their faces glowing with a sense of achievement and gladness. A 'sod' was a casting that was warped or distorted; the metal was not sufficiently tensile and had cracked under strain. Some 'sods' had too many blowholes, cracks, lumps and swells to rescue them. Others might be straightened out. There was always a feeling of tension and drama in the air until a good clean casting emerged. If it did, we'd troop off to the lavatory for a smoke, and at night to the boozer for a beer.

I used to love the visits to the Crown and Anchor – there

was always lots of beer, leg-pulling and companionship. Nobody drank like foundry workers. Some of them drank all their earnings. No matter how much we imbibed, we knew it would be sweated out of us the next day: people who work in a steambath don't have any trouble with alcohol. I suppose the prospect of a beer or two at the end of the day helped us to put up with the gruelling work.

Pouring metal was always dangerous, hence the face-guards, the leg-pads, the heavy gloves and the heavy boots. Workers were always tripping over things, scorching their clothing, cooking their feet, or banging themselves on moulds and machinery. Freshly poured metal might look like crusty bread straight out of the oven, but it could roast, scald, blind or cripple in seconds. I never stepped over the golden stream as the moulders did. Put your foot in there and it was gone. It took a 'sand rat' to survive.

Being shut up all day in an inferno, mostly on my feet, often squatting to get relief, was hard going. I survived because I indulged in what Bobbit called 'daydreaming'. I watched what I was doing, but often my mind was elsewhere. Yet I did eventually have the satisfaction of seeing what my sweat had helped to create. Out of the chaos at Bow Bridge came an unending stream of metal products. Some were useful things like pipes and boilers; others were lace-like works of art. All were known for their quality. The work of the Bow Bridge Iron Foundry can be seen to this day on the bridges over the Thames.

---◇---

One day, Syd Bates took me to join the Transport and General Workers' Union. A trade union was the only thing my father had ever joined, so I thought I owed it to him. For somebody who had only his labour to sell, I knew I'd be better off in a union; everybody in dockland knew that.

I went to my first meeting on a Monday night. It was in a ramshackle room in a fusty old building on Bow Road. I told the secretary, who was sitting at a blanket-covered table, that I'd like to join. He shook my hand, told me his name was Albert Eastead and dusted cigarette ash off his suit. Pushing a ledger aside, he helped me to fill out a membership form. I paid my dues. He lit another cigarette, shook my hand again and called me 'brother'. I knew that the first principle of trade unionism was that all men are 'brothers'. 'Tyke a seat,' he said.

Clutching my card, I joined Syd and several others on a bench. There were about twenty of us – two of us from the foundry. I was the youngest.

Mr Eastead called the meeting to order and introduced me. There was a murmur of approval; I felt the searching eyes.

The meeting began and one item after another fell to the secretary's chant: 'Do I have a motion?' 'Proposed.' 'Seconded.' 'So moved.' 'Questions?' 'All those in favour say "aye".' 'To the contrary?' 'Motion carried.' When the members couldn't make up their minds, he would urge, 'Git on, can't stiy 'ere all night.' It bothered me that the 'brothers' were so wishy-washy.

We then heard reports. A bearded man spoke of a meeting he'd been to on unemployment. 'For the fust toim in six years, the number of unemployed is dahn.'

This was greeted by jeering and clapping. 'The figures are cooked. Go and look at the unemployed on the streets!'

Another member had been at a meeting to consider the growing threat of the Black Shirts. 'Oswald Mosley is using the same tactics as fascists in Germany and Italy. 'E wants to persecute Jews and communists, like they do there.'

'What did the meeting decide?'

'Nuffink.'

There was more laughter and clapping. The speaker shuffled uncomfortably and sat down.

A young man sitting next to me jumped up and yelled, 'While you're laughing, the bastard Black Shirts are opening a branch office two streets from here. The way to stop 'm is to go out now and bash 'm. That would teach 'm.' There was a passionate wildness about him that was exhilarating. He was so intense as to be intoxicating.

Everybody sat up.

'Who's coming with me?'

Syd Bates signalled with his eyes for me to keep my head down. An embarrassed silence filled the room, the secretary hid himself behind a veil of smoke. There were no takers.

The youth looked around, 'I'd chuck the lot of you, that I would,' and stormed out.

The discussion continued as if he had never spoken. I didn't know what to think. George Lansbury had said that fascism was being exaggerated. I'd met fascists in Lancashire but they'd been looked upon as a mad fringe. I didn't want to go out and bash fascists, but I did feel that something should be done.

I walked back to my lodgings that night asking myself how on earth Labour could win an election when the workers didn't know what they wanted and couldn't agree. Was socialism going to finish up with nothing but words?

At work the next day I told Syd that the meeting had struck me as dead. He laughed. 'The trouble with you, Woody, is that you think London has been waiting for you to get 'ere. We're in the union because it helps us to get better pay. We're not in it to get a broken 'ead and change things. Forget about a world socialist commonwealth in which all men are "brothers". The communists and the chapel-socialists will never agree among themselves.'

A week later, after my next branch meeting, I talked with the young man who had proposed bashing the fascists. Syd had already told me that he was a communist. He was small and angular with a round, clean-shaven face and a pair of thick-lensed spectacles. He earned his living from a back-breaking job in the rag trade. His name was Peter Levine.

'You didn't get very far last week.'

'I despair of this crowd. They won't do a damned thing.'
I waited for him to go on.

'Anyway, what are you doing here? You're not a Cockney.'

'I'm from the North.'

'Were you in the Labour Party up there?'

'Yes, I did a lot of speaking. I hope one day to represent the party in Parliament.'

'You've got a nerve. You won't get to Parliament from here. Cockneys don't take to outsiders. They're scared you might be another northerner going to do them harm like Ramsay MacDonald. The party will never get on as long as they fight among themselves. Everybody should join together in a popular front. It's our only hope.' When Peter said 'popular front', his eyes flashed.

It didn't take me long to learn that the trade union 'brothers' thought him an extremist who deserved watching. Afraid of communist subversion, the official trade-union line was to keep the communists out.

Chapter IV

Back to School

One day in a crowded underground train I found myself staring at a notice from the London County Council. Stuck between advertisements for Brylcreem and Watney's beer, it looked out of place.

> Do you want a better job?
> Education is the key.
> Join a London County Council night school.
> There is one in your area.

As the train rattled on, the light alternating between the tunnels and the bright sunshine, I wondered if this education business wasn't worth a try. A little of it could hardly do any harm. I didn't want to remain a labourer in the foundry for the rest of my life. Much as I liked Bobbit, I was stuck with a job without any prospects. Grandma Bridget had said that 'larnin'' was the key to all doors. 'The one with the most knowledge has the longest reach,' she used to say. It was ironic coming from her: with all her 'larnin'', she'd finished up in the workhouse.

By the time I reached my destination, my mind was made up. I'd take a look at this night-school business. There was a school only minutes away from the foundry in Denbigh Road, off Bow Road. I'd seen the students coming and going with their books.

The next night after work, I waited my turn before the supervisor of admissions. He gave the impression of having had a long day. I told him I'd seen the poster in the train. Stubbing out his cigarette among a pile of dead stubs, he nodded in a way that told me he had heard it all before.

'What schooling have you had?'

'Elementary.'

He explained what the school offered for people like me. I became so enthusiastic that I wanted to register for everything.

'First do the three R's,' he advised.

He then turned to money matters. He asked about my earnings, about my family and about myself. Retiring into a cloud of smoke, he played with some figures on his blotter. 'Nobody's going to ask you for anything. Books too will be supplied.'

I enrolled there and then; I filled in the forms and was given vouchers for books.

Back on the street, I wondered what on earth I'd got myself into.

———◇———

Three nights later I attended my first English class. Apprehensive, I sat at the back. The teacher was Miss Hesselthwaite, an elf-like, bespectacled spinster. She wore a tightly buttoned grey jacket and skirt, and laced-up black boots.

I fell under Miss Hesselthwaite's spell from the start. She taught me the magic of words. 'The active tense is the stuff of good writing,' she would say in a gentle voice. 'Write clearly, the right words in the right order. Don't use unnecessary words: not "it is my understanding", but "I understand"; avoid vague language like "could, should, might, maybe" – they weaken your message.'

Several nights later, she criticised my first one-page essay as 'unbecoming'. She rewrote it on the blackboard, killing most of its adverbs and adjectives on the way. She corrected me in such a gentle way that I wanted to go to any length to please her. It became a matter of honour.

Henceforth most of my nights were given to 'larnin''. I used to get away from the foundry at about five-thirty, race to The Cut, wash my hands and face, get a quick meal, and go to night school still wearing my overalls.

Miss Hesselthwaite taught me how to use words, and Mr Charlie Duke taught me to enjoy literature. He was a small tweed-wrapped, pipe-smoking fellow. Wet or fine, he would make the journey through the dark streets on foot with his books in a knapsack on his back. Mr Duke regarded the make-belief of fiction as one of the greatest consolations known to the human race. He only recommended classics. To be approved by him a writer had to be long since dead. He knew the works of Sir Walter Scott, Henry Fielding and Charles Dickens by heart. He introduced me to Honoré de Balzac. 'There's a man who makes his characters live,' he said. I liked Balzac; he described people I knew. Mr Duke read so movingly that he carried us off to a different world. Even a whisper from him could fill the room, he could have been playing a flute. It was the sound that moved my heart.

The books he recommended fired my imagination and quickened my pulse. I read them in all sorts of places and at all sorts of times; completely absorbed, I would become involved in the unfolding of the story. I wasn't the only one in the world who had had to struggle and who was down on his luck. I couldn't work out the plots fast enough, and took everything I read as gospel truth. Not that I enjoyed everything. Jonathan Swift's *Tale of a Tub* I thought dull and said so. 'Greater men than you have thought differently,' Mr Duke reproached me. In his light a classic was inviolable.

The third R that the supervisor of admissions had wished on me was arithmetic, taught by Mr Westerman. He was a good teacher and I'm sure knew what he was doing – numbers poured out of him – but his subject never stirred me. I knew all the basics from having been a newspaper boy with George Latham, the newsagent on Revidge Road, Blackburn. He used to say, 'We're businessmen, Billy.' Logarithms, calculus and algebra I thought an abomination. I shall never know why writing and reading possessed me, while arithmetic left me wooden. Anyway, I did my best and did well in exams. But as soon as I could, I dropped arithmetic and gave more time to writing and reading.

I was seventeen when I went back to school. It was the autumn of 1934. At the foundry they thought I was tackling something of little value; the Tinkers thought I'd gone 'batchy'.

Learning aroused my curiosity and imagination. There was wonder in it and adventure – an entirely new way of looking at life had opened up. My desire to learn became so great that I could hardly wait for the next class. I progressed by leaps and bounds because I was doing what I wanted to do. My mind was unworked, fertile soil.

Not everything was plain sailing. I had to do my homework under a poor light in Ben's room with Mrs Wheeler's radio blaring through the wall. I'd been tossed off the corner of the living-room table because I was in the way of the three women. They thought it odd for a healthy young man to be bothering with books. Mr Tinker didn't interfere, he invariably disappeared behind his newspaper and stayed there without saying a word.

At night school I met and was befriended by Alex Hargreaves, a small intense fellow, about my own age. He had brown eyes, slicked hair and the beginnings of a moustache. He was studying finance and accountancy and was contemptuous of my studying literature. We used to share breaks between classes and make our way home together. I thought him very clever.

———◦———

One night when I was returning some books to Miss Hesselthwaite in her back-street lodgings where I often visited her, she suddenly put her knitting down and looked at me as if she was seeing me for the first time. 'You did so well in your exams, have you ever thought of going to a university?'

'Goodness, gracious, no.'

'Well, I hope you will.'

The idea of becoming a scholar could not have been farther from my thoughts. It made me feel slightly giddy. Other than Grandma Bridget all my forebears had been labourers. A mental abyss separated the likes of us from universities. All I knew about Oxford and Cambridge was that they rowed against each other on the Thames.

At the end of the year Dr Cord, the principal, sent for me. Like my sister Brenda before me, I had shone in examinations. He asked me about my subjects, my family, and what I hoped to do with my life. My telling him that I hoped to become a Member of Parliament caught him off balance. 'I'd like to continue my education,' I confessed. When compared to working in a foundry, the idea attracted me; learning had opened up an entirely new world for me.

I went back to my classroom feeling that the principal was a bit flummoxed by the kind of fish he'd caught, but was definitely out to help me.

Prompted by Miss Hesselthwaite, I began to attend a Workers' Educational Association (WEA) evening class in world affairs, held once a week by Reg Sorenson, MP for West Leyton. We met in a little room over a shop in Westminster. He used to come to us straight from Parliament on foot, lay his briefcase aside, take off his hat and overcoat, and plunge in.

It was an unforgettable experience to listen to such an

articulate, stimulating teacher. His jumping from country to country widened my horizons immensely. He described the circumstances in which Lenin, Mussolini and Hitler had come to power; he told us about the Japanese occupation of Manchuria. I had no idea where Manchuria was, but invading it seemed the wrong thing to do. He also spoke of the turmoil in India, Ireland and Palestine. He was convinced that a war between the democracies and the dictatorships was inevitable.

Another night he dealt with the socialist writers Sidney and Beatrice Webb, who had been to Russia and had described conditions there in their book *Soviet Communism, a New Civilization?* I had bought a copy of the book very cheaply at my last trade union meeting. For many of us, the Russian example had become the only hope for the working class. While the structure of capitalist society was breaking down, Russia was forging ahead in trade and industry. At least, that is what they led us to believe.

The Webbs were food and drink to young socialists who couldn't swallow Marx. We were captivated by their simple answers. They painted a glowing picture of the society we ought to build. From them we got our belief in the nationalisation of industry as a panacea. Their *History of Trade Unionism*, which was also distributed through the unions, defined the object and purpose of trade unions as comprising 'nothing less than a reconstruction of society by the elimination from the nation's industries and services of the Capitalist Profitmaker'. The book confirmed what many of us already believed: that private enterprise was a predatory animal that had to be tamed.

I was so worked up about the Russian experiment that I took my turn shouting the Webbs' ideas from a soapbox in front of Poplar town hall.

One Sunday morning I woke up to find that there was no Ben in bed. As far as any of us could reckon, he'd gone off on Saturday night for his beer and eels and had vanished. We started a search for him. My fear was that he'd fallen into the canal.

The truth was almost as bad. When I got home from work on the Monday evening, the coppers were all over the house. All the Tinker family looked grey. Before I could get my dinner, I was bundled into Ben's room where I was questioned by a plain-clothes detective. He wanted to know who I was, where I'd come from, where I worked and what my relations were with Ben. He ended up asking me more questions about myself than about him.

'What has this got to do with Ben Tinker?' I eventually asked.

'Ben Tinker is being held in Pentonville on criminal charges.'

'What charges?'

'Of being in possession of a deadly weapon – a revolver – and of discharging the same at the police with intent to kill. A most serious charge, you will agree.' His eyes searched my face.

I was speechless. Ben . . . firing at the police! There was something wrong.

'That's not the Ben I know. He wouldn't know one end of a revolver from the other. His head doesn't work that way.'

'There was a robbery in Stratford on Saturday night. We arrived to find the accused standing outside the premises holding a gun. He'd been drinking. Shortly before we arrested him, a shot was fired. After he'd sobered up he confessed to everything. "That's me," he said, as I read out the charges. Full of regret, he is. Wonder he wasn't killed. It should be a lesson to you.'

'I still don't think it could have been Ben. It's beyond him to plan a break-in.'

'The evidence against him is overwhelming.'

The detective wrote everything down in a book. He said he would return the next evening for me to sign a statement. He also said that I might be called as a witness for the defence.

His parting shot was, 'I don't suppose you were with Ben Tinker that night, by any chance, were you?' For a moment I felt a chill. There was no telling what Ben had said.

'No,' I answered.

The copper smiled stiffly and left.

A couple of nights later, after I had signed the statement, we learned that the minimum sentence Ben would get would be five years. The Tinkers took it badly. Mr Tinker asked me if I'd go with him to see Ben to cheer him up.

Come Saturday, Mr Tinker and I visited Ben. We had a long wait in a dreary room with peeling walls. We sat on a bench facing people who looked lost and who kept a still tongue about their troubles.

Eventually, with a warder listening, we spoke to Ben through a wire screen. He was glad to see us. He looked well, and was scrubbed clean. I think he was enjoying his turn of fate: it was a rest from stone-breaking. I thought for a moment he was about to say, 'Can't beat it 'ere,' but he didn't. He asked for nothing and made no complaints. We'd been told not to discuss the circumstances of his arrest. I'm sure he didn't realise that he was in deep trouble. We said we would return.

About a month later, on condition that he underwent psychiatric treatment, Ben was discharged. His case didn't go to trial. He would have agreed to everything had they tried him. I suppose the authorities eventually got the measure of the man: given his mental condition, he couldn't have fired and hit a building, let alone a police officer.

Ben went back to his stone-breaking, and his Saturday-night feasts of beer and jellied eels.

Chapter V

From Stratford to Bow

It was the grand finale of a dreadful day at the foundry. I'd started back to the Tinkers late; the traffic was awful; to cap it all, a cloudburst almost washed me away. I eventually reached Ben's room looking like a drowned rat. Nothing else can happen now, I thought, as I parked my bicycle in the corner.

Fate decided otherwise. I bumped into the aspidistra stand, sending Mrs Tinker's hidden jug of beer crashing to the floor. Horrified, I watched a brown tide flow across the oilcloth. I forgot that I was wet through.

Mr Tinker put his head round the door. 'Yours?' he demanded, pointing at the beer, his one eye flashing.

'No, no,' I faltered, trying to mop up.

I heard him ask Mrs Tinker the same question. Their voices rose one above the other. Suddenly, something hit the wall. Battle was on. It was one of the rowdiest fights I'd heard.

The next morning Mrs Tinker burst into my room before I had time to get up. She had a black eye.

'Yer can sling yer 'ook,' she yelled, slamming the door.
Where could I sling my hook to? I worried.

I was still worrying when I went to night school that evening.
Appalled at the prospect of my being thrown into the street,
Alex Hargreaves, my night-school friend, promised to speak
to his stepmother. He was as good as his word. The next evening
he took me to his home in Addington Road, Bow.

I was impressed by the great stone houses, with their
wrought-iron railings and large front steps. Closer up, they
didn't look so good: stonework was cracked, windows were
stuffed with rags and paper, chimney pots were broken. The
scraps of garden at the front were covered with weeds and
littered with junk. Dogs and cats wandered about.

To get into Alex's house we had to squeeze past a great
oak hallstand. 'Must have cost a mint,' I said, admiring the
intricate carving, the mirrors and the china figurines.

'Got it for a song in Petticoat Lane. Look at the worm-
holes. It's been stuck here for years; can't get it any farther.
How's this for more junk?' He threw open two glass-panelled
doors. Sagging chairs and couches, lace-covered tables, worn
rugs, knick-knacks, and large, chipped Persian vases filled
the rooms. 'These are the "best rooms". Used only at Christmas,'
he said, shutting the doors.

At the end of the hall an impressive staircase with a carved
handrail wound its way upward. We went downstairs, our
fingers trailing over the smooth wallpaper, grey with people's
hands. Generations of masters, mistresses and servants had
worn the staircase hollow. Voices and laughter reached us
from below.

In the living room, Mrs Hargreaves greeted me. I recognised her; I'd seen her stocky figure at Bow Labour meetings.
Her cheeks were as pink as a girl's and her grey hair was
pulled back in a bun. Alex's stepfather sat by the fire. One
glance at him told me that he was very sick. 'I'm the fellow
whose train is going out,' he said, shaking my hand.
Everybody talked to him as if he would be returning to his
job as a street sweeper the next day.

I was introduced to Alex's stepbrothers Chris, Denny and Bernie, and his stepsister Carol: they had all been adopted by Ma Hargreaves when they were infants. They were now in their twenties and looked alike. Finally I met the two lodgers, Milton and Dick.

Dominating the room was a picture of a smiling, close-cropped soldier. This was Nick, the Hargreaves' only son, who had perished at Ypres in Flanders in 1916. He looked so full of fun that I expected him to wink at me. Woven into the fabric upon which the picture was mounted were the words: 'The War To End All Wars'.

A large cupboard ran down the length of the outside wall. Above it was one small window that looked up to the weed-filled garden. It was open a crack to allow flies to escape. Someone tapped on the glass and grimaced through the grating.

Avoiding any preliminaries, the Hargreaves offered me a whole bed and full board for the same money I was paying at the Tinkers. 'It won't profit us, but it might 'elp yer,' Mrs Hargreaves said. I couldn't believe my luck.

Tired of sleeping with Ben's feet in my face, I jumped at the offer. I went straight back to The Cut, said goodbye to Mr Tinker, Sarah and Ben, grabbed my few belongings and fled.

'Didn't like the looks of yer from the start,' Mrs Tinker flung after me as I went through the door. Her conduct severely tested my belief that there is a residing virtue in the working class.

On my return to Bow, I was taken in tow by Emily Tracy, the Hargreaves' daughter, a tall, thin woman in her thirties, who showed me round the house. I was to share a bedroom with Milton, Dick and Alex on the top floor, the old servants' quarters, which had been divided into three rooms, all painted a faded green. I stowed my belongings under my bed, which stood in a corner against the sealed window. A black stocking filled with sand on the window ledge kept out the cold. A bed to myself with clean sheets – I'd come up in the world.

Chris, Bernie and Denny occupied the middle bedroom. It had a skylight. Their door stood ajar to let in air. Carol slept in a windowless converted storeroom at the end of the corridor. It was suffocating in there and smelled of stale cheese.

As we walked down Emily pointed out the family bedrooms, which were above the two unused 'best rooms'. There were two indoor toilets.

Halfway down the stairs I was introduced to Emily's husband Clem Tracy, who had just rushed in past the hall-stand. He was small in stature, had bright eyes, and a face that looked like a polished apple. After shaking hands with me, he dashed upstairs.

'Clem is forever in a rush,' Emily sighed. 'He works in the laboratory at Poplar general hospital.' I learned later that he was good at giving injections and would sometimes help his father-in-law out if he got into trouble over the weekend.

I soon settled down to the Hargreaves' routine. After a hurried breakfast of tea with tinned milk, two rashers of bacon, one pale fried egg, tomatoes and as much bread and margarine as we could eat, all of us, except Mr and Mrs Hargreaves and Emily, rushed off to work. We snatched a wrapped bread and cheese sandwich off the hallstand as we went through the door. Cut and prepared by Emily the night before, the sandwiches were stiff and stale by lunchtime.

Except on Saturday and Sunday, the family reassembled at night for the evening meal. We ate what was put in front of us or we went hungry, but the food was so much better than at Mrs Tinker's that I never complained. Dinner done, some would go out for the night, the rest played shove-ha'penny or Wilkie Bards (cards). Most nights Alex and I would do our homework in 'the best room at the back'. Before going to bed, we held post-mortems of the day's dog and horse races. This is where Mr Hargreaves came into his own, gasping out the name and odds of the horse we should follow. We started the day with 'What 'orse are you on?' Emily organised the bets with a bookie who had a pitch on the pavement in Bow Road. I never heard of a copper intervening. Later on, in 1938,

Pa Hargreaves won me a princely sum on an American horse called Battleship.

No one in their right mind ever missed the Hargreaves' Sunday dinner, which was eaten at noon when the men came back from the 'rub-a-dub' (pub). There never was any alcohol in the house: 'The scourge of the poor,' old man Hargreaves used to say with a sigh, though I noticed his moral rhetoric stopped when whisky was about. The meal was a feast of roast beef, several vegetables and, strangely enough, lots of Yorkshire pudding. On Sundays we all sat down clean and washed, the week's grime behind us. Pa Hargreaves always ate alone by the fire. When he'd finished his soup he'd fish in his pocket for his false teeth to eat the beef course. The meal always ended with rice pudding and a cup of tea.

Sunday dinner was much more important than Sunday church, which only Dick attended. Dick was the one who really believed in God. He belonged to a queer sect over in Poplar who thought that all religions were equal. The rest of us were either unrepentant pagans, or God-fearing Christians who didn't go to church. Most of us were comfortable in our disbelief – so comfortable that we never discussed it. Dick's 'You don't ask the question that matters: what is the purpose of life?' didn't interest us.

The Hargreaves household was a happy one. We knew we were happy, which is half the battle. Not that life was all laughter. Occasionally there'd be a crackling of lightning and a crash of thunder. One moment there'd be peace, the next there'd be a roaring fight going on, with everybody leaping to their feet and leaning across the table shouting. With Pa Hargreaves calling, "Arf a mo. 'Arf a mo,' and the dog barking, and Ma Hargreaves yelling, 'What kind of socialists are you?' the battle would rage on.

But, with the exception of Alex, whose nature was unforgiving, verbal blows were soon forgotten. Most of us had come from worse conditions and were glad to have found food, shelter and companionship. We had somewhere to eat and sleep. It was enough for me that I didn't need to go on the dole or into the street to beg. Compared with the Tinkers, life at the Hargreaves' was very good.

Mrs Hargreaves had dedicated her life to helping the poor. It was her sense of commitment that gave her the energy to work endless hours, day after day, as a member of the town council. I was surprised by the activities she could squeeze into a single day. The Juvenile Court and the Public Assistance Committee took most of her time. She also worked with local orphanages and shelters for women. Her idea of Utopia was England with the worst abuses against the poor left out. 'Socialism,' she'd say, 'means no more wars, no more want, no more wickedness.' Homeless children and the condition of the old saddened her most. What she couldn't understand was why a supposedly all-merciful God didn't do something about it. 'Either 'e don't exist, or 'e don't care,' she concluded.

Pacifism was her strongest cause. I don't think she'd ever recovered from losing her son Nick. The tenderness and affection with which she mentioned his name told me that she had lost her greatest love. "E went to France believing that 'e was doin' the right thing. 'E came 'ome on leave, disgusted. 'E said, "The war is the biggest sodding lie, Ma. There can't be a God." I knew when 'e left that 'e wouldn't come back, and 'e didn't.'

The Hargreaves household was a happy one. We knew we were happy, which is half the battle. Not that life was all laughter. Occasionally there'd be a crackling of lightning and

Emily looked after everything and everybody in the house. She even made my bed. She was rarely still except during a game of cards at night. Her brother's death, her father's suffering and her childlessness all weighed heavily upon her – she had a gaunt appearance, which her cropped hair made worse. Gone were the days when she and Clem had danced in the Palais de Dance in Mile End Road. We used to say that Emily was stronger than any man – she had to be.

Fortunately she could always rely upon Clem. He was so able that we always said, 'Leave it to Clem.' He made the decisions for the household and saw them through. He never seemed to relax, even when playing cards, he'd get up and walk about. He would rush home at five, wash, eat and if the weather was fine, potter in the back garden until the light failed. He never looked up when he was out there, and he didn't welcome visitors. His crops of vegetables and flowers were prodigious. Most of them he sold to the hospital.

It took longer for me to become familiar with the four siblings: Chris, Carol, Bernie and Denny. They were small, wiry creatures, with eyes set too far apart. At first I couldn't tell one from the other. Chris, with his protruding Adam's apple, was the oldest. Everybody liked him because he was good-natured and kind. He worked with Clem at the hospital and was the tail on Clem's kite.

Chris's brother Bernie was a combination of rascality and goodness. He was a porter at the hospital and turned everything that happened there into a farce. They tolerated him and his ever-rasping cough because they knew – as I didn't – that he was dying of tuberculosis. His emaciated face and flushed complexion should have alerted me to that. Later, Emily confided to me that Bernie had been married, but that his wife had taken off with a gypsy pedlar. Perhaps Bernie's clowning was meant to conceal his sorrow and his need for love.

The younger brother Denny puzzled us all. He kept to himself. Strangely enough, he was the only one who had a regular 'Judy' (girlfriend).

Carol was brittle and had no time for the lodgers – Milton, Dick and me.

Thanks to Ma Hargreaves' political influence, and the victory of Labour in the local elections, Clem and all five adopted children had jobs in local government. Nobody threw a fit of conscience about it.

◇

During the week we were in bed by ten-thirty. Ma Hargreaves, Clem and Emily were the last to retire, bringing Pa Hargreaves with them. Milton, Dick, Alex and I usually ended the day yarning and smoking upstairs. There was always something to laugh about before going to sleep. The football rivalry of Tottenham, West Ham and the Arsenal was our standby. Because of the shortage of space, we stuffed our clothing between the bed and the wall. Occasionally, garments slipped on to the floor and were dragged around the house by Emily's dog.

Sometimes before going to sleep, I would sit up in bed and stare at the lighted windows below. I used to wonder what was going on under all those glistening roofs. With a mist, the scene could be magical. Occasionally, a storm crashed down – flashes of lightning lit up the sky; gale-strength winds rushed past the house shaking it fiercely.

Dick's bed was next to mine. He was a tall, powerfully built, fair-haired youth with a face that could have been carved out of stone. Scars ran down his back. His right arm was tattooed with a snake. He had the largest hands, which he was forever opening and closing to make a fist. Energy came off him in sparks; everything about him was wild and passionate. His piercing blue eyes could flash with anger. We all feared his temper. 'I wouldn't start anything wiv 'im, if I was you,' cautioned Emily. Sometimes I'd see his long knife lying on his bed.

In his late teens Dick had arrived at the London docks from Pitcairn Island. His only possession was a locked tin box that he kept under his bed. I didn't know that Pitcairn existed until I met him. In a strange English he would sometimes talk to us at night about his birthplace: about the wind, the cliffs and the crashing surf, and about sunsets more beautiful than any of us had ever seen. I think it helped him to cover up his self-consciousness and his innate nervousness.

'London's a dark hole,' he once said, 'full of mouldy mist. Everything is swallowed up by buildings, smoke and fog. Everybody's a stranger.' Sometimes I thought of him as a great fish that had become stranded on the mud banks of the Thames. The astonishing thing was that he couldn't swim.

He told us there were no beaches at Pitcairn, only cliffs hovering above a heaving, pitiless sea.

One night I asked him why he had left.

'Simply happened. I wanted to know what was beyond.'

Because of him, we knew all about the mutiny on the *Bounty*, and Captain William Bligh long before we saw the film. Fletcher Christian was one of his forebears.

Dick intended to make his fortune, sail back to Pitcairn, find a wife and raise a family there. How his dream could be fulfilled on a starvation wage as a knock-about on the docks was beyond us. Yet it almost came true.

Every Tuesday night several of us would go over to the Hackney Wick Greyhound Racing Track and place a bet or two on the dogs. The place was always packed. Coarse-looking men stood about handling thick bundles of pound notes. You wondered where all the money came from. It was enough to turn your head.

I had so much on in those days – night school, union meetings and homework – that I rarely had time for the races. When I did go I loved everything about it: the vast arena, the banks of faces, the restless crowd, the pageantry and the races themselves.

Noses pressed against the wire, the dogs scrabbled and whined until the hare flashed by and the gate of the traps flew up. There followed thirty seconds of bedlam while the dogs raced round the track, leaping the hurdles, neck to neck. The yelling and shouting only stopped when the hare had gone to ground and one of the dogs was declared the winner.

One night Dick struck it rich. We watched in awe as he recklessly threw back into the next race every penny he had won. He dashed about like someone possessed; there was no stopping him. We brought him home that night in triumph with thousands of pounds in his pockets. When he piled his winnings on to the table, everything in the house stopped. Pa Hargreaves even stopped gasping for breath. Ma Hargreaves just stood there, hand over mouth. Only Clem, who worked for the bookies, had ever seen so much money. What comfort it gave us to run our fingers through the piles of one, five and twenty pound notes. The wonder is we didn't pinch some of them.

'Dick,' gasped Pa Hargreaves, raising his shaking hands, 'you must never go near the track again.' There were tears in his eyes. 'You can go 'ome to Pitcairn now. Your luck is in, boy; you're a free man. Find a ship and go.'

Everybody agreed, but Dick had other plans. He'd tasted blood and was not to be put off. Against our pleading, he went back the next racing night with a shoebox full of money under his arm. 'He's dotty,' Pa Hargreaves despaired.

Dick came home that night richer than ever. We couldn't believe our eyes. Like a madman, he shovelled the pile of bank notes from one end of the table to the other, shrieking. He'd had a few drinks, and his speech had become incomprehensible. His face glistened with sweat, his distended nostrils twitched with excitement. Between hiccups, he shouted that he loved us all and embraced us one after the other. He even danced with the dog. Each time he calmed down, he counted his money again, placing it in stacks. This time Pa Hargreaves said nothing. Instead, he held out his steel-rimmed spectacles and rubbed them closely. The following day Dick bought himself some coloured silk shirts and a pair of the wildest red velvet corduroy trousers. We roared with laughter when he put them on.

The next racing night, except for the Hargreaves, Emily and Milton, who opposed betting, we were all at the track. For one night I skipped night school. Even Clem joined in. If Dick could make a fortune, so could we – all we had to do was to follow him. We were too poor not to want to take advantage of his miracle.

Alas! On the third night Dick lost heavily. So did we. 'I hope you're not angry with me,' he said as we came home.

After that, he went back night after night, determined to renew his lucky streak. Three weeks later he was broke, self-tormented and self-destroyed. Shorn of money and pride, he walked out with his tin box on his shoulder and was never seen again. 'God 'elp 'im,' muttered Pa Hargreaves. We could only think that he had slipped back into the shadows of the docks from which he had come. It was odd how much we missed him. To cheer us up, Emily used to say that anybody as handsome as Dick would be sure to find a nice, rich widow. But we didn't believe her. Often in the bedroom, especially on a starlit night, we'd talk about Dick and wonder if he'd found his ship. It was curious that the only one in the house who believed in God should have been deserted by Him.

———

Milton, a quiet courteous middle-aged bachelor, was as steady as Dick was wild. His steadiness was reflected in his round boyish face, wise eyes, and the perfect proportion of his brow, nose, cheeks and chin. His sleek brown hair was still unmarked by grey. He was the best-groomed among us: without fail, he shaved every day. He didn't drink, smoke or swear; he never got worked up. Heavy showers and dirty pea-soup fogs seemed to wait until he was safely indoors. Where he'd come from nobody knew. If they asked, he looked at them with a slow, watchful stare. He took no part in family rows and refused to discuss politics or religion. I think there was great kindness in him, but he didn't like Emily's cocker spaniel and he avoided women. He reined us in if the sex talk became offensive at night. He always struck us as a bit squeamish, the one way to turn his stomach was to squash a bug on the wall in front of him.

Furled umbrella in hand, Milton left the house at precisely the same time every weekday dressed like a banker. ''Ere comes a swell,' we used to say. 'He's probably just a button-hole maker,' said Clem. We never found out. With a neatly folded newspaper under his arm, Milton returned at exactly the same time every night. On approaching the front door he would take his watch out of his waistcoat pocket. 'Always-on-time-Milton' we called him. We set our watches by him.

One night in the bedroom, Alex started needling him for

being an 'old maid' and to our astonishment Milton exploded. For half an hour words poured out of him. He revealed that he had once lived a licentious life soaking up the drink. His family had cut him off. He'd lost his job and become a drifter. Half mad, he had been committed to an asylum. After a year, he emerged a different man – one who would fear alcohol for the rest of his life.

We never teased Milton again. Behind that façade of calm was an extraordinary vulnerability. For the first time we understood the meaning of the words chiselled into a piece of wood above his bed:

> With midnight always in one's heart,
> And twilight in one's cell,
> We turn the crank, we tear the rope,
> Each in his separate hell.

Later in life whenever I was close to going over the edge, it was the memory of Milton that pulled me back. I could not forget his warning: 'Don't take to drink.'

"E was lucky, 'e was,' Emily said. 'But 'e's afraid of falling back into the pit from which 'e's crawled.'

The fourth person in our bedroom was Alex. He was kind to me, but difficult to live with. He had been abandoned as an infant on a bench in Bow. Instead of being grateful to Ma Hargreaves for adopting him, Alex held it against her that he should have been cast with the poor.

They were daggers drawn over socialism. 'You and your like are a no-good rabble with too much power,' I heard him say to her one day. 'You're ruining Britain. You're handing out money to people who've already made up their minds to be helpless and destitute. All they want is to sit on their backsides.'

She was too simple and kind to handle him. "E'll be the death of me,' she'd say.

'Couldn't whimper when we took 'im in,' the old man grieved. 'Now 'e's breakin' our 'earts.'

Clem would have thrown him out but for Emily, who forgave Alex all his faults. They'd grown up together and her affection for him was unconditional.

Highly intelligent and motivated, Alex set himself to capture what he thought was his proper place in society. Money was central to his plans and he proceeded to acquire it. At night school he studied accountancy. 'It's where the numbers are,' he'd say. 'Numbers is money.'

Alex clung to his cherished gentility. Every Saturday and Sunday morning, weather permitting, he headed for the West End, armed with a cricket bat or a tennis racket. After playing tennis or cricket with the nobs he presumably had his weekly bath there.

Milton, Dick and I used the public baths on Roman Road. Apart from the occasional bather who spat on the floor, the baths were fairly clean. They were hosed down before you stepped in. There was unlimited hot water and no restriction on time. Thanks to the Labour government, they were cheap (threepence for a bath; sixpence with soap and towel). We carried on a shouting match from cubicle to cubicle. To lie back in hot water and bawl and laugh was exhilarating.

Carol gave us the shakes one night when she walked in with strangely shining eyes and announced that she was going to get married. She must have been wanting to tell us for days for it all came out in a rush. For a moment we were struck dumb. We'd never heard of Mike, the would-be groom. The next day Ma Hargreaves showed us a letter from a nurse telling us that Mike was in hospital dying of cancer. The young fellow was too ill to reach the altar. Carol was not put off by what anybody said. She intended to marry her bloke.

Except for Pa Hargreaves, we all went to the town hall to witness the marriage. Nobody dressed up, not even the bride. We hadn't met Mike and we didn't like what we saw. He was on his last legs: he had a sunken face, his clothing hung on him like a scarecrow and he talked as if he'd just run up a long flight of stairs. He'd given up his job as a mug-faker (photographer) months before. It bothered us that Mike didn't seem to have anybody there from his side. The tenderness Carol showed him was more like a mother's than a bride's.

The happy couple spent two days at Southend on their honeymoon, after which they took up residence in Carol's storeroom on the top floor. I thought they might have set up home in one of the 'best rooms', but they didn't. I used to wonder whether there wasn't something sinister about those rooms.

A week later Mike collapsed. Whenever he tried to get out of bed he fell over. For two months Carol excelled herself as wife, nurse and cook. She ran up and down the stairs as if they didn't exist. She gave all her time to him. What little savings she had, she spent on buying the best food, nobody could convince her that love and diet alone do not a cure make. She flew off the handle when Mum suggested that all the money she was spending wouldn't help. She never lost the stubborn will to go on.

'I can get 'im back into 'ospital,' Ma Hargreaves suggested. 'That's something I can do.'

But Carol wouldn't budge. If Mike was going to die, he was going to die in her care at home. She was so defiant that we thought it best to keep out of her way. 'Let 'er be,' said Mum, weeping.

We did what we could to cheer Mike up. Not that it was easy. It pained him to talk and his coughing fits left him breathless. His brow and dishevelled hair were always drenched with sweat. His face darkened, his eyes dimmed; he seemed all skull. Although Carol kept cleaning him up, there was always dried foam on his lips and flecks of blood on his chin. His bedside table was a mess of medicine bottles, cotton wool, slop basins and crumpled towels. As his agony grew, he became difficult to handle and much more demanding. It was easier on all of us when his mouth fell open and his voice became a feverish whisper. Eventually he became too sick for us to visit.

In time, his wheezy breathing could be heard throughout the top floor: it sounded like a cow in labour. It was astonishing that a dying person could make such a din. We had to shut our bedroom doors and put up with the fog to get a night's sleep.

Early one morning I woke and listened for the bellowing. There was none. Other than the gritty scraping of somebody's feet passing down the corridor, everything was quiet. Carol, a bride of two months, was a widow.

Mike's death taught me something about the special circumstances in which two people will come together and pledge their troth. Carol lost, but not before she had given us an example of self-sacrifice, faith, hope and charity. Mike was the only person who ever gave her life meaning.

For a couple of days Mike's coffin stood in the 'best room at the front'. Except for those of us in the house, nobody came to see him. When I tiptoed in to say goodbye, Carol was sitting by his head in silence. The room was as still as the grave. Mike lay there, his face a frozen mask. His cheek and chin bones stuck out; his ears seemed uncommonly large; his hair was flat and lifeless; his hands, folded across his front, bore little flesh.

Later, we all went out and had him buried. It was a miserable funeral in wind and rain, not July weather at all. We walked in pairs behind the black-plumed, horse-drawn hearse, Mum and Carol leading. Each blast of wind threatened to tear our umbrellas out of our grasp. Several ragged-looking pallbearers followed. Here and there a passerby nodded or raised his cap, or made the sign of the cross. Some thought we were burying old man Hargreaves. 'No,' we called, 'not 'im.'

We were met at the cemetery by a pair of gravediggers wrapped in wet sacking and a priest soaked by the slanting rain. The mound of wet earth gave off a mouldy smell. In the distance rooks sat on gravestones, watching. The bottom of the grave was full of water, its surface peppered with rain-drops. It seemed wrong to bury anybody in a puddle; and in such a polished, expensive coffin, too. The only thing right about Mike was that he had been insured.

Ignoring the wind and the pouring rain, the priest spoke of death as 'coming to us all'. He talked about the 'last trump and the resurrection and the life. Out of death comes life.'

His remarks were lost on me. All the resurrection and trump business made no sense: Mike was dead, none of us thought we'd ever see him again. Yet there had to be more to life and death than a rain-soaked cemetery.

The coffin was lowered into the water with a splash. On the lid was a bunch of anemones, which Carol had put there. We all took a lump of wet earth and threw it in. Bent double, the gravediggers did the rest. The wind shook the evergreens and wet us still more.

As I left the graveyard, I decided that death and funerals were not for me. I felt there was something awful about Mike lying in the wet earth.

After the funeral, Carol sat among us mute and expres-sionless. She was insensitive to what was going on, recog-nising no one, scarcely seeming to breathe. Sad lines etched the corners of her mouth. Everything about her – from her dress to her unkempt hair – suggested that she was about to go to pieces. It took time before Mum got her to eat prop-erly. 'You won't do Mike any good by dying.'

It was just as well that the Hargreaves took their summer holiday a week after the funeral. It wasn't much of a holiday – three weeks in the fields of Kent picking hops – but it took them from a sad house. They'd picked hops during August and September for as long as they could remember. Lodgers and neighbours who could get away also went; Clem arrived with a hired lorry into which they all climbed.

Ma Hargreaves' brother Len, his crushed mopstick wife Sheila and their daughter Miranda, came along too. Miranda was a big-breasted, brown-eyed beauty with a mane of shin-ing chestnut hair done up in a thick, smooth braid. It was the first time I'd seen her and I was struck by her beauty. Her red lips were full and sensual. She was wearing blue overalls and a nebbed cap with artificial daisies around it. I learned later that her real name was Daisy. She'd seen the name Miranda in a magazine and had liked it, and kept it.

Miranda's father Len was a scarlet-faced fellow and an outstanding drinker. Perhaps that's why he liked to pick hops. He was fat to the point of being interesting. Long, sickly faced Sheila, who loved to tell you her troubles, was always worrying that Len would drop dead in the house and that they would not be able to get his coffin out. I watched as they levered him aboard the lorry.

Pa Hargreaves went along too. Nobody thought it odd that they should take a rattling skeleton with them. 'If 'e 'as to die, 'e might as well die in t' fresh air,' Ma Hargreaves said. Bleary-eyed, crumpled cap on his head, he sat in the back on a collapsible chair covered with a blanket. He preferred the lorry, where he was surrounded by relatives and friends, to going by train or bus. Everybody cheered when the lorry started. I waved to them until they were out of sight.

Several weekends later I took a special bus from Poplar town hall directly to the hop fields. I arrived at night. A light smoke hung above the fields. The paraffin lamps and the campfires made it look like an army bivouacked in the bush.

Moving among the scattered huts, I found the Hargreaves family eating hot beans and pork around a rough table. Pa Hargreaves was propped up in a deck chair. They greeted me warmly and gave me a plate of food. After cleaning up, we played cards. From across the field we heard people calling and the sound of an accordion. The moon hovered among the clouds.

The next morning I went hopping. It was like entering an impenetrable jungle. The plants were entwined around wires supported by tall poles. We moved through the maze pulling down the bines and picking the silky, sticky, yellow-green hops as we went. We were paid by the bushel. Most pickers earned ten to twelve pounds each for three weeks' work –

sunup to sundown. From our wicker baskets the hops were poured into large sacks, which were carted away to the cone-shaped oasthouses where they were spread out to dry. Later they would be pressed and sent to the brewery. The picked field was like something the locusts had left behind.

The job was relatively easy, and we talked and sang as we went:

> Where have you been all day,
> Henry, my son,
> Where have you been all day,
> My beloved one?
> In the fields of nature, in the fields of nature.
> Make my bed, I've a pain in my head,
> And I want to lie down.

That night Miranda and I wandered off from the camp-fire into a hop field. It was full moon and the smell of the hops was heavy. We'd hardly sat down when Chris tapped me on the shoulder, 'Ma wants you to play Wilkie Bards with the rest,' he said darkly. Had a dragon appeared at that moment and devoured him, Miranda and I would have cheered.

I was sorry when my weekend was over and I had to take the bus back to Poplar.

The Hargreaves returned after three weeks with rosy cheeks, freckled noses and sunburned hands. The fresh air and sun had done wonders for them, especially for Pa Hargreaves. He came home full of beans.

————◊————

Several months after Mike's death, Denny was cast off by his girlfriend Bonnie, who went off and married a brawling drunkard. Denny and Bonnie had had an on-off relationship for some time and we all thought him much better off without her. But that was not how he saw it. He became extremely nervous, flaring up over trifles and finding fault with everybody. He was forever telling us that one day he'd get away from us all. Without us knowing it, he must have been fighting a dark fate.

One night Clem came rushing into the house, passed the hallstand, and went slap-bang into Denny's legs swinging in front of the glass-panelled doors of one of the 'best rooms'. Wearing his Sunday suit, Denny was hanging from a rope tied to the balustrade at the top of the attic stairs. He was quite dead when Clem cut him down. His body had been removed by the time I got home. Several heavy-coated policemen were there. It sent a chill down my back when I stumbled into the darkened house and was told the news.

Nobody ate that night. We spoke in whispers. Old man Hargreaves kept blowing out his cheeks; Ma Hargreaves sighed and dried her eyes with the corner of her dress; Chris, Bernie and Carol wept for their brother. Dry-eyed at Mike's funeral, Carol cried her eyes out for Denny. Strange people came and went. We knew Denny had had woman trouble, but it had never occurred to any of us that he would kill himself. Chris told us that the night before Denny died he had rushed into the bedroom as if he intended to say something, but had left without saying a word. He left neither note nor money.

We all had to pitch in to bury Denny, whether we liked it or not. Without insurance – suicides don't get insurance money – we could only afford the bare bones. Chris and I were in charge of the finances and we had a lot of trouble making ends meet. I don't know what we'd have done had someone not put us on to a cut-rate funeral parlour in Poplar. It was a mean little place with two flashing signs in the window: 'The Complete Inexpensive Funeral Service' flashed one. 'The Dignified Death', flashed the other. In the circumstances, the gravediggers also promised us a discount. Because it would have cost us too much to pretty him up, the coffin lid was kept on.

For a day or two Denny lay in the 'best room at the front',

candles and all. The black trestles on which the coffin rested had been included in the price.

We buried him in a corner at the end of the cemetery in unconsecrated ground. He was on his own next to the gravediggers' hut and the empty flowerpots, only a thick hawthorn hedge prevented him from slipping into the canal. It was a beautiful spring day with the sun warming the land and the sparrows chattering. A gentle breeze ruffled the trees.

A black-veiled stranger joined us at the graveside. It was Bonnie. 'We made the rope and he used it,' she sobbed to a shocked Ma Hargreaves. Carol covered her face and wept.

The preacher didn't do as well for Denny as he had done for Mike. He dwelt on the need for God's mercy and eternal rest. 'There is no such thing as death,' he ended. Well, Denny looked dead to me.

I joined Clem in his garden that evening. We sat silently on the bench together. I'd never known him to sit still for so long. He was like a pricked balloon. Although it takes a lot to surprise a Cockney, Denny's death had taken the wind out of him.

Emily always held a grudge against Denny for having hanged himself in her house: 'Right there against our front door. For Gawd's sake, why couldn't 'e 'ave 'ung 'imself at Bonnie's? 'Umiliating, that's what it is.'

—◦—

The memory of Denny hung about the house for a long time, saddening us all. Only gradually did we get back to our normal routine. One morning about dawn I heard the phone ring. Emily answered. 'Yes Ruth . . . no Ruth . . .' There was a muffled conversation, after which Emily dressed quickly and dashed out of the house on 'an errand'. She returned shortly afterwards with a large parcel. There was more telephoning. Close-mouthed neighbours and friends arrived during breakfast and were closeted with Emily. A little shame-faced, with bundles under their coats, they left the house as quickly as they'd arrived.

Later, one of Emily's secret packages provided me with a new suit, which was altered the same day by a Jewish tailor in the next street. From Ruth came shirts, underwear, ties, socks and Sunday shoes – all at giveaway prices, pennies instead of shillings, shillings instead of pounds. For the first time in my life I wore a silk singlet and silk underpants. I felt a different man.

Everybody was casual about the arrangement, least said, soonest mended. I raised the matter with Miranda. 'Stolen,' she said. 'Pinched at night and sold to lucky devils like us before sunup.'

'Does Ma Hargreaves know they're knocked off?'

'Don't be silly,' she tittered. 'Next thing you'll be telling me you don't want the bleedin' stuff. You get the lolly while someone else gets nicked for it. What more do you want?'

Who Ruth was and where she lived I never found out.

If Ma Hargreaves supported these shady deals, she didn't do it for money. When I came to know her better, I realised that she was a kind of Robin Hood. Her ethic was to help the poor, even if it meant stretching the rules. With a religious passion she believed that life was a wrong that had to be put right: 'It's no sin to steal, if it's not for yourself or from your own.' Her concern was suffering, not sin. 'We was poor,' she'd say, 'but we was 'onest.'

Chapter VI

Finding My Way

I used to accompany Ma Hargreaves to the meetings of the
Labour Party in Bow. One night she introduced me to
George Lansbury, whom I had admired for years.

"'E's a Lancashire weaver's son,' she said, "'oo thinks 'e
knows 'ow to run the country.'

Lansbury greeted me as if I was someone important. I felt
his great warmth. He was a tall, heavy old gentleman with
a broad brow and a fine head of white hair, some of which
straggled down the sides of his face. His blue-grey luminous
eyes were smiling. He looked at peace with himself. His
double-breasted, blue-serge suit was buttoned up. His bowler
hat and his clipped white moustache conveyed a sense of
being in charge.

I knew he was one of Britain's leading pacifists. In World
War I he had refused to carry arms. When visiting Russia in
1920 he had disagreed with Lenin over the use of force. He
opposed rearmament. The basis of his teaching was love. It
is not surprising that he should have risen when he did;

poverty, anti-feminism, militarism, imperialism and colonialism – all of which he fought – were rampant at the time of his rise. War was his greatest fear. Chapel-reared, he had a passionate religious conviction that the application of Christian principles would save the working class and the world. He challenged my disbelief in a Christian solution. I was captivated by him.

Lansbury was not the only one who feared another capitalist war. One Saturday morning at the beginning of 1935, my trade-union friend Peter Levine told me about an anti-war film that was to be shown in a Poplar cinema. He told me to keep the meeting to myself and to arrive without attracting attention.

I wandered into the crowded cinema at the given time. Peter was already there; we sat together. The lights went out; the hubbub ceased. After several minutes, the film had made its point: we were there to learn how to bring the government down in case of war. We were shown how to disrupt communications and bring munitions factories, electricity, gas and water works, docks and railways to a standstill. Given the will, one could wreak havoc with wire-cutters and a spanner. The film also told us how to infiltrate the military to prevent them firing on the workers. Finally, it showed how to organise a general stay-in strike. The idea of overthrowing the British government stunned me. This was 'incitement to disaffection', for which you could go to jail.

No one at the meeting took responsibility for the film. When it was over we dribbled out in ones and twos as unceremoniously as we had dribbled in, with an eye open for the coppers.

Sedition was heady stuff to Peter. He said the film had been made in Moscow, from where we got all our Russian propaganda. Glossy magazines showing how good things were for the masses in the Soviet Union had persuaded Harold Watkins and me to volunteer to go to Russia as weavers years before.

Throughout the 1930s, the challenge of fascism in the East End grew. Against Labour's pacifism, the fascists preached the cult of the warrior; against Labour's divisions they demanded unity and absolute obedience to their leader, Oswald Mosley; in place of Labour's vacillations, they promised decision and authority. The Black Shirts made no threat to private property or capitalism. In 1931 Mosley had resigned from the Labour Party. He abandoned socialism and international brotherhood for a policy of 'Britain first'.

With their bands and flags, the fascists began to parade in the East End, where half the Jewish population of Britain lived:

> Onward Black Shirts! Form your legions,
> Keep the flag for ever high.
> For a free and greater Britain
> Stand we fast to fight or die!

The Cockney response was:

> Hitler and Mosley, what are they for?
> Thuggery, buggery, hunger and war!
> Two, three, four, five,
> We want Mosley, dead or alive.

The deteriorating economic situation and the growing flood of German Jewish refugees into Britain gave the fascists a rallying point. They claimed that Britain was being overrun by the Jews. By 1934 all grievances were being blamed on them. In Stepney, Shoreditch, Hackney, Poplar, Bow and Bethnal Green the Jews became alarmed, especially after hooligans smashed Jewish shop windows in Mile End Road. They feared that they were about to be subjected to the same brutal treatment as Jews in Germany.

'Stay away from the fascist meetings,' Ma Hargreaves warned me, 'you are only providing them with publicity.' The official trade union and Labour Party policy was to ignore them. This was asking too much of young people like Levine and me; we couldn't fight fascism by pretending it didn't exist.

Out of curiosity Peter and I, and a crowd of 15,000 others, went to the fascist rally at Olympia Hall, White City, in June 1934. Slogans about the meeting had been going up in the East End for weeks. Along with hundreds of opponents we managed to get into the hall with forged tickets. Outside thousands of shouting and booing anti-fascist demonstrators fought with foot- and mounted-police. As we entered the brightly lit hall, I looked back on the surging crowd with its banners and flags. Snatches of the Internationale and the Red Flag could be heard. The air was full of passion and uproar.

Inside the hall, columns of black-shirted men and women stood guard. One felt the suspense and the air of expectancy.

We had been there about twenty minutes when there was a general stir. Orders rang out; the spotlights were swung to the entrance, where flag-waving supporters were greeting Oswald Mosley. He looked insolent and self-assured. His dress reminded me of the Italian fascists and German Nazis I had seen in newsreels. He made his way to the platform, which was ringed by Union Jacks and fascist flags. I had to concede that he was one of the most striking figures I had seen on any platform.

He had hardly begun when the loudspeaker wires were cut. The cry 'Down with Mosley!' was taken up in different parts of the hall. The searchlights swung to the fights between demonstrators and stewards. Some people made for the doors. Until the last protester was thrown out the atmosphere was chaotic.

The wires repaired, Mosley began again. Striding up and down, he called for a renewal of British life. It was a Hitler-like performance: the angry glances, the contemptuous stare, the pointing, stabbing finger. He'd spoken for about ten minutes when another uproar broke out. The speaker stood silent while the second batch of protesters was ejected. On and off, the disturbances continued for the best part of two hours.

Suddenly Peter jumped up and began howling at Mosley. Before I could pull him down he was seized, punched, kicked and carried out. I picked up his spectacles off the floor. When I reached him in the corridor, he was still fighting and getting the worst of it. Without his glasses he could hardly see. As I forced my way to his side, I was punched for good measure. Peter had come for a fight; I hadn't, and I resented being knocked about.

I got Peter to a First Aid post to have his cuts and bruises treated. His face was a mess for weeks. He could thank his lucky stars it was not worse. The papers said that truncheons, knuckle-dusters, razors and iron bars had been used. With bruises to show for it, I vowed never to sit next to him at a fascist meeting again. Miranda thought me out of my mind to have gone at all.

In September 1934 I attended another fascist rally in Hyde Park with Harold Watkins, with whom I was always in touch. This was one of the few times we had been able to get together. We never saw Mosley. The police kept the fascists and anti-fascists well apart.

It was wonderful to be with Harold again. He was working in a timber yard at Southall. I expected him to be frustrated with all the setbacks he'd had since coming to London, but he was his old bright self – convinced that everything would work out in time. We were both going to night school now and exchanged news. One way or another we were going to get an education.

———◇———

Peter Levine was my first Jewish friend. He guided me through the maze of East End politics. He showed me how Jews were active throughout the east London trade-union movement and the Labour Party. 'Action is our life,' he said.

I had never lived among Jews before. I sensed a current of

envy and resentment of them among the Cockneys. Because the Jews dressed differently, sometimes spoke a different tongue, and kept themselves to themselves, the Gentiles thought of them as foreigners in a way that was not true of a migrant such as myself. To the Cockneys they were Yids or Jew boys. We were Goys. As long as one side did not try to lord it over the other, Goy and Yid got on well together. Clem Tracy worked for the Jews at the dog track at Hackney. 'They pay well,' he said.

One night after Peter and I returned from a meeting, I was looking at a book in his bedroom, the state of which reflected his habitual untidiness. We would sit until midnight sometimes telling each other how we would change the world. Peter was watching me from the bed where he was lying, hands clasped behind his head. 'Woody, why don't you join the Communist Party?' he suddenly asked. I could tell from his calculating look that his question was premeditated. I knew enough about Peter to realise that if I answered 'Why not,' I'd quickly become a card-carrying member.

Instead I said, 'I'm not a revolutionary. I don't share your apocalyptic vision. Nor am I sure that God is dead.' At heart I was an evangelical and humanitarian pacifist like Lansbury. It was the pacifist streak in me from my mother's side, the Kenyons. 'I don't want to go round bashing people. I don't see why I should go round bashing people if communism is – as you keep telling me – inevitable.'

'You're squeamish,' he answered. 'The working class can only improve its lot through the strike – by violence. Appealing to a sense of justice or humanity, or even long-term capitalist interests, is futile.'

'Employers can be persuaded.'

'Rubbish!' His voice was rising. 'Power is the only thing the bosses take stock of. Do you imagine that things can go on as they are? There has to be revolution. You can't tinker with the system; you have to dig it up by the roots. I don't know who is the more naïve: you with your belief in democratic persuasion, which simply means replacing one group of capitalists with another, or Lansbury with his "Blessed are the poor" business. You both have to learn that those who control the means of production control everything else. We want action, not dreams.'

I didn't answer his tirade.

He did not hold my rejection of his offer against me. On the contrary, he did everything he could to help me in the labour movement. Neither Peter nor anyone else ever asked me again to become a communist.

There was another reason why I didn't take up Peter's offer to join the Communist Party. Only a week before, I had attended a lecture in Poplar town hall given by Father Leo O'Hea. The labour movement had given the meeting its blessing. O'Hea was one of the few priests whose ministry lay with the poor. As an Irishman, he was particularly friendly with the Catholic Irish leaders of the East End. Ma Hargreaves had praised his strength and sincerity.

His topic was 'The Social Problem'. He gave a good talk, saying that neither communism nor fascism was the answer to our problems – Christianity was. Despite the length to which he went to tell us why that was so, I came away unconvinced. Yet he'd said enough to increase my doubts about a communist solution.

Actually, I was struck more by the person than by the speech. He was tall and straight, with a granite-like face heavy with experience. His deep-set grey eyes were sympathetic. His firm mouth and aquiline nose expressed strength. He had a natural manner and a clear, powerful voice. He gave the impression of being good and godly without being remote.

I told Peter I'd been to O'Hea's lecture. 'Do you know him?'

'He's like all Jesuits, dark and sinister; all that incense swinging and candles stuff . . . He sings the same song as Lansbury, only worse.'

Italy's invasion of Abyssinia in 1935 provoked a crisis in the British labour movement. It forced us to ask ourselves what we were going to do about aggression in international relations. It was a moment of truth both for the Labour Party and its leader George Lansbury.

Through the efforts of Albert Eastead, my trade-union secretary, I became a delegate to the Thirty-fifth Annual Conference of the Labour Party held in Brighton between 30 September and 4 October 1935, where policy toward Italy was to be threshed out.

The issue before the conference was whether the Labour Party should support the imposing of sanctions against Italy for its aggression against Abyssinia. As leader, Lansbury was confronted by a dilemma: if he agreed to the use of force against Italy, it would contradict the pacifism he had stood for in the past; if he didn't agree it would undermine the League of Nations and the idea of collective security, which the party endorsed.

Lansbury – still the most loved of all the Labour leaders – began the meeting by admitting that it wasn't logical of him to accept the obligations of the League, while refusing to use force to uphold them. Yet, as a true pacifist, he could not support the League in using force. In the past he had met the problem of his pacifism either by keeping quiet or, as leader during the past four years, doing the best he could for the party as a whole. 'It was inconsistent of me,' he said. 'I have always been inconsistent. Life demands it.'

The assembly may not have agreed with Lansbury, but it was obvious from the applause that the audience admired his honesty and piety.

Ernest Bevin, head of my own Transport and General Workers' Union, spoke next. A skilful, ruthless trade-union leader, Bevin had risen through the ranks and was steeped in the power struggle. Everybody knew that he despised and distrusted Lansbury's misty preaching.

In an irritable tone, Bevin told the audience that they should not be influenced by sentiment or personal attachment to Lansbury, whom he accused of being irresponsible and contradictory. 'Lansbury's attempt to serve two masters – his own conscience and party policy – is dishonest. The labour movement is being betrayed.'

Although there was a confused murmur of protest against Bevin's fierce attack, the audience didn't need persuading that Lansbury was in the wrong. Making no allowance for his age, for the service he had rendered the party, for his recent accident and the death of his wife, Bevin proceeded to destroy him. The conference voted overwhelmingly in favour of sanctions against Italy, and later for armed deterrence to back it up. Lansbury's leadership of the Labour Party was ended. I opposed the use of force over Abyssinia as Lansbury did. But then Lansbury was old and should have known better. I was young and my sense of rightness was typical of the pacifist and anti-militarist stand of many of my generation. I felt wholly right. Time would prove me – and I think Lansbury – wholly wrong.

Several weeks later the Poplar Labour Party gave a party for Lansbury on his retirement. Ma Hargreaves got me an invitation. It was a small affair made up of East Enders and one or two visitors, including Father Leo O'Hea, whom I had heard lecture. Lansbury said a few words. 'I've come home,' he ended, wiping away a tear with the back of his hand. Ma Hargreaves thought the old man was delighted to be out of office. ''E's a saint,' she said. ''E should never have been persuaded to accept the leadership. It was 'is greatest mistake. 'Is stepping down don't make the slightest difference to us. We'll always love 'im.'

She introduced me to O'Hea, who had heard of me through her and Albert Eastead. 'They expect great things of you,' he said. He asked me about my work in the foundry. We spoke about Bevin's criticism. 'The important thing,' he said, 'is that Lansbury's resignation marks a turning point in Labour's attitude towards foreign policy. Bevin was right in insisting on uniformity. In foreign affairs, Labour must speak with one voice.'

Looking at me intently, he asked: 'What are your own plans?'

'I hope one day to become a Labour Member of Parliament.'

He smiled.

'My immediate concern is to get an education. My wildest dream is to go to a university.'

'You'll do what God intends,' he said, as if the matter was settled. 'God will reveal to you what you should do and which way you should go.' Until then I hadn't thought that God was involved. 'Learning,' he went on, 'is of less importance than what you do with it. If you intend to become a leader, you must know how to act. I'll put you in touch with an old friend of mine, Mr Philip Stone, who might help you with advice.'

I thanked him and we said goodbye. Father O'Hea left the meeting, tramping in with his heavy boots. There was a loneliness about the retreating figure.

A week or two later I received a letter from O'Hea's friend Philip Stone. The envelope had Pan Am printed on it and it was crisp and new. My name was typed in capitals; I might have been somebody important. He invited me to dine with him. It was the first written invitation to dinner that I'd ever received.

We met in the City at an expensive restaurant, where I was addressed by the waiter as 'Sir'. I was spiffed up in a new shirt and tie, and a suit that Emily had got from Ruth. I remember it was the day King George V died. The doleful sound of guns could be heard in the distance.

Mr Stone was a middle-aged man with eyes full of laughter. He was an affable host. Just as well that he was, for the amount of cutlery and china on the table made me nervous. I noticed him looking at my hands. He was more astute than I realised. I discovered that he was an executive of the Pan American Airline.

After dinner he offered me a cigarette. He smoked his own

in an elegant cigarette holder. He asked about my work in the foundry.

'Father O'Hea tells me that you have hopes of going to university?'

'I do. The trouble is that my qualifications are not good enough. I've already been rejected by the London School of Economics.'

'Unless you can be excused entrance examinations, you don't stand a chance of getting in.'

'What about the Central Labour College in London?'

'All you will get there is class-war propaganda.'

'What about Oxford?'

'The university proper will not accept you. Your only chance of going there is to be admitted to either Ruskin or the Catholic Workers' College, which is run by Father O'Hea. Both offer a two-year course for working men and women who give promise of becoming leaders. Ruskin was founded by three American admirers of John Ruskin. The Catholic Workers' College was founded by Father Charles Plater.'*

'Are the colleges part of the university?'

'They are and they aren't. Their students cannot graduate in the university. Nor can they wear a gown. In all other respects they are members of the university.'

'I find it baffling.'

'So does everybody else.'

'Does one have to be a Catholic to go to the Catholic Workers' College?'

'The crucial question is: are you the kind of person who will eventually put a university education to good use in the labour movement?'

The next night I wrote to both colleges. I also wrote to Harold Watkins, telling him what I was doing.

*The Catholic Workers' College changed its name to Plater College in 1965.

I had further meetings in the East End with O'Hea. Christmas 1935 came and went. Eventually I had a request from O'Hea to write a ten-page essay on 'Why I joined the Labour Party'. Stone had forewarned me that he used it as an entrance examination.

I wrote the essay in Ma Hargreaves' 'best room at the back'. She encouraged me in every way. 'It's one of the things I regret, never 'aving 'ad an edication.'

'My joining the Labour Party,' I began, 'was an act of protest against the social conditions of my childhood. I have not forgotten the armies of unemployed and the utter demoralisation of my father and those around us as workless month followed workless month. If the Tories are responsible for Britain's decline, as I think they are, then I must fight to replace them with Labour.'

I went on and on, talking glibly about Labour's mission to end exploitation, unemployment, ignorance, and war and want.

Having sweated endlessly over several drafts, and chewed several pencils in the process, I went up to Bow Road and posted the essay before I changed it all again.

The next night I visited Miss Hesselthwaite. She knew nothing about Ruskin or the Catholic Workers' College. 'Get to Oxford, no matter what,' she said. 'There's no telling what might happen to you there.'

After Miss Hesselthwaite I talked to Reg Sorenson, my WEA teacher. 'Go and be educated,' he said. 'The labour movement needs men like you.' He undertook to write testimonials for me and advised me to accept whichever college offered me a place.

He thought I'd be wise to get the help of Harry Graves, an East End politician. I already knew him as a leader in Labour circles and I'd been to his house several times. He was a bachelor. I called him and arranged to meet him at home the following Thursday at seven in the evening.

When I got there nobody answered my knocking. Finding the door unlocked I wandered in, and continued to wander until I came upon two naked figures on a couch. It was too late to turn away, nor would my feet respond. Rigid with fright, I was frozen to the spot. The lovers couldn't believe their eyes when they saw me. We just stared at each other – bewildered. I wondered why they hadn't locked the door. That was the end of any help I would get from Harry Graves, I thought. Wrapping a towel around himself, he prodded me to the door. He had forgotten all about my appointment.

I didn't dare tell the Hargreaves. A thing like that would have been blabbed all over the East End in a day.

When I met him a few days later, neither of us mentioned our last meeting. It might never have happened. He willingly wrote a testimonial for me; he helped me ever after. I was beginning to discover that life is very strange.

Finally I had a long talk with Peter Levine. 'You're crazy to think of going to Oxford, Woody,' he said. 'Oxford is for the nobs. They know nothing about the class struggle. The only worthwhile education is one governed by Marxist ideas. For that you have to go to the Central Labour College.'

———o———

Some time before I dined with Stone, I had seen a notice of a vacancy for a job as an administrative assistant with the Thames and Lea Conservancy Board. The job attracted me. I knew the rivers; I lived within a stone's throw of the Lea, and I liked the idea of working out of doors. Compared with the foundry, the terms of the appointment were regal. I told Bobbit that I was applying for it. 'It's the gint's job that I've been looking for all my life,' he laughed. With nothing to lose, I sent in my application and forgot all about it. Weeks later, to my surprise, I was called to the head office of the Board at Brettenham House, Lancaster Place, the Strand.

Wearing my best clothes and speaking my best English, I arrived on the day, at the time stated. There were two other shortlisted candidates. We took a written test in the sunlit boardroom at the top of the building, sitting on red leather chairs. Everything about the room, including the long, polished oak table with its pewter inkpots, was tasteful. Except for the rumble of traffic on the Embankment below, all was quiet and orderly. I looked out across the Thames, above the treetops and Cleopatra's Needle to the south bank of the river and thought what luck some people had to be able to work in a place like this.

Although I had trouble with the arithmetic, I was saved by the one-page essay on the Thames. I'd read an article on the Thames in the train that very morning. When the examination was finished the other candidates and I sat about and waited.

Eventually the door opened and I was called before the board's second-in-command, Mr Charles Ives. He interviewed me, and then the other two candidates. I waited. After an hour or so Ives came back for me. He spoke encouragingly and took me to the chairman's office. Sir William Desborough, a benign, white-haired gentleman, wasted no time on me. It was obvious that Ives was making the appointment anyway, and that I was his choice. 'Are you one of the Woodruffs who operate the wharf at Wapping?' was Sir William's last question. A fine pickle, I thought. If he is a friend of the Woodruffs of Wapping, I'm in; if he hates them, I'm out. 'No,' I answered, 'no connection whatever.' 'Thank goodness,' he said, dismissing me. Perhaps because I knew Oxford was in the offing and I was relaxed, I got the job.

I returned to Bobbit and told him of my success. 'I knew you'd come good,' he grinned, wringing my hand. 'Fust ryte.' That night, with much beer and many toasts, I celebrated my success in the pub.

<><

Before leaving the foundry a week later, Miranda and I went on the works' beano to Southend. We joined the foundry men and their families on the embankment near Westminster Bridge, with Big Ben tolling nine o'clock and the traffic eddying and swirling about us. Everybody was dressed to kill.

Miranda was wearing a chic leather beret and an expensive black leather coat that had 'pinched' stamped all over it. We were in high spirits and up to every kind of trick. It's amazing what a day off will do to folks. These were different people – there was no cursing, everybody smiled and showed off their children.

We boarded the steamer at Westminster Pier, larking and joking as if we were going to America. We cheered when the steamer hooted and cast off. We joined a great concourse of vessels making their way to the sea. We passed under Tower Bridge and all the other bridges on our way to Wapping and Limehouse. Some of the workers waved to relatives on shore. Beyond the Isle of Dogs we steamed past moored ships from the ends of the earth. All around us were cliffs of warehouses, power stations, gas works and refineries and factory chimneys; everybody on shore was scurrying about trying to make a living. It gave us a feeling of superiority to stand back and watch other people work. We were breaking loose.

After leaving the city and the crowds behind we floated on a quieter stretch of river, past ancient wharves, green fields and a few trees, and felt better for it. Farther down, the shore was marred by ugly petrol storage tanks looking like giant silver mushrooms, and higgledy-piggledy buildings from which flashed advertisements for gin, whisky and beer. There was a bar on board and Miranda and I took time off from staring at the ships and the shore to show that we were really enjoying ourselves.

It was low tide when we reached Southend. You could smell the salt, the fish and the fresh air. It was all space. We faced a vast expanse of mud and a crowd of other holiday-makers eating ice cream. As the mud looked so forbidding, everybody flocked to the pier, the longest in the world, lined with shops. At one booth there was a wooden effigy of a man who bore a surprising resemblance to Bobbit. I'm sure it was meant to look like him. 'Tyke a pot shot at 'im,' the barker yelled, handing us the wooden balls, ''ee can't 'it yer back.' Miranda and I did.

You needed eyes at the back of your head; cheats were everywhere. The gold watch Mr Harding the storeman bought for two shillings and sixpence was tin. 'Lor lumme, matey, yer aht awf a crown,' was all he got when he took it back. We drank heavily and gorged ourselves on seafood and vinegar. No one outdrank Mr Bobbit.

Later we wandered along the front, past lodging houses, squinting into shop windows. We listened to the barkers at the fair and the boatmen on the beach, and had a donkey ride against the incoming tide. With the sun setting we heard a military band. Afterwards we sat on deck chairs and pretended we were at Monte Carlo. Miranda thought she was.

The fresh air must have done us good because at the end of the day the foundry workers, some a little far gone, sang their way back up the river. Other steamers were coming up on the tide. Accompanied by an accordion, we sang such favourites as 'My old man said follow the van, and don't dilly-dally on the way . . .' and 'Nelly Dean', and 'Down at the Old Bull and Bush'. You can't stop a Cockney singing. Bobbit led us and was on his feet till the end.

From the great bend of the Isle of Dogs, all through Cockneyland, Miranda and I danced, while others spread themselves on the benches and slept. She would have been happier had the boat turned around and we had danced all the way back to Southend. The closer we got to home, the more the lights blazed: on the river a confusion of green, red, amber and white colours glittered. It was magic to sail under the bridges with all the illuminations reflected on the water. Crawling across London Bridge was an unending line of car lights. From shore, signs winked at us extolling the benefits of Schweppes Tonic Water, Gordon's Gin, Haig's Whisky and Wrigley's Gum – 'Keeps you alert'. Lit up, Big Ben and Westminster looked just like fairyland. Before we disembarked we all stood and held hands while Bobbit led us in singing 'Auld Lang Syne'.

All that remained was to dodge the rumbling traffic and

catch the District Line with its draughty carriages and its advertisements flapping in the breeze. Exhausted, with our arms around each other we pretended to sleep. When we got out at Bow Road, we passed the same fellow whom we'd seen strumming on his banjo when we set out that morning. With a charcoal-covered face and a few pennies in the cap at his feet, he was still playing at the kerb with the traffic roaring by. I took Miranda home.

I stayed in touch with Bobbit for years, never forgetting his decency. I can't imagine what might have become of me had he not shown me such sympathy in my early days in London.

———◇———

The following Monday, I put on a suit, collar and tie and reported at Brettenham House for duty. My hours were from nine until four – a great change from the seven-thirty to five in the foundry. I started late enough to avoid strap-hanging in the Tube.

I began by working under Mr Ives, who taught me how the Board worked, how to communicate and how to use my time. Later I would learn about actual operations on the rivers. He was the first man I'd met who set me an example of reticence and reserve. I needed it. I never knew him to raise his voice.

'Did you shout for me?' I asked him one day on entering his room.

'I may have called, Woodruff, but I certainly didn't shout.' That put me in my place.

Often he would reply with one word. I found myself imitating his demure 'indeed' and 'really'. I began to use 'doubtless' and 'rather' on the telephone and felt better for it. Ives was always well groomed, efficient and considerate of others. I could not have had a better boss; the chemistry between us was perfect.

After being appointed, I never spoke to Sir William again.

I came to like him and respect him, but only from a distance. He would have been surprised had he known that at lunchtime I occupied his chair in the boardroom. I ate my sandwiches looking out over the Thames; I thought it a shame for such a beautiful room to be unused. It pleased me that Sir William's chair could spin round and round. There were times when I imagined myself facing the members of the Board. 'The meeting will come to order,' I would silently call, raising Sir William's gavel and peering at the shining expanse before me. Having made sure I left no crumbs, I would then walk along the tree-bordered Embankment from Cleopatra's Needle to Westminster Bridge and back. Always I was accompanied by a procession of trams, buses, lorries, carts, cars and people.

There followed three extraordinarily happy months. For weeks I simply couldn't believe that my job was real. I thought I'd wake up and find it gone. After the foundry, the conditions were unbelievable. No din, no dirt, no danger, no straining, and a clean office to myself. I had guaranteed holidays, guaranteed sickpay, and a guaranteed pension. Morale at the Board was high. Conduct was beyond reproach. Nobody said, ''Ey you!' 'Stop jawing!' ''Arf a mo!' or 'Wot's doin'?'

Ma Hargreaves and the rest of the family couldn't believe my luck either. Overnight, my weekly income had jumped from twenty-five to fifty shillings. I could afford to buy a daily newspaper, which I read like a proper bureaucrat going to and coming from the office. The workers used the trains several hours before us and we toffs sat there later with washed faces and starched shirts, feeling very important and self-satisfied. Clem worked out to a penny what my pay would be in ten years' time, and how much I would get when I retired. He thought I'd gone barmy when I told him I'd still go to Oxford if I got the chance. No Cockney gave up a job like that. Only Ma Hargreaves and Alex supported me.

Getting the Water Board job was the cause of my first big row with Miranda. With the extra money she thought me a good prospect for marriage. But until then there had never been a suggestion of marriage in our relationship. We'd been too poor to talk about it. Besides, our lives pointed in different directions – I wanted to get an education and go into politics; she had no interest in politics. Happiness to her was having more money to spend, especially on pleasure. If the toffs could go to glittering balls, why couldn't she?

To talk about the possibility of giving up the Water Board for Oxford made her madder still. 'Oxford is not for the likes of us,' she said. I ended the argument with her the only way I could: 'If I get the chance to go to Oxford, Miranda, I'm going to take it.' Oh, how she raged!

—◇—

Miranda almost got her way. One Saturday we went on a trip up the Lea. It was a hot summer's day. I did the rowing, she steered. We'd hired a large boat with canvas awnings, which could be let down if it rained. Miranda was looking her best. She was wearing bejewelled sandals, a pair of Bermuda shorts and a cotton shirt tied at the waist. It was so loosely buttoned that her breasts were more outside the shirt than they were in.

About noon, we pulled over and fastened the boat to a willow tree. The fields were ablaze with wild flowers; black satin cows, tails swishing, eyed us. A great silence prevailed; nobody else was in sight.

Reaching out for an oar that had got loose and was in danger of floating away, I was suddenly given a push from behind which landed me in the water. While I struggled and spluttered, Miranda sat on the cushions rocking with laughter. I didn't think it funny at all.

Back in the boat, with Miranda still in fits, I tried to get my sodden clothes off, watching her over my shoulder because I knew she was capable of pushing me in again. I dropped the awning on the riverside for privacy and when I turned to get my towel, Miranda was standing there before me naked. Her hair was down. She slid her hands around my neck and gently pulled me to her. I was overwhelmed by the sight and smell of her nakedness. 'I love you,' she said, her voice liquid and soft. Holding each other, we sank on to the cushions. She tossed her thick hair over my head.

Only when it was too late did I realise that I'd forgotten to put on the condom Chris had given me. I fished in my clothing for it. 'Don't put that bleedin' thing on,' she said, pulling me back on to the cushions. The outside world ceased to exist.

Miranda was as tempestuous about making love as about anything else. She could not have enough. When I fell back on to the cushions exhausted, she slid over me sinuously until her mouth, legs, arms and breasts held me down. My exhaustion soon fled.

Eventually even she was satisfied. We dropped the awning on both sides, curled up under our towels and slept. When I awoke, I saw the light through the strands of Miranda's hair. The angle of the sun had changed, it was late afternoon. All I could hear was the lapping of the water against the boat, the drone of insects, the chink of a blackbird and the sound of a boat engine far away. I shook Miranda. 'It's getting late, we'll have to go.' She responded by embracing me again.

All the way back she lay on the cushions and purred like a cat.

It was dark when we returned the boat. Wearing my wet shirt, pants and shoes, we walked to Ma Hargreaves', where I changed into my overalls and then took Miranda home. She clung to me at the door. Her mother's penetrating voice called from the kitchen: 'Bring 'im in!' Miranda giggled and tugged at me, but all I wanted to do was to go home and sleep.

I woke on Sunday morning much before my usual time. The others were fast asleep. Daylight was approaching. As I studied the ceiling, I worried about what had happened the day before. Would Miranda become pregnant? I'd had plenty of warnings about her from Chris, which I'd ignored. For the first time it struck me that making love to Miranda – or to anyone else for that matter – could be perilous. I wasn't ready to have a family and was uncertain of my love for her. The more I lay there, the less I liked my predicament: ecstasy had turned to worry. I didn't dare tell Chris I hadn't used his condom.

In the following weeks I went on worrying. If Miranda were pregnant, as she hoped, I'd have to marry her. That was the code. 'We can always live with Mum,' she said. Living with Mum was the last thing I wanted. Luckily, as it turned out, I was spared.

After that, I did my best to avoid Miranda. I didn't trust her, or myself. 'Look,' she said. 'We don't have to get wed now if you don't want to. If you're worried about a child, I can use some pessaries Mum gave me.' I sensed a note of desperation. I already knew about those particular pessaries from talk among the lodgers. An East End company made them. If they didn't work and you complained, they sent you a book called *Bringing up Baby*. I hoped *I* wouldn't get stuck with having to bring up a baby.

<hr>

One day in the middle of summer I picked up the letters from behind the front door to take them downstairs, and saw a letter addressed to me with the Oxford postmark. My spirits rose, I was so excited that I turned the envelope over and over in my hands. I didn't open it until I'd run back upstairs to my bedroom. It was a short letter from Father O'Hea, but it was all I wanted to hear: I could go to Oxford – the Catholic Workers' College had offered me a place! The financial assistance of the London County Council would be helpful, but O'Hea would take me with or without their help. He needed to know my response quickly.

I read the letter two or three times before running downstairs to show it to Ma Hargreaves. She might have been my mother the way she hugged me: 'Wonderful! Billy, I can't tell you 'ow 'appy I am.' I detected a tear. When Clem came home that night he was incredulous at the thought of my giving up the Water Board job. 'You've got to be mad,' he said. 'Only a madman would exchange books for cake. One day, when it's too late, you'll realise that books are for blockheads.' ''S right,' said Chris. 'Can't eat books.'

The next day I used Ma Hargreaves' phone to call Ruskin College. I spoke to the secretary, asking if he might let me know where I stood with my application. I was to learn that educational bodies don't make that kind of decision on the telephone. He advised me to take O'Hea's offer while it was going. Remembering what Miss Hesselthwaite and Reg Sorenson had said about a bird in the hand being worth two in the bush, I committed myself to O'Hea. It was one of the best decisions I ever made.

I dropped a note to Philip Stone. He wrote back congratulating me, and saying how fortunate I was. I also wrote to Brenda. She answered at once on a postcard. 'Lucky you, luv.'

It remained for me to tell Charles Ives. Not wanting to burn my boats, I put it off for several days. He was genuinely disappointed when I told him; so was Sir William. It helped that they were both Oxford men. The Conservancy Board was hundreds of years old; no doubt it would struggle on without me. Uppermost in Ives' mind was whether I'd take up rowing. As an old rowing blue he was always telling me what a fine sport it was, and how I'd benefit from it. To please him, I said I would certainly try. Our harmonious relations continued until the day I left and we parted good friends. It was a privilege to have worked with such a man. Even though my stay at the Water Board had been brief, it had strengthened my self-confidence and given a tremendous lift to my ego. I wasn't about to ride in triumph in the Lord Mayor's coach, but in joining the Water Board I'd come a long way. It taught me that – regardless of the odds – I could win through.

Miranda was speechless for days at my decision.

In July 1936, two months before I went to Oxford, General Franco rebelled against the legitimate Popular Front Spanish government. The long-awaited death struggle between fascist and anti-fascist forces, which Peter Levine had been talking about for ages, had begun. Germany and Italy at once identified themselves with Franco, the Soviet Union with the Republic. Britain and France remained neutral.

In his WEA lectures, Reg Sorenson was on about Spain all the time. He showed us how Spain had become divided between the forces of the Right and the Left: between the military, the monarchists, the large landowners and the Church on the one hand, and the socialists, the communists and the anarchists on the other. Anybody looking for a cause – romantic or heroic – had now found it.

The Spanish Civil War was a moment of truth that affected us all. Until then most of us Labour activists in the East End had not given a thought to Spain. Why bother about a country so far away? Two communist East End garment workers, Sam Masters and Nat Cohen, were the first to organise a British group of volunteers, which eventually became the International Brigade. Peter Levine was one of their first recruits. 'You must come to Spain, Woody, it's a chance to hit back. Oxford can wait,' he said.

It caused me to examine my conscience about pacifism all over again, but ultimately I was too much of a pacifist to follow Peter, and he should have known that.

I saw him off at Waterloo Station. He was to meet up with other volunteers in Paris and from there go on to Spain. It was a sad parting. Peter had been a good friend.

Chapter VII

To Oxford

The day of my departure to Oxford in September 1936
arrived all too soon. I was close to tears when I said
goodbye to Ma Hargreaves. The whole family stood at the
door shouting their good wishes. Miranda and Bernie came
as far as Paddington Station to see me off. Miranda was
dressed to kill in a smart, brown costume. You'd never have
guessed she was a factory hand. 'If Oxford throws yer out
tonight, we'll pick yer up tomorrow,' Bernie said, beating my
shoulder. Miranda made up for her silence by giving me a
hug.

I was nineteen and in the highest spirits. The prospect of
a sixty-mile journey through the English countryside, rushing to a place I'd only dreamed of, filled me with excitement
and a sense of freedom. Once more, I was gladly venturing
into the unknown.

As the empty train began to rattle and twist its way out
of the station, I waved goodbye through a cloud of steam.
Three years earlier, when I had run away from northern

England, the idea of my going to Oxford University would have been preposterous. Now the absurd was happening. I had no fears of the future. I was convinced that if I worked hard I would win through.

As I stared through the window, I fell to thinking about Miranda. I was glad we were parting. Our relationship had become very unsettling to me; I felt I was being pursued. Only the week before, she'd come unexpectedly upon me in one of the Hargreaves' 'best rooms', where I had been working alone. She was wearing a red dress with big white buttons down the front. Before I had time to get up from the table she had thrown her hands around my neck and kissed me. 'How much do you love me?' she asked. I put my hands on her thighs; she was not wearing panties. Suddenly she lifted her dress until it sat on her shoulders. Despite all my good intentions to avoid her, we embraced passionately and sank to the floor. Almost when it was too late, I withdrew, coming all over Ma Hargreaves' 'best rug'. 'Shit!' Miranda said, and went off in a flaming huff. Embarrassed, on hands and knees I tried to clean up the mess with my handkerchief.

I came out of my daydream as the train approached Reading. The sunlit river, hills and meadows captivated me. The September weather was holding up. All the time I'd been in east London I'd never lost my love of the land. Now I was rattling across the open country as if I owned it. I saw trees and fields and woods and hills and animals as if for the very first time. I remained glued to the window until the train slid into Oxford, where I caught my first glimpse of the university's towers. It was a week before term.

I surrendered my ticket at the gate and made my way out of the station. As my bag was light, I decided to walk to the Catholic Workers' College.

As I went along, I became conscious that I had reached a quieter, cleaner and more confident world. There were no crowds of noisy cloth-capped workers, no dirty gutters. I saw no beggars, no slums, no barrowboys, no screevers, no griddlers and no long procession of lorries. There was a light, expectant mood in the air. Compared to Bow Road it was like being in church. In place of factory chimneys there were college spires; in place of workshops and warehouses there were great stone-fronted colleges with manicured lawns. In the sunlight, the stone looked golden. Trees, shrubs and flowers lined the streets. The private houses were built on a grand scale. They had a settled, comfortable, orderly appearance. For me Oxford was love at first sight.

Half an hour later I was standing in front of No. 1 Walton Well Road, the Catholic Workers' hostel. It was a four-storeyed, self-assured Victorian dwelling, with a large entrance and four great bay windows overlooking the street. Fronted by elegant wrought-iron railings, the building conveyed a feeling of strength and spaciousness.

I was greeted by the matron, Mrs Padmanabha, a buxom woman who led me up a wide staircase past a print of Titian's *Madonna and Child* to one of the bedrooms at the front, which I was to share with another student. I then joined other students in the common room downstairs. The room extended all the way from the bay windows at the front to a large window overlooking an extensive wooded garden at the back. Shadows from the trees flittered over the colourful loose-covered couches. The walls were covered with books. A fire burned in the grate. Later I reported to Father O'Hea in his office. It was a packed, well-used room smelling of tobacco.

At tea, I was introduced to my roommate Jim Foggerty, a coal miner from New Silksworth, County Durham. Jim was the most handsome of men. He was of medium height, muscular, brown-eyed, with delicate features. He had a down-to-earth quality. He spoke his Tyneside dialect with a shy, gentle voice, which took me days to get used to.

We were both delighted with our bed-sitting room overlooking the street. Light flooded through the bay windows. It was a much larger room than the one I had shared with three others at Ma Hargreaves'. The furniture was simple; there was nothing polished or off-putting. There was so much space that the room seemed empty, even after we had unpacked. The bathrooms and toilets were steps away. We could have a bath every day if we wanted to. To us it was luxury.

To my surprise, my ears picked up the rhythmic blows of a drop hammer. I was told that there was an iron foundry beyond the back garden; the hostel had once been the foundry owner's house.

Sometime before supper, Jim and I took a short walk to nearby Port Meadow, through which the Thames flowed. The Thames was much cleaner here than in the East End. Slowly our eyes took in the trees, the river, the towpath and the endless grassland lost in a distant mist. The stillness of the scene was overwhelming. We heard only bird-song and the sound of distant bells. Later, we learned that flooding had preserved Port Meadow down the ages. It was this unspoiled countryside that I had yearned for in London. Eyes closed, I reached out to the enormous unoccupied space. I could breathe again. I went to bed that night feeling very much at peace.

The day after our arrival, Father O'Hea brought us together in the common room. There were ten of us: eight men and two women. All of us had working-class backgrounds. Foggerty was a miner. The other six were a weaver, a bricklayer, a docker, a clerk, a factory hand and a railway man. They ranged in age from their late twenties to late thirties. Some of them were married. I was the youngest. Several had been unemployed for long periods. The women, Miss Dempsey and Miss Humphries, lived in lodgings elsewhere.

The principal began by introducing Mrs Padmanabha, who talked about the running of the place. The house followed the university practice of not locking doors within the hostel. The front door would be locked at eleven at night. She asked us not to drink in rooms; there was a pub opposite the college and another next door.

O'Hea then explained the purpose of the college. 'Education for leadership is our goal,' he said. 'You are here because of your origins and experience. I look on you as "the spark in the clod". There is no better way to develop that spark than to spend two years here. The influence of even a small group who wants to do something socially useful can spread far and wide. Oxford itself started from small beginnings. I hope that your coming here will eventually help those from whom you have sprung.

'In the next couple of days, I shall give each of you the names of your tutors and their colleges. After that it is up to you. Books, lectures, essays and term examinations are matters settled between student and tutor. Tutors will advise on lectures. Although lectures are not compulsory and only loosely connected with examinations, I think it would be foolish not to take advantage of them. It is not every day that one can listen to some of the brightest minds in Britain. Those of you who stay for a second year will be required to sit for the university's diploma in economics and political science.

'It will not be easy for you to change from using your hands to using your heads. You are going to have to learn how to argue with pen and ink. The university will make no allowance for your deficiencies, whether in assimilating or analysing material, or in reading or writing. There will be no factory hooters to tell you when to begin and when to stop. The university never stops. You will be constantly lured from your work by lectures by speakers of world renown. To try to take in everything would be adding to your already heavy burden. In past years some students have been unable to keep up and left. You'll have to get used to working with the middle and upper classes, which will be an education in itself.'

He explained that the academic year was divided into three eight-week terms: Michaelmas (October–December), Hilary (February–March) and Trinity (April–June). Vacations were for catching up with reading. As our scholarships only covered term work, we'd have to find a living between terms.

'However hard it is going to be,' he ended, 'I can assure you that the effort is worthwhile. For the past seven hundred years students have benefited from coming here. You must take the university on trust. You have a great challenge and a great opportunity; what you learn here you will never lose.'

A day or two later O'Hea took us on a tour of the university. We all rode bicycles. For several hours we visited college after college. Our last stop was the magnificent hall of Christ Church. I returned from the tour with a blurred vision of ancient, weather-beaten buildings with leaded-glass windows, of proud spires, of silent quadrangles, of emerald-green lawns with borders of colourful blooms, and of elaborate steep-pitched vaulted roofs with dormer windows. I saw Oxford that day as I would never see it again.

———<o>———

My first week of term stood me on my head. I didn't know what I was doing. Joining a flood of students wearing caps and jacket-length, sleeveless black gowns with streamers flapping in the wind, I raced this way and that; I pedalled furiously from lecture to lecture. Not having matriculated, I had no right to wear a cap and gown and I did not like being stopped at the entrance to a lecture room for not wearing one. It gave me the feeling of being an intruder.

A good deal of the lectures' content was beyond me. At nine o'clock one morning I listened to a professor extolling the virtues of the Renaissance (whatever that was). He couldn't say enough about the Renaissance having given vibrancy and energy to the whole of Western civilisation. At ten, in the same room, I learned from another that in discarding the dogma of Original Sin, the Renaissance had blurred the lines of Western thinking. He blamed it for all the faults of Western society and held it responsible for the worst aspects of the present-day mechanistic, secular civilisation. What was I to think?

Accustomed to working with my hands, I was overwhelmed by the amount of thinking and writing I had to do. And I had to do it on my own. I was used to following orders or working with a crew. Here, no one ordered me about; nor did anyone give me help. I think there was a conspiracy to deny it. If you didn't know what to do, you had no right to be there. Tutors spent no time on the intellectually lame. Had I not fallen under Oxford's spell, I would have fled.

The first tutor I visited was A. B. Rodger, dean and tutor in History at Balliol College. I was wearing a tie. As I crossed the quad, bells tolled. I wondered what was in store for me. In answer to my knocking, I received a bellowing response to enter. I stepped into a large, book-lined study. The ivy-framed windows looked out on to a quadrangle swarming with students. Lamps burned overhead and on the tables. A heavy-bodied, middle-aged man of medium height stood with his back to the fire. He was wearing a tweed jacket, grey flannel trousers and a plaid shirt. His flushed face and large, bald head, which was cocked quizzically to one side, gave the appearance of a bulldog about to bite. At one end of the mantelpiece was a wedding picture of the man I faced. 'Yes,' he said fiercely, squinting at me over his half-moon spectacles.

'I'm Woodruff.'

'Ah, yes, Woodruff,' he answered, sceptically. 'So you want to do some work, do you?' He ignored my outstretched hand.

'Yes,' I said cautiously. I had made up my mind that the bulldog was not going to bite. As bidden, I sat down on the edge of a chair.

'Done any history at an upper level?' he asked, shaking the loose change in his trouser pocket.

'No, sir.'

'None?'

'No.'

'Where did you go to school?'

'Blackburn, Lancashire.'

'When did you leave school?'

'At thirteen.'

'Thirteen,' he repeated, staring at me in a bemused way, while whistling under his breath.

'What do you hope to do in life?'

'To be a Labour politician.'

He rattled his coins some more.

'Tell you what,' he said, his eyes challenging mine, 'why don't we break the ice with a paper on the Enclosure Movement of the eighteenth century ... you know ... when a lot of people were chased off the land . . . Material and moral loss of the poor, etc. You might not think so, Woodruff, but it has a lot to do with what has been happening in Russia lately.'

Although I knew a little about the collectivisation of agriculture in the Soviet Union, I hadn't the slightest idea what the English Enclosure Movement was. 'Yes,' I agreed, my voice breaking.

'Well, that's settled,' he said, striding about the room, shuffling papers as he went.

I sensed he expected me to leave. I didn't dare – I either spoke up now or I was lost. 'Where might I find the details?' I ventured.

'Details, details?' he started, as if it were improper of me to ask. 'Well, you might look at Slater and Beresford, and Fisher and Johnson for a start,' he said grudgingly. 'If you look at them, you'd better look at the Hammonds, and Cole, and Fay, and Prothero.'

I scribbled names down in my notebook as fast as I could. He seemed puzzled and a little put out when I asked him for the authors' initials and the titles of the books. I didn't dare ask him which parts of the books I should read.

By now I wasn't even talking right. How on earth was I going to find eight books, read them, and produce an essay in a week's time? 'Will it be necessary to read all eight volumes?'

'Gracious me, no, Woodruff,' he boomed. 'You'd be mad to. You don't read books, you gut them; it's the gist you're after. If you feel that an author has nothing important to say, drop him. You'll get to the nub of things pretty quickly, you'll see. Anyway, you won't find half the books I've given you. There are other students preparing essays, you know.' Smiling, he waited.

My face must have registered consternation.

'Even looking for a book you can't find will teach you something, Woodruff.' He whistled under his breath again, shuffled his papers, and indicated that I should go.

I stayed. I had to – I was desperate. 'How long do you expect the essay to be?'

'Well, Woodruff, that depends on you, doesn't it? Some do it in ten pages, others with nothing to say, dawdle it out to twenty. The standard rule is to start at the beginning and to go on till the end. You're a sensible fellow, Woodruff, I'm sure you'll know when you've reached the end.'

While I gathered my papers to go, he gave me some advice on lectures. 'You might try Rowse . . . everybody does. Good on Tudors. I'd look in on Clark too, while you're at it. Sound on the seventeenth and eighteenth centuries is Clark. What you are after is the gist, remember.'

I really was not listening. I was wondering why he was recommending Rowse and the Tudors when the Tudors preceded the dates of my examinations. I thought he must have made a mistake and I said so.

'Ah,' he answered, smile on lips. There was a pause while he whistled some more. 'Woodruff, you have not come to Oxford to take examinations, you have come to learn. The whole purpose of Oxford is learning.'

I stared at him, bewildered. How on earth was I supposed to recognise the 'gist' he talked about. To ask him, I realised, would be a reckless thing to do. Flight was the only wise course.

Mumbling my thanks, I made for the door. As I stumbled out into the quad, I wondered how I was going to cope. Dazed, I made my way past the porter's lodge into the street. I jumped on to my bike and rushed off in search of the recommended volumes, to gut the 'gist' from them.

Later that day I visited my economics tutor, Dr Eric Dowdell of St John's. I found him sitting by the fire. He had expected me and did not get up or turn towards me when I entered the room. With a wave of his hand he indicated where

I should sit. His tone and dress were sombre. This time I didn't even try to shake hands. Compared with Rodger he seemed a younger, frailer, quieter body, devoid of eccentricities. For some minutes he questioned me about my background and my knowledge – if any – of economics. Addressing the fire in a quiet voice, he then set me a topic: 'What are the primary factors of production?' He provided me with an endless list of books, advised me to attend James Meade's lectures at Hertford College on economic analysis and policy, and waited for me to leave. Not once had he looked me in the face. Only when I was leaving did I realise that he was blind. No one had mentioned it.

It remained for me to see G. D. H. Cole at University College whose lectures I would attend and with whom I would work closely in my second term on the theory and practice of trade unions (labour movements). I'd heard of him long before I came to Oxford. I knew him as the leading labour theoretician and historian. I was also curious to meet an academic who had written detective stories. I was already familiar with his *The Common People*, and *What Marx Really Meant*, and knew that he was opposed to revolutionary methods.

I found Cole in his rooms. He was a tall, austere figure, well and neatly dressed. He was a friend and supporter of O'Hea, and had expected me. I knew from the first moment that I was in the presence of a most informed and penetrating mind, and that I was fortunate to be there. Again, there was no shaking of hands. In fact he hardly emerged from a deep leather chair. I expected him to ask me about my experience as a foundry worker, but he didn't. He stuck to his topic, going off like a gun. I felt that he was not as happy with people as he was with books; he talked like a book. Avoiding digressions, he talked about labour movements and gave me a reading list. Not another word.

As he talked, my attention was drawn to his hands. Since my arrival in Oxford I had been fascinated by people's hands. Unlike the scarred, shovel-like hands at the foundry, Oxford hands were delicate-looking, with long, bony fingers.

Cole's signal for me to leave was to put his head into a book.

───◦◦◦───

Oxford at the start was an unending race, which absorbed me from morning till night. In the mornings I was at lectures, in the afternoons I looked for the books needed to write the essays. Nights I spent preparing my papers. Rarely did I get to bed before midnight; nor did my roommate Jim.

For the first time in my life I was challenged to think. I was no longer an ox under a yoke. I had never known such freedom, even if it was the freedom to drown. At least I was working for myself.

I must have lost ten pounds during those first frantic weeks. I didn't seem to have a second to myself. The idea of going for a walk was out of the question. Snatching a nightly pint of beer with Foggerty in the smoke-filled Golden Hart opposite was all I managed. Smoking seems to have been my only recreation; my consumption of tobacco doubled. There wasn't even time to get my hair cut. The only way I could cope was to rise at five and study the whole day. I had never worked so hard, that was the truth.

The fiction was that no one exerted himself. Undergraduates pretended to toss off work in a nonchalant manner. I don't think the women students were as blasé, but the idea of success without visible effort was widespread among the men. I would have gone hungry had I tried that at the foundry. Workers knew that life was work, and were proud of it. Toffs, I discovered, had a different code: kill yourself, but don't mention it and don't show it.

In contrast to the hammer-and-tongs-way of the working class, the atmosphere of the university was peaceful and orderly; life moved along in a discreet and gentlemanly way. I'd never known so many people going out of their way to be polite. The first time I was addressed as 'Sir' in Oxford, I felt two inches taller. Public-school manners were in charge; rules on study were lax; rules on conduct were stern. Honour mattered; character mattered; but conduct mattered most of all. No one got rattled; no one was rude; no one bawled. Resentment against us working-class students who had managed to scale the walls of privilege was about, but it was muted. The aristocrats rarely snubbed anyone on grounds of class; the middle class was too industrious to waste time discussing it.

----<o>----

No matter how stressful those first weeks were, I could always escape to the hostel. I was at ease there among my own kind. Class support was important to us, the presence of each of us supported and reassured the others.

Life at the hostel followed a simple routine. The day began with Father O'Hea banging away in the cellar, raking out and stoking the boiler. With crashes and thumps enough to waken the dead, and oblivious of the fact that we were trying to sleep, he shovelled the coal like a proper stoker. We always knew when he was through: the shovel would be dropped with a clang, the furnace door thrown to with a crash. We called him the 'boilerman'. Reluctantly, we admired his strength. He would then take an ice-cold bath in the bathroom on our landing. For some reason, he always left the door open. I agonised every morning until he took the last of three plunges – I felt for him in his spluttering and coughing. Why his bath water had to be ice-cold, I never worked out. The rest of us were delighted to be able to have a hot bath.

Father O'Hea rang a bell at seven for Mass. I never went down to the chapel without being moved. Life was magnified in that unadorned room. The stark simplicity of the altar heightened its effect. We might have been in a cathedral, with the prayers and responses rising to the vaulted roof. As I watched the candles flicker, I was amazed that the turning of bread and wine into the body and blood of the Saviour could take place in such a humble setting. I know that the service brought meaning to the lives of the other students; it made sense of their existence. Christianity after all was a religion of hope – addressed to the poor and the downtrodden.

I shared in the worship, though I could not share my companions' commitment. Sometimes during Mass my attention would wander and I would find myself studying the feet hurrying past the cellar window, or the face of a stray dog looking in.

Breakfast, at which the principal read *The Times* and *The Daily Herald*, and no one took any notice of anyone else, was at eight. One rarely talked to the other students until dinner at one, or supper at seven. Every meal was superb. The day ended with O'Hea going upstairs to his small bedroom under the roof. It was usually long after midnight, long after the last bus had ground its way past our window.

At Oxford I felt I was in a world into which I did not naturally fit. I had little in common with the urbane, privileged schoolboys who had come up from the public schools. More class-bound than I, they struck me as being very young and immature. They knew little about the real world. They were always overdoing it a bit – a bit too languid, a bit too indifferent. It was an entirely new experience for me to meet youths of my own age, who told me in an affected tone of voice how they were 'awfully happy', or for whom things were 'too stunning'. Every time I sounded my flat northern vowels, I pronounced my difference. I stood out in speech, dress, emotions, tastes, manners – even the way I ordered a drink – and movements. My lack of schooling was most evident. I was an outsider, with a deep-seated feeling of social inferiority.

Regardless of their immaturity, the intellectual self-confidence of these students surprised me. With their lightning plays on words and an easy assumption of nonchalant superiority, they knew much more than I, and they knew it effortlessly. Nor did they tiptoe about as I did; they walked about as if they owned the place, which they did.

I may have been a fish out of water – insecure and sometimes laughed at for my gullibility and my accent – yet I was in no doubt about the advantages of my new life. I'd never lived in a society in which people could afford to do nothing but sit and stand around, read books and linger over coffee, eat and drink their fill, and talk – especially talk. Words were the legal tender. I was amazed that nobody thought it unusual, and that the university had got away with it for so long.

Still, with all these frightening beginnings, Oxford conveyed to me a sense of security, permanence and order. I didn't need to bow and scrape. The clocks I saw and the bells I heard were there for my pleasure, not to repress me. If I pleased, I could ignore them and I wouldn't lose a penny or go hungry. For the first time in my life I was not living from hand to mouth. I didn't have to worry where the next shilling was coming from, or whether I was going to be thrown out of a job on to the street. I bought on credit. I didn't have to stand in queues and wait my turn. Gentlemen did not wait their turn.

After Blackburn and the East End, it seemed unreal that I should live in a town as beautiful and as mellow. The only towns I had known were dirty-brick ugly. In awe and wonder I studied the buildings, the clean sky, the verdant fields and the river. The beauty of the place grew on me and as it did I came to love its every nook and cranny. Many was the night I stood outside the Camera captivated by its dome against the starlit sky. I came to know the splendour of Magdalen, Christ Church, New College and Merton, all of them 'miracles in stone'. I marvelled at the tranquillity of the cloisters of New College, and the peace of the Botanic Garden, the gardens of St John's, and Merton's 'Mob quadrangle' – all of them oases of peace. To attend evensong in Christ Church Cathedral or New College Chapel was an unforgettable experience.

It was equally unreal to listen to lectures in Christ Church

Hall on a wintry morning, with a great log fire crackling in the hearth, the light flickering through the windows of the tall vaulted bays and the past looking down at me from the portraits on the walls. Not even the icy bench on which I sat or the freezing table on which I took notes deterred me from appreciating the magnificence of my surroundings. When the beams of the immense timbered roof were raised, English colonists were founding the New World. I felt in them the spirit of another age. What other students took for granted, I regarded with awe. The red-cheeked, long-legged girls added immeasurably to the scene.

Oxford's sense of history seeped into me through my pores. Wherever you went you breathed the past – which gave meaning to the present. On visits to Balliol I hurried across the spot where Bishops Ridley, Latimer and Cranmer had been burned at the stake during the Reformation. At five minutes past nine Great Tom of Christ Church tolled 101 strokes, representing the number of students when the college was founded in the sixteenth century. It signalled the closing of its great iron-studded doors. Perhaps it was mystique, perhaps a spell, but I felt privileged to be there.

———◇———

Somehow or other I came to terms with lectures and tutorials; I wrote my first essays. Rodger of Balliol criticised my essay on the Enclosure Movement with 'Good *Daily Mail*, Woodruff,' which I knew was a nice way of saying it was journalism. He then elaborated: 'You're looking to history for easy answers, Woodruff – to confirm your idea of right and wrong. You're another clever Dick condemning the past for being shortsighted. What generation has ever looked beyond the end of its nose?'

Having knocked all the wind out of my sails, in a few spellbinding sentences, he proceeded to show me where I'd fallen down and what was required of me.

Dr Dowdell's comment on my first paper was, 'Thank you,

interesting' ('interesting' meant you might pass, 'very inter-esting' meant you were coming along fine). With a sniff he gave a masterful résumé of the kind of paper I should have written. Neither Rodger nor Dowdell needed to tell me that I was out of my depth. Had I been able to sit around and become introspective, I suppose I might have despaired. What saved me was my sense of purpose. I had to succeed. What immature schoolboys could do, I could do. I remembered Miss Hesselthwaite's warning that the beginning would be hard. It was.

But it got better. The quirks of tutors gradually ceased to bother me. Although I was unable to toss off essays – for me each one was an ordeal – I began to reap the benefits of the tutorial system, where knowledge is shared rather than used as a stick to beat the student. I learned how to benefit from the coaching of distinguished scholars. Teaching was para-mount. 'Never write a book, Woodruff,' Rodger used to say to me, tongue in cheek. 'If you do, make sure it is a slim volume. There are already too many books.'

The trick was to stay wide awake, ready to catch the sprats of wisdom thrown offhandedly in your direction. It called for intense concentration and a heightened appreciation of the subtle, rarely repeated digressions and idiosyncratic, some-times waspish anecdotes. Let your mind wander for a second and you were lost.

By a solid effort rather than intelligence, I made sense of the books I was told to study. My working-class colleagues called them 'the big books'. I avoided chasing books by study-ing in the Camera, the reading room of the Bodleian Library; this way books were brought to me. I was there when it opened at ten and, except for meals, lectures and tutorials, stayed until it closed at ten at night. It meant that Foggerty, who didn't mind when others barged in on him, could have our room to himself. The sound of drop hammers coming from the back of the building did not disturb him as it did me.

If I worked late at the Camera, the pubs would be shut and

Foggerty and I would drink a beer in our room. Against all regulations we kept a box of warm beer under his bed. Sometimes Jim played his harmonica: the beer and the music smoothed us down.

The Camera reading room was as silent as the grave. A respectful hush prevailed. Staff members spoke in whispers; coughs and sneezes were admonished with one *sh-sh*. If flirtations took place, they were silent and unseen. There was a sense of greatness and challenge about the place. Those who sat there were not just any old flotsam and jetsam, they were readers for life at one of the oldest and greatest libraries in the world. They were sitting where famous men had sat. I knew that the students around me, however languid, were among the brightest in the country. Their superiority was infectious. When the dreaded time of 'Schools' came at the end of my course, it was with these that I would have to compete.

I followed Rodger's and Dowdell's advice and attended the lectures by A. L. Rowse, G. N. Clark and James Meade. I took few notes. Rowse drew a great crowd. Peacock-like, he was brilliant and colourful. Clark was magisterial. The doors of his lecture room were locked when he entered on the stroke of ten and were kept locked until he was done. I think this was to prevent his listeners from running away rather than to preclude latecomers from getting in. Meade was the most stimulating. Unlike Dowdell, who dealt with economic theory as an end in itself, he was concerned to use theory to improve public policy. There was always a moral element in Meade's thinking. He had everything in his favour: youth, good looks, knowledge, intelligence, modesty, good manners, human sympathy, wit and energy. His enthusiasm was infectious. Yet, surprisingly, he usually had a small audience – so small that often a lecture became a seminar. I had the good sense to stay silent.

The lectures given by the famous Father Martin C. D'Arcy, university lecturer in Moral Philosophy and Master of Campion Hall, introduced me to an entirely new field of knowledge. Brow furrowed, gown rustling, eyes focused on his toes or half-closed as in a trance, D'Arcy would often stop his pacing to study the floor or the ceiling in search of the exact word to express his meaning. Meanwhile I was suffocated by his 'oughts', 'ifs', 'buts' and 'howevers', which floated above me like a dense cloud. Having grasped what he was saying, I was thrown off when he questioned what I thought we had already agreed upon. I was also thrown off by the way he kept the dogma of Original Sin up his sleeve. He left us in no doubt about the limitations of human nature. He was fond of quoting Immanuel Kant: 'Out of the crooked timber of humanity, nothing straight was ever made.' Fat lot of good that was to someone like me who intended to rebuild the world.

I never managed to get a handle on his subject. In a foundry I knew what I was doing; with philosophy everything hung on a verbal thread. His discussion of topics such as 'What is the Good?' or 'What is the true end of man?' or 'What is truth?' left me floundering. This constant worrying about doing the right thing sounded unnatural to me. The people I'd come from just *did* without 'feelosophising'. The working class didn't have time to reflect whether or not they'd done the right thing. They either followed the rules or lost their job and went hungry. It amazed me that I could stand around discussing the 'moral imperative' and get three meals a day. I listened wide-eyed as D'Arcy turned his words inside out and upside down. His crowded audiences loved his brilliance, his wit and his word play, but I have to confess that he was wasted on me.

I don't know what he would have said had I told him that the clothes I was wearing had been obtained from a 'fence'. D'Arcy's philosophy didn't seem to me to have much to do with life in east London.

I understood the lectures of Father Lewis Watt from Heythrop College on Catholic Social Doctrine much better. An ex-lawyer, Watt was as lucid as D'Arcy was vague. A crisp little man in a black suit, with a convict haircut, a pale face and a pinched nose, he never wasted a word or a second. There was no 'iffing' and 'butting' and wandering around the room looking for the right word. He stood stock-still and shot his points at you as if they were bullets.

In a short space of time Watt taught me a great deal about Marxism, totalitarianism and the state. The danger of Marxism, he used to say, is that it is temptingly simple. He considered it a half-truth. While all the other great religions (he called Marxism a secular religion) dealt with the secular and the sublime, with life and death, Marx dealt only with life. In place of the Marxist doctrine of class war, Watt advocated cooperation based on Christian charity and recognition of the dignity of labour. Not that he refused to give Marx his due. He considered Marx's protest against the social conditions of the time and his grandeur of conception admirable.

Watt also introduced me to the papal encyclicals *Rerum Novarum*, On the Conditions of the Working Classes (1891), and *Quadragesimo Anno*, On Reconstructing the Social Order (1931). The aim of both encyclicals had been to close the gap between the Church and the working class. In modern industry the worker had become a replaceable part, tied to the machine and the clock.

Watt could not only handle the grand sweep of history, but as a lawyer he could handle the details. He introduced me to the teachings of Thomas Aquinas on private property: 'It is one thing to have a right to the possession of money, and another thing to use money as one wills.' Property implied a function. I hadn't heard of Aquinas, but I had heard of the nineteenth-century French anarchist Proudhon who had declared, 'property is theft'.

On returning to our room, Jim and I would sometimes debate the points brought up by D'Arcy and Watt. We found ourselves holding different views. I think I must have been a complicated person compared with him. For Jim everything was simple and clear. There was a self-assurance about him that I lacked. To Jim, faith in God was everything. Peter Levine had lamented my lack of faith in communism; now Foggerty was lamenting my lack of faith in Christianity.

'I can't love God as you do, Jim,' I told him. 'I am not religious. I recognise Christ's passage across history as of extraordinary importance, but my mind is torn by difficulties and contradictions. I don't understand what is meant by eternity. I don't need a God to tell me that hatred is evil and love is good; that tolerance is preferable to intolerance; that to help the poor is right; and that to ignore the misery of the poor is wrong. These things I know from experience and feeling. I'm unable to take things on faith. Instead, I want to get to the heart of things. I want to look everything and everybody straight in the face. I want to see things as they are. The freedom to think like that is surely one of our most precious freedoms. My attitude does not arise from stubbornness or false pride, Jim, but from downright spiritual confusion.'

'You want to know everything, Billy, and you can't.'

'Why can't I?'

'Because there is a door in life beyond which you can't go; there are things that you cannot see and touch. There are things that are too big for you and must be left to God.'

'What are these things?'

'I don't know, except there wouldn't be life without them. That's where faith comes in. You can never define love or beauty, yet you know they exist. You're in a bad way, Billy, you're questioning the word of God. If the world has meaning it must have a mind. I think the mind that directs life is God. God is inscrutable. You must trust God. Find Him, Billy, before it's too late.'

'How am I to find Him?'

'You can only find God through grace. "Seek first the kingdom of God which is within you."'

'I've done it and He doesn't answer.' Jim didn't realise how much I felt the weight of my own inner doubts and conflicts.

'Stop thinking of yourself as somebody special. If you

142

approach God with your heart and not with your head, He will answer. God's grace is like a moonbeam. It will find you:

> Amazing Grace! How sweet the sound
> That saved a wretch like me!
> I once was lost, but now am found,
> Was blind but now I see.'

My trouble was that I believed in this life on earth; I believed in things that I could see and touch. Jim believed in the unseen and the eternal. To him the Lord God was a kindly father and everything more or less fell into its right place.

'Follow your conscience and do the decent thing,' he ended.

I gained some relief from my spiritual problems by attending debates at the Student Union and the Labour Club. The pacifism of certain speakers sat well with me. Although there were more conservatives and liberals, the socialists made the most noise and gained the most attention. To my surprise, some students had suddenly discovered a new loyalty to 'the people' and 'the masses'. Their efforts were bent on climbing down rather than up. According to them 'the masses' were doing wonderful things; ordinary people were wiser than their leaders.

Outside of Ruskin and the Catholic Workers' College, I don't think I ever met a genuine socialist at Oxford. What I did meet were intellectual socialists who had a negligible effect on the life of the masses. They were all head. They collected working-class experiences as others might collect stamps or butterflies. We working-class students called them 'pretend socialists'.

Instead of worrying about 'pretend socialists', I extended my friendships elsewhere. I started going to Ruskin's Friday-night hops (the dance halls in town were out of bounds), where Foggerty sometimes played the piano. For an hour or two I took my brain out of my head and put it in my feet. The difference between Ruskin dances and those elsewhere in the university was that at Ruskin you danced and danced;

elsewhere, you stood around and talked and talked. When it was time to go, instead of playing the National Anthem, Jim used to bang out the Red Flag, smiling. Few of us intended to live and die beneath it, but we sang it anyway.

O'Hea's way of turning us into civilised human beings was to subject us to the cultural evenings put on by two dear old ladies who lived in a large, sepulchral house in south Oxford. Each week we would straggle after him to visit them.

Dressed in silk and buttoned up to the chin, our hostesses greeted us as if we were returning prodigal sons. They'd spent the whole week preparing for the occasion and fussed over us until we were seated on their unhappy-looking Victorian chairs.

The elder of the two ladies played the piano. Mozart sonatas were her favourites. As she played the same pieces week after week, we became familiar with them. She always finished with a final flourish of her hands. She would then stand, eyes sparkling, and bow with great dignity as if it were a London concert. We stood and clapped. We would not have dreamed of hurting her feelings. Her sister read Shakespeare sonnets. With great dramatic gestures, she lived every line.

The last word said, the last note sounded, we were served supper fit for a king. The fine china looked out of place in our hands. Our fairy godmothers were always astonished at our appetites. I used to wonder what they thought of us: their easy-going chatter left us tongue-tied. Foggerty was the charmer because he could talk about music.

I'm convinced that our unfamiliar appearance and speech brought light into their lives. I can only hope that they thought us worth the trouble they'd taken.

◇

When I could find time, I wrote to my family in Lancashire and my friends in the East End. There was talk of my father finding a job with Rolls Royce in Derby. I also kept in touch with Harold Watkins. Both my sisters had set up their own homes by now and were busy raising a child – Brenda a daughter, Jenny a son. Bobbit, who wrote encouraging notes, but declined my invitation to visit Oxford with a 'not bleedin' loikly', told me that the foundry was still 'a sodding place occupied by lunatics'. Miranda wrote loving notes. Her greatest worry, I think, was that I might become religious. Miss Hesselthwaite and Ma Hargreaves always cheered me up. Although more people were finding jobs, they told me that conditions in east London were still bleak. Hunger marchers were still pouring into London.

On a quick visit to Bow at the beginning of October I didn't see Miranda, but I did meet my old trade-union secretary, Albert Eastead, who had become mayor. 'Didn't realise there was so much bad abaht,' he said cheerfully. ''Ardly time to get a pint.'

The clash of secular ideologies and the growing menace of war were never far from our thoughts. Sir Alfred Zimmern, who occupied the Montague Burton Chair in International Relations, was a political oracle who opened our eyes to the world scene. He was stocky, with a large head; his bright eyes peered through thick lenses. 'The problem of our survival,' he stressed, his finger stabbing the air, 'lies more in the foreign than in the domestic sphere.' He was convinced that a confrontation between the liberal Western democracies and the fascist states was only a matter of time. The world was arming to the teeth; another Great War threatened.

With war clouds gathering in Europe (the British government had ordered forty million gas masks) it didn't take much for him to persuade us. As a constant visitor to the continent and a strong supporter of the League of Nations, he always had first-hand knowledge of the growing political crisis. He used to say: 'If children can decide how they will act together, why can't we?' I was surprised one day in 1937 to see Heinrich Brüning, the ex-Chancellor of Germany, enter the lecture hall with him. Brüning's picture had been in all the papers, there was an air of distinction and authority about him. I sat directly in front of him while he expressed his worst fears of Hitler and national socialism. I came away impressed, but hardly surprised that such a civilised, gentlemanly person had been outmanoeuvred by the Nazis.

Zimmern also dealt with the emerging nations in Asia and Africa. Although he usually left his audience to make up its own mind – 'you either support the colonial peoples in their struggle for independence, or you support the colonial powers in putting down the national movements . . . which?' – his sympathy with colonial peoples in their struggle was manifest.

After lectures Zimmern would invite discussion. He was interested in my origins and found it fascinating that a foundry worker should be attending his class. Yet he poured cold water over many of my favourite ideas. My belief in a world socialist state was a nonstarter with him. 'A dream,' he said, 'and not even a beautiful dream. If the problem of international relations concerned our ability to move sacks of potatoes about, we'd solve the problem tomorrow. Moving human beings about and obtaining mutual understanding between them is, however, a problem of an entirely different order. Neither international socialism nor international capitalism can bring about world unity. World systems, whether we like it or not, go against the grain of human nature. Those who try to build a heaven on earth fail to understand human psychology.' He also poured cold water on my idea that socialism was the alternative to compulsion. 'You wouldn't get far in the world without compulsion,' he said. 'Society needs government and government needs power. Without power you have anarchy.'

Zimmern's lectures may not have improved my examination chances, but they provided me with a wonderful education.

The coming of examinations took my mind off world affairs. I'd worked hard during the past eight weeks – perhaps too hard. I was hanging on by my teeth, but I was sufficiently confident to believe that I would get by. In the examinations I did the best I could. I came away neither elated nor depressed. I would not know the results until the beginning of the next term.

To celebrate, the students at the hostel swept the furniture aside and put on a dance, to which many Ruskin friends came. Our 'orchestra' was a gramophone.

The last thing I did before leaving for the Christmas vacation was to have a long talk with O'Hea. He thought I was settling into the new life very well. He had heard nothing but good about me from my tutors, and expected I'd do well in the course and get a great deal out of it. I never mentioned spiritual problems, nor did he. He had a wonderful way of not intruding into one's private life. Except for going for a walk up the river with him now and again, he had left me entirely to my own devices. There was nothing petty or mean in the man, nothing slipshod. Behind the gentle, outward appearance lay a shrewd mind and great inner strength. After eight weeks, my trust in him was complete. No one who knew him doubted his integrity, or his vocation. He devoted his weekends to the spiritual needs of inmates of a prison in the Reading area, or to workers' meetings elsewhere in the country. I was not surprised that the Church allowed him the scope it did.

O'Hea was a doer as well as a thinker. He taught by example. I once witnessed two students arguing about whose turn it was to carry the buckets of coal upstairs. Without a word O'Hea picked up the buckets and carried them himself. The way he carried them, they might have been full of air.

One had to think twice before accepting an invitation from O'Hea to go for a walk. For him, a walk was a test of endurance in which hedgerows, streams, brambles and bogs were ignored. He went through them like a buffalo. He was the only man I knew who could walk past a bull and keep the conversation going. One day I was about to cross a field with him. A bull was bellowing at the other end. As it came towards us, I vaulted over the fence. 'Look out,' I shouted. O'Hea took not the slightest notice. Instead he continued to study the birds through his binoculars; he seemed oblivious to the lowered head and lashing tail. I had visions of him being carried away on the horns. Not at all. The bull halted some yards away, confused; eventually it wandered off. I caught up with O'Hea several fields later. He never said a word.

I left Oxford to share Christmas with my parents in Derby, where they had resettled after leaving Lancashire. I intended to spend the next six weeks at home studying. It was a happy homecoming after three years away. I found my parents well. Mother, now grey-haired, stretched out her hands to greet me. My parents could not understand what I was doing at Oxford, or what Oxford meant. But whatever I was doing was evidently better than what I had been doing, and that's all they cared about. My suggestion that they should visit me there embarrassed them. Mother cared only for her new house. It was smaller than the one in Livingston Road, but for her it was the ship that had come home. Father was either at work or nursing plants in his greenhouse. Because Britain had begun to rearm, he worked day and night helping to make Spitfire fighter planes for the Rolls Royce Company. My people no longer knew the penury they had known in Blackburn. They had money to spare. Even so, I'd got so used to them being poor that I would not have dreamed of imposing additional expenses upon them.

Late on the afternoon of my arrival I went for a long walk in the snow-covered countryside. It was a bitterly cold December day. I was out for several hours and went to bed that night exhausted. I woke in the early hours in a high fever, unable to breathe. My face was on fire, I had intense pain in both lungs. The sheets were wet with sweat. Somehow I roused my parents. Realising that they were facing something quite abnormal and perhaps dangerous, father went out into the sleety night to fetch a doctor. I have a vague memory of his arrival. He diagnosed pleurisy and advised my immediate removal to the central hospital in Derby; neglect could cause suffocation. My parents objected; they had not lost their fear of hospitals. The physician agreed to return in an hour and if there was no improvement, I would either be admitted to hospital, or he would refuse further responsibility for my care. Fortunately my temperature had fallen by the time he returned, so I was left in bed at home, where he visited me on and off for the next three weeks. All these things I learned later. At the time, other than the look in my mother's eyes, I had little idea what was happening. Encased in a hot mud poultice, all I could do was to lie there and feel sorry for myself.

Sometimes when the hours grew long I felt that I was swimming in a still lake in which I was sinking and rising again. I heard the ticking of the clock, a timid bird pecking at the window, muffled sounds and voices coming from the kitchen. I watched the sun's rays going around the room. I heard the sound of Christmas bells and shouting in the street. I had no visitors, for I knew no one in Derby.

As I improved, I listened to the radio. There were reports of the Spanish Civil War. I thought of Peter Levine. The war made me face up to the weakness of my convictions: what kind of a pacifist was I? I was beginning to suspect that I was too self-willed and too self-centred to be a true pacifist. There was a combative streak in me.

After several weeks I tired of sorting out my own and the world's problems and turned to reading. Once I was up to it, I did nothing else but read. When I got tired of my university texts, I drew upon a list of books, which Charlie Duke had given me when I left the East End. Mother ferried books to and from the public library. I was a glutton, devouring one volume after the other.

Eventually the time came for me to return to Oxford. Still

feeling wobbly, I paid a last visit to the doctor. After being indoors for so long, the fresh air and the street noises were unfamiliar. He told me to keep my mud waistcoat on for several weeks. 'You probably fell ill because your body and mind have been subjected to too much stress. Regardless of the work you have to do, you must set aside part of every day to get out of doors into the fresh air. At this point there is not very much I can do for you that you cannot do for yourself. If you follow my advice, you will make a complete recovery.'

Chapter VIII

Second Wind

My return to Oxford for Hilary Term 1937 was like coming home. I came out of the railway station glad to be back. Although it was a wintry afternoon with trampled leaves and some snow about, I walked to the hostel. My footsteps crunched on the frozen pavement and I arrived in Walton Well Road glad to escape from the cold. Appetising smells came from the kitchen; everything was scrubbed and clean. We might have been her own children the way Mrs Padmanabha welcomed us back.

I joined Jim Foggerty upstairs. He had spent his vacation working down the mine. To catch up with each other's news we went for a walk on Port Meadow, where a heavy mist covered the river.

The next morning I woke to the murmur of voices and the tinkle of the altar bell. The foundry whistle blew at the back of the house.

I spent an hour that morning with the principal going over my first term's papers. He was pleased with my progress. My assignments for the new term were labour movements with Cole, political science with Richard Price, and Rodger and Dowdell for further reading in history and economics. I'd already decided to attend Zimmern's lectures. His recently published *The League of Nations and the Rule of Law* had impressed me.

Once term began my life was dominated by writing essays. Every one remained a trial. There were times when I was overwhelmed by the sheer volume of material; I had never heard of some of the ideas tutors threw at me. I could only keep up by cutting back on sleep. Reading essays was no easier than writing them: by page three of my first paper for Price, I found myself whispering in a strange, husky voice. I couldn't believe that I was mouthing such wild ideas in such an idiotic way.

My first tutorial with Cole was on the socialist movement in Britain. 'Socialism here,' he began, 'is different from that on the continent. It places greater emphasis upon evolutionary rather than revolutionary methods.' Hardly pausing for breath, he then surveyed the history of the labour movement. 'Do you have any questions?'

'Yes,' I said, for I was not afraid of Cole, 'I notice that you say little about the class war. Is the idea dead?'

Again he went off like a gun – his tongue racing to keep up with his thoughts. 'The idea of class warfare was the invention of Marx. It was the product of the Industrial Revolution with its factory system, its wage labour, and its growing proletariat. Marx held that everything is primarily economic. In real life everything gets mixed up. I do not underestimate Marx, he had a formidable mind, but his talk of class warfare is unconvincing. Labour's problem is class unity.'

Overwhelmed, I could hear him rushing on. 'British workers have not followed Marx, because they do not like theory. Socialism here grew like topsy, undefined. What's more, almost all of our early labour leaders were devout churchmen. They sought respectability.'

I listened to him, wide-eyed and open-mouthed as he went

on and on, until someone banging on the door told me it was time to go.

Price, with whom I had an appointment immediately after Cole, was known as a holy terror. My friends looked at me pityingly when I mentioned where I was headed. 'Well, all the best,' they said, wringing my hand.

On entering his study I found a strange little fellow sitting with his legs tucked under him. He reacted to my entry like a cat disturbed from its favourite spot. He had an effeminate voice. His hands were so white and so fine that I was mesmerised by them. He wasted no words.

'You Woodruff? Come in, find a seat,' which was impossible without moving stacks of books and papers. Giving me no time to get out pen and paper, he outlined my assignment: 'Using Rousseau's *Social Contract* as your text, write a paper on the theme that man is by nature good and is only corrupted by the development of civilisation. The object of the exercise,' he said, rubbing his head, 'is to get you to say something intelligent about the nature of society and its origins. Good day.'

He gave me a look that defied me to stay. I was completely overcome. I croaked 'Good day,' and fled.

As I dashed out of Price's room another victim stood waiting at the door. 'Moody?' he queried.

'Don't linger,' I advised as I escaped into the quad.

In the weeks that followed I did a number of essays for Price: 'Summarise Hobbes' political theory'; 'Criticise the work of John Locke'; 'Do you agree that Machiavelli's *The Prince* is a primer on self-interest?'

For Price there always had to be an answer. I thought him brilliant. The drawback was that he took a sadistic delight in throwing mental fireworks into your lap, and watching your reaction: 'The innermost principle holding society together is the very opposite of reason,' he said during one tutorial. 'Right? Hume says so.'

No sooner had I got over that hurdle than he delivered another blow. 'How can a statesman remain faithful to his principles as long as other statesmen are trying to undo him? Machiavelli says he can't. What?' Any remaining sign of life in me only encouraged him to add to the torment.

'Why bother with political science to decide what we should do? The Marxists argue that it will happen anyway; the non-Marxists put their trust in a dictator or the market system; the true Christian leaves it to God; many think that fate decides everything. What need is there for us to do anything? What?' Many's the time he made my collar tighten.

After being raked over three times, I no longer knew or cared 'What'. In my haste to get out of the room, I knocked over a pile of books. Back on my bike, I fell to wondering what the Price household was like. I'm sure there wasn't a Mrs Price. How could there be when he never smiled? Perhaps he had a dog. What?

—◇—

I got on well with Dowdell, with whom I did a half-term's work, but thought he lived in an impenetrable world. I never got to know what he was really like. He had a way of lapsing into a preoccupied silence, which made me feel tense. He was devoted to teaching, but seemed so lonely. Perhaps that is why O'Hea dragged him across bogs and ditches to listen to the song of migrating birds. It was just as well that Dowdell was blind to the bulls and other perils which he faced in O'Hea's company. I thought it preposterous for two fully grown men to stand up to their ankles in icy water discussing the finer points of a bird's call.

Sometimes when I was early for my tutorial I would wait for Dowdell by the fire. On the mantelpiece a clock patiently ticked the time away. Silently the door would open. Having greeted me solemnly, he would cross the room to take a seat at my side. He knew where I was sitting. I knew he was wary of me, wariness entered the room with him like a mist.

That term I wrote papers for Dowdell on value, capital, competition and monopoly, rent, wages, interest and profit. He believed in the virtue of free-market capitalism, relying upon Adam Smith's 'hidden hand' to automatically direct self-interest to a higher good. I told him what free-market capitalism had done to my birthplace. He made a quiet response and left it at that. I used to think him cold and bloodless; at first I thought him asleep. Not likely – he never missed a point. He had a remarkable capacity for committing to memory everything I'd said. Looking back, I was lucky to have had such a foil to my socialist arguments. It made me think.

Of all my tutors, Rodger was my favourite. I did several essays for him that term. He taught me that history is always alive and can be thrilling. It did me good to visit him. He was always vibrant, self-assured, expansive and exciting. For other tutors I had great respect; for Rodger I had affection. A happily married man, he seemed to live in the best of all possible worlds, doing precisely what he wanted to do.

He had the knack of summarising what we had discussed in a few short sentences – short enough that I could grasp their meaning. His explanations were rapt and vivid; he understood the nuances of words and used them like fine tools. 'You are immature, Woodruff,' he would chaff. 'All socialists are. You are sensible of the past only in so far as you want to change the present. You think the past can be chopped up like a piece of meat; that you can measure it; that everything is known; that there is no mystery. The past is not a clearly discernible rung on a ladder leading towards some future Utopia. Your vision of the future is not based on the past, but on odd things going on in your head.'

I always came away from his rooms having learned something. He was forever questioning me, forever forcing me back on my own thinking. 'Mustn't treat you like an empty bucket waiting to be filled, must we, Woodruff?' He brought home to me the extent to which the Great War had been a watershed in world affairs. He also challenged the Marxist idea that history is a science. 'To generalise about matter is one thing, to generalise about human beings is another.'

I would sometimes quote one of the sources he had given

me. 'Yes, yes,' he'd reply. 'Stone does say that, but what do you think? Use your common sense, man.' I found being asked to think (when previously no one had ever had the slightest interest in what I thought) an overwhelming experience. I always knew when he was becoming exasperated: he would gently turn his wedding picture to the wall. His hands grasping the mantelpiece, he'd mutter: 'That's not so, my boy; that's not true, my boy.' Later, 'my boy' would become 'old boy'. His tone of voice was always warm.

Rodger was a big man; there was nothing petty or mean about him. He was more a patrician than an intellectual. With all his learning, he never lost sight of everyday life. One summer's day I turned up for my tutorial without my essay. I confessed that for once I'd played truant and had spent my time canoeing up the river. His response was immediate: 'Oh, I say, sensible fellow, sensible fellow, Woodruff. Not often we get weather like this. I wish I could have joined you.' To me, he was one of Oxford's great personalities.

———◇———

In my second term I was still an outsider looking in. I didn't have the college tie or blazer to be accepted as one of the crowd. Some mannerisms – however minor – I never mastered. To attend receptions where we balanced cups and plates on our knees and indulged in loose chatter was an ordeal for me. I couldn't use a saucer without making it rattle. The silver sugar tongs went berserk when I touched them. I had the same trouble with the cutlery at formal dinners. The first time I was given a finger bowl I stared at it incredulously.

I was helped to overcome my awkwardness by Hans Thiel, whom I found one day on Ruskin's staircase addressing a group of students. '"Pretend socialists" are mingy little people with sniffish, superior middle-class ways,' I heard. I stopped to listen. He gave me a friendly nod and continued. He might have been a professor the way the others hung on his words. His manner of speaking had an uncanny, penetrating force.

After he had finished, I was introduced to him. He was dark-featured, of medium build, and about my own age. His thoughtful face and shining eyes intrigued me. There was an air of mystery about him. As he talked, he kept running his long, nervous fingers through his thick, black hair. Repeatedly, he adjusted his spectacles.

I discovered that Hans Thiel had an incisive mind and the quickest flash of wit. He loved the intellectual pleasure of conversation. He was so eloquent that he usually led the discussion, interjecting a bright quip whenever anyone paused in answering him. His family had fled from Germany and his parents were living in New York, but he rarely talked about his past and I never probed. We were both birds of flight: he from German anti-Semitism, I from poverty. We became friends.

Perhaps Hans overcomplicated his life by trying to know everything, but had he not done that I'm sure he would have died of boredom. He was interested in revolutionary socialism, but I knew at heart that it was the last thing he wanted. His socialism was intellectual.

He was at his best when relating some dashing irony about university life. Gossip was his tonic. He loved to tell tales of back-stabbing among the dons. He was full of fun – fun serious, fun farce. He'd go to any length to cause a commotion among the stiff-lipped academics.

One day he persuaded three of us to dress up as women and float past the sunbathers at Parsons Pleasure. As we approached in our punt, I saw what looked like a heap of sea lions gathered on the bank. Sleep hung over the still bodies. A whole island of male nudes sunbathing shocked my working-class feelings. Even the free-living Soviet people kept their pants on.

We were almost alongside them when one of the nudes stirred, looked at us with a disbelieving eye, and raised the alarm. With a great shout, white tails bobbing, the sea lions took to the water. Doubled over in laughter, we lowered our parasols and drifted by.

Until I met Hans I didn't realise that I had been worrying unnecessarily about studies and examinations, and that the immense effort I was making was rather bad form. He thought that my flitting from lecture to lecture was lunacy. With quick-silver brilliance and great sophistication, he assured me that there was absolutely nothing to worry about; university work was quite manageable. He scorned the worker's talk of 'big books'. For him it was all so effortless. He didn't stay up all night finishing essays. I envied him his self-confidence.

Hans loved to socialise. Whereas I was reluctant to attend receptions (especially as I was still wearing the thick, itching mud plaster), he would saunter off and hold his own, glid-ing in and out of functions like a bird. Neither people nor occasions intimidated him. While I was dropping saucers, he would be directing the conversation.

One sunny day, instead of having tea in his rooms, he insisted that we carry the teapot and cups and plates and knives and sandwiches down the street and picnic on Worcester College lawn, which beckoned invitingly from his window. 'But Hans,' I said, 'we're not members of Worcester . . . and such things are not allowed.' Five minutes later, my protests swept aside, we were eating tomato sandwiches on Worcester's precious lawn.

'Mustn't be inhibited, Woody,' he said as he basked in the sunshine and drank his tea in royal style. 'Wouldn't do.'

Hans was good for my ego and my studies. If I met him in the street with a pile of books under my arm, he'd stop and advise me what to throw away. 'Absolute rubbish this one,' he'd say, taking a book off my stack. 'Can't imagine why he recommended it.' Yet close as our friendship became, there were times when our interests differed. At Friday night hops at Ruskin, I never saw Hans dance. He preferred to stand and talk. I never saw him in football or cricket garb. Rowing would have been an abomination. Exercise for him was lying in a boat floating down the river. His idea of a walk was going from bookshop to bookshop.

Some weeks after returning from vacation, I decided that it was time to remove the mud waistcoat that I had been wearing since my illness at Derby. By now it was thoroughly stuck to my skin and the itching was damnable. The choice was to soak it off bit by bit, or wrench it off in one go. With Jim hanging on to the end of the dressing, I counted one, two, three, and pirouetted across the room. The effect left me speechless; I had to sit on my bed to get my breath back. I was convinced that Jim was not only holding the dressing, but my skin as well.

Having got rid of my straitjacket, I began to play football. It was one of the things I did really well; I had been playing football since I was four. I played so well that colleges used to borrow me if they were a man short – all I had to do was change my jersey. I preferred to play centre-half, which allowed me to wander all over the field.

The game was played for the unadulterated joy of playing. At best you might have a man and his dog watching, or a crowd of three or four who had nothing better to do. A game fought in a frenzy of energy, regardless of weather, was what lumbering youths like me needed. Afterwards, we'd stand about – physically exhausted, half-dressed – discussing the match. Few were brave enough to take a freezing cold shower in a little draughty hut called a pavilion. After downing a shandy (half beer, half soda), we'd leap on our bikes, and disregarding the rain, pedal furiously back to a hot shower. Football helped me to be at ease with the toffs. They were not all head, as I had thought at first.

As the vacation approached, Jim invited me to his home at New Silksworth. 'Nothing fancy, but it will give you a chance to see how coal miners live.' It sounded exciting and I accepted.

Term work finished, Jim and I took the train to the North. We set out early in the morning, travelling through a damp, cold countryside, and reached New Silksworth at dusk.

The Foggerty family received us with great warmth. Jim's father had died of silicosis years before. The rest of his family were soft-spoken like Jim. There were so many people in the house that I wondered where I'd sleep.

I'd hardly been made to feel at home when two of his brothers came in from the mine. They cleaned up in a tin bath before the fire. That evening we all sang around the piano. Oh, how a mining family can sing! Later, as if it were the most natural thing in the world for eight to sleep where there was only room for four, we all found a corner.

At dusk two days later I walked with Jim and other miners down a narrow country road to the pithead. In the distance screeching buckets were tipping slag on a pyramid of waste. At the pithead the miners put their pipes, matches and cigarettes into lockers, and changed into rougher clothes. We were given Davy lamps. We then mounted a steel stairway and made our way past miners and coal tubs to the shaft. We crowded into a packed, narrow cage like herrings in a barrel. It smelled of sweat and dampness and danger. The gate fell, fastening us in.

With no warning we suddenly dropped like a stone into the earth. For a moment I thought I'd lost my stomach. Had the cable snapped? My companions showed no concern; they continued to mutter to each other, while glistening cables, slimy beams and flashing lights shot by. Two thousand feet down there was an awful jolt, which made me think that the cage was rising again. A dusty burning smell filled the air.

We stepped out into a low main road. The grime-covered dayshift stood waiting to go up. A strong draught of air came from rattling ventilating machines. At a signal we climbed aboard a line of empty coal tubs headed to the coalface under the sea. After about a mile Jim waved for me to get off – the din was so great that speech was impossible.

Entering a gallery we stumbled forwards along a rough, wet track. The only lights were the Davy lamps and the lights on our helmets. Without my helmet the wooden beams would have felled me. Foggerty was able to move with his head down, yet see where he was going. As I staggered after him, wondering how much farther, I had my first feelings of claustrophobia. Ominous cracking noises came from the beams above my head. My back, neck and thighs were aching. The glamour of going down a mine was beginning to fade.

At the coalface Jim joined his team, leaving me to watch from a distance. Through the coal dust I saw a shadowy group of men. Some wore only clogs and kneepads. The temperature was over 80° F. In the flickering light the men looked tough. I watched them break up lumps of coal that had just been cut and blasted out of the wall. New holes were drilled and explosives inserted. Everyone took cover. There followed a tense moment of waiting. The signal was given and with a crash that stunned me, down came a seam of coal. As soon as the dust settled miners dashed in to prop up the roof with pitprops as thick as a man's calf. They worked as a team; each knew what to do. I wondered how a gentle dreamer like Jim could do such Herculean work.

Sometime during the night the pandemonium stopped and I was offered a little food that I washed down with cold tea. Jim introduced me to his mates. They nodded; they probably thought I was a nuisance.

After seven-and-a-half hours I groped after Jim down the endless galleries to the railway. There was no conversation on the way up. The men stood like sheep in a pen.

Light was coming when we reached the top. The air was sweet. As we shuffled out of the cage, the day shift shuffled in. We changed our clothes, handed in our equipment, gargled to rinse out the coal dust, and fell in with a stream of miners trudging across the bleak landscape. An east wind blew in from the sea.

163

Back in the house we stripped to the waist and, kneeling over a large tin bath in front of the fire, took turns washing. I cleaned Jim's back; he cleaned mine. It took several days to get rid of my aches and pains.

The next day Jim and I cycled to Hadrian's Wall, the north-west frontier of the Roman world, and explored its earth-works. I'd heard so much about the wall as a child that I was thrilled to see its ruins. The ruts of Roman chariot wheels were still there.

After several days I said goodbye to Jim and his family and took a train back to Oxford, stopping off for a night at Derby to see my parents. Jim went back down the mine. I left behind a courageous, generous, light-hearted people.

<hr />

Before Trinity Term began I spent a month reading in the Camera. I stayed with Mrs Padmanabha, who lived next door to the hostel. My savings and the money from the LCC scholarship kept me going. I was happy to forget that 'Schools' would come in June. There were times when I slipped away from my books to lie on flowered lawns with rose scent in the air and have tea, or sleepily sunbathe at Parsons Pleasure, or doze over endless cricket matches in the sunshine in the Parks, with bees in the grass and muffled bells sounding far away. What bliss to paddle a canoe to the Trout at Godstow, to linger over a beer and talk and watch the fireflies; how wonderful to dance in bare feet on lawns in moonlight with soft music coming through open windows; how easy to venture out into the enchanted Cotswolds, returning with the stars; and have enough shillings to rattle in your pocket to pay your way.

No wonder I loved Oxford. I was completely captivated by it. I loved it for what it was: a great centre of learning; I loved it for the challenge it presented; I loved it for the freedom and the wonderful life it offered; I loved it for the opportunity to enrich my life; I loved it for the teachers who had accepted me and who tried to help. They would never know what it meant to me. My only fear was that I would wake up one day to find that I was back with Charlie Bobbit at the Bow Bridge Iron Foundry.

I loved Oxford so much that I finally discarded my stolen clothes and bought a tweed jacket and grey flannel trousers like any respectable undergraduate. Before doing so, I pondered which was the more ethically correct: to wear clothing that I knew had been stolen, or to buy clothing with money for which I had not worked.

———◇———

Trinity Term begun, I worked hard at my studies. Somehow or other everything was beginning to come together. I also played hard. I rented a canoe called *Ruby*, which I regularly paddled to Godstow or Kings Lock. There I stripped off and swam. It was pure animal pleasure. 'You's a silly, bloody fool you is. You'll break your bloody neck, you will,' the lock-keeper bawled as I dived into the roaring water which flung itself over the weir into a rock-studded pool. Deaf to all caution, my body shot across the bottom like a trout. There are moments in life, like diving off a weir gate, which you never forget. Youth and spring together invite madness. I wallowed in the bliss of being alive. In those days God was everywhere. Every morning, while Jim was in chapel, I cycled to Port Meadow, stripped off and swam with the swans as my companions. Only those who have bathed in the crowded lake in Victoria Park would know the joy.

———◇———

Springtime is the time at Oxford when visitors fall from the sky. Dear Miss Hesselthwaite came from Bow. I met her at the station, found her a place in a house on Walton Street for the night, and spent the whole day with her going from college to college, and dining her out. She wore a starched print frock, a new hat with red glass cherries and a flowery scarf. She must have thought that the sun was stronger in Oxford than in London, for she held a parasol in her white-gloved hand. A few days before, she had seen the new king and queen in their gold coach on their way to the coronation at Westminster Abbey. Oxford had celebrated with dancing and champagne. She was thrilled at everything, and said all the right things to the people we met. What surprised me was that she said them in a superior tone of voice that I'd never heard before. She was thrilled to see the places where C. S. Lewis taught. She was familiar with *Dymer*, Lewis' book-length poem. She was so honest and good, so pleased at everything that was happening to me, that I felt like having a good cry when she left. 'Do well, Billy, for Bow,' she called as the train drew away.

The Mayor of Poplar, my old trade-union leader Albert Eastead, also paid me a visit. He arrived at the hostel in a shining limousine. ''Is 'Oner' was sitting next to his liveried chauffeur. O'Hea knew him well and was delighted to see him. From the letter that had preceded the mayor, I knew he was pleased to find an excuse to take a day off. 'Blimey,' he said, on getting out of the car, 'you 'ave become a toff, Billy.' I noticed the blue pouches under his eyes, his slight stoop and his shortness of breath. But he struggled on around the university and was interested in all I showed him.

When I introduced him to anybody of note, he'd invariably say the wrong thing in the direst Cockney accent. He answered Rodger when talking about Hitler with: 'If yer arsks my opinion [I honestly feared he would say 'old cock'], there's gonna be a war. Ye can't ply arahnd wiv people like 'Itler. Not 'im, not 'alf. 'E needs turning off, 'e do.' Eyebrows raised, Rodger had the good sense not to incite ''Is 'Oner' any further.

Late that afternoon ''Is 'Oner's interest in Oxford colleges began to wane. 'Look 'ere, Billy,' he said, mopping his brow, 'hedication is ahl right, but hain't it time we wets our whistle?'

''S right Albert,' the chauffeur agreed.

I prayed that the mayor and his chauffeur would not wet their whistles too much on their way home.

Harold Watkins also came as term was ending. He was still working in a woodyard. He came all dressed up wearing a starched shirt and a suit and shiny shoes. He had the same jolly eyes; his teeth flashed white under his dark moustache. He stayed at the hostel so that he might be closer to O'Hea and me. It was as moving to have Harold with me as it had been to have Miss Hesselthwaite. He and I had been together since we were children. For old times' sake, we drank and talked about the past most of the day and night. It was all nostalgia. We went into fits of laughter when we talked about the time we went looking for Betty Weatherby in a blizzard, and wondered what would have become of us had we gone to Russia. He had no news of Betty and little news of Lancashire. As we walked through the colleges, he marvelled at university life. 'Nobody working and three meals a day, Billy! You've arrived.' I introduced him to all the right people, to try to encourage him to get in, but he never did. It would have been wonderful if we could have been at Oxford together. He would have worked hard and done well. Harold was a good man, right down to his heels.

There was a note of sadness at our parting. Would we meet again, and in what circumstances? It was obvious that our lives were drifting apart. Unspoken, we both wondered how I had got to Oxford while he'd failed. We swore everlasting friendship. 'Billy,' he said, clasping my hand, 'Ah'll tell thee sumthin'. It's for thee own good. When tha famous, don't forget me or where tha's cum frae. Tha can get that in thee noddle.' My hand wilted in his clasp.

———◇———

And then one morning, unawares, came the dreaded thought of examinations. Gracious! How many weeks were left? How cruel that one could not go on enjoying the spring! I knew that failing was not an option. I'd no job to go to; I had to

167

pass. So back to the Camera I went, back to the books; further dancing on lawns in the moonlight would have to wait.

———◇———

One evening, on coming back from the Camera, I found a note from the principal asking me to see him. I went to his office and, late as it was, found him at his desk.

'What do you intend to do during the long vacation?'

'I have no plans. I haven't given any thought to it.'

'How would you like to spend the summer at the Ecole Sociale at Louvain University in Belgium?'

'What language do they speak in Belgium?'

'Flemish and French.'

'I don't know either.'

Ignoring my remark, he went on. 'A group of students from the Ecole Sociale are about to make a study-tour of the industrial centres of Belgium, Luxembourg and north-west Germany. The experience would be valuable, and it would help you to make connections abroad.'

I knew nothing about Belgium, except that my father had fought there. Although I had seen the word Louvain in learned articles, I didn't know that it was an ancient university. Later I discovered that O'Hea had studied there. 'What about money and how will I make myself understood?'

'The money can be worked out between Louvain and Oxford, the languages are your worry.'

'When do you want my answer?'

'Now.'

I took a deep breath. 'I shall be very happy to go, and am most grateful.'

'You've made the right decision,' he said returning to his papers. 'I'll provide you with details later.'

I was just about to leave when I blurted out a bit shame-facedly: 'I don't have enough money to keep me going until September.'

O'Hea was like Hans Thiel, nothing ever stumped him.

There was a perfectly simple way of doing everything.

'There's a man named William Cockerill,' he said, 'who was at Oxford a hundred years ago. He founded an armament industry and, among other things, the Cockerill Shipping Line. Their headquarters are in Liège, where the business started, but they have offices everywhere. There's one in London whose address I'll give you. Write to them, tell them who you are, and what your plans are. They'll put you on the continent and take you off without any trouble. Won't cost you a penny. It's something the founder thought would be a good idea for Oxford men. It's still done. I heard of someone getting a passage to North Africa the other day.'

I began to think of magic carpets.

'As for pocket money, there are half a dozen sources. Look up the ice-cream people, Tom Wall's. They're very generous to students like you who want to travel. Yes, I think Tom Wall's will do. Better get on to it tonight; there's not much time left.'

'No, there isn't.' I left in a daze. Going to Europe had been beyond my wildest dreams Yet here it was all settled – in minutes. It was overwhelming. O'Hea and I had discussed sums of money equivalent to my annual wage at the foundry.

I returned to my room and told Foggerty about my windfall. His first comment was that the principal must have felt pretty sure that I was going to pass my examinations. I thought so too. We toasted my luck with a glass of warm beer.

I wrote to the Cockerill line and to Tom Wall's. It bothered me to write to strangers for money. Any money I'd ever had, I'd had to work for – which I'd been brought up to believe was the right and proper thing to do.

Everything worked out as O'Hea had said. Cockerill sent me a card and a letter. The card was addressed to the Captain of the *Ghent*, which would take me from Tilbury to Antwerp. The letter told me to write to them in Hamburg for my return passage. Tom Wall's sent me a cheque almost by return mail. I studied that cheque for a long time. It was stiff and crisp and new. I'd never received money like that. I'm sure Tom Wall's knew what they were doing, yet the amount worried me, especially as I hadn't earned it. Ever after that I bought Wall's ice cream.

I also obtained my first passport. Its arrival at the hostel caused quite a stir. Foggerty and I thought its embossed golden lion, unicorn and crown most impressive. Imagine His Majesty requesting the whole world to allow me 'to pass freely without let or hindrance and to afford [me] such assistance and protection in [my] travels as may be necessary'. I didn't think anyone, least of all the King, would go to that trouble on my behalf. And for a mere seven shillings and sixpence.

Meanwhile I kept my nose to the grindstone. The examinations came and went. By luck, or industry, or both, I could not have done better. Rodger wrote across my papers: 'This would get a First in PPE' (Politics, Philosophy and Economics). O'Hea gave me the scripts to read for myself. He offered no praise. Foggerty passed, much to my joy, which meant we'd be together again in the autumn. He told me his plans were to spend the summer down the mine.

To celebrate the end of examinations, a group of us drank our way across the town. We started at a pub in North Oxford and downed a half-pint at every pub all the way to Magdalen Bridge. The thirst I had acquired as a 'sand rat' stood me in good stead. Foggerty and I were the only two sober enough to walk across Magdalen Bridge and take a drink at the pub at the other side. Our friend Thiel was nowhere to be seen.

The next day, dim-eyed, but excited and joyful at the prospect of my first sea voyage, I took the train to Tilbury to join Cockerill's freighter *Ghent*. I called in on the Hargreaves, but kept well away from Miranda – to whom I'd not written for a long time. I carried my very first pair of pyjamas in my bag.

I smelled the sea the moment I got out of the train. I found the *Ghent* tied up among a huddle of masts. Sailors were leaning over the rail. The ship was a scarred, battered work-horse of the seas. A wisp of steam rose from the funnel, the hatches were battened down.

I presented my card to the captain. He was a tall, bearded Scot with the beaked nose of a hawk. He was not pleased to see me or his company's card, and addressed his comments to his stubby pipe. The founder's intentions notwithstanding, students and other free riders were an abomination to him. Having assigned me a cabin, he waited for me to leave.

Disregarding the sullen reception, I went looking for my cabin. It was a tiny cell containing the bare essentials: bunk, seat, hand basin and a porthole. There was a smell of engine oil and burned soup. A lifejacket hung on a hook. I put my suitcase under the bunk and went up on deck. Darkness was falling.

Beneath a damp, leaden sky I watched the seagulls fighting for food. I knew that Romans, Saxons, Danes and Normans had been at Tilbury before me. Vikings had come to plunder. The fear of the Spanish Armada had run through its streets. Hunters for spices, gold, souls, fame and adventure had passed this way.

I was brought down to earth by a sailor who sidled up to me. 'So you're a student, are yee?' He eyed me in a jaundiced way. '. . . from Oxford?'

I said I was.

'Ah weel,' he went on, 'there's no tellin' what some people will do for a livin'. You are a good sailor?'

'I've never been to sea.'

'The pity,' he laughed. 'There's a storm brewing in the Channel and the old man has decided to sail on the night tide. He's at his best when water is coming over the gunnel. He has the record with Cockerill, he has, for the number of ships he's lost. We'll reach Antwerp about sunrise.'

My sense of adventure was coming under serious attack.

An hour or so later, the same sailor brought a large bowl of onion soup and some bread to my cabin.

'There's a poker game going on below deck,' he said as he laid out my food. 'I'll come for you if you wish.'

I said I did wish. Having eaten, I joined three others in a smoke-filled cabin at the stern. They all had weather-beaten faces. There was lots to drink. I didn't touch it; my face was swollen from the excesses of the previous night.

The speed with which they started to take my money scared me. I could see myself getting off the ship naked. I had to work myself into a lather to win it back. At cards my East End training stood me in good stead; I was not the dimwit they took me for.

While we were playing, the engine-room bell rang; boots clattered along the deck. With a slow rhythmic dipping movement and only the slightest suggestion of a roll, the *Ghent* glided out to sea. The night was quiet, the sea calm. For me, it was a moment of disbelief. Born on an island, I was sailing out into the world, as many of my forebears had done. Before turning in, I went on deck. I felt as free as a bird.

————◦————

With a crash that sounded like the end of time, the storm struck soon after midnight. I woke to thunder and a howling wind. I felt my bunk rise, only to drop to the floor again. For a moment I didn't know where I was. I struggled out of my cot and clung to the bulkhead. I put on my lifejacket. Knees bent against the heaving floor, I lurched to the porthole and looked out. An angry, white-capped wave rolled towards me; there was a blinding flash of lightning. I saw leaping mountains of water and shivered with cold. Every time the bow came crashing down, the ship groaned with me. I hoped that those on board knew what they were doing.

That night I was sicker than I thought it possible to be. When I was not clinging to the taps with my head over the basin, I was lying on my bunk contemplating the merits of free travel on the Cockerill Line. Exhilaration had left me. I vowed never to drink my way across Oxford again, or to eat onion soup. Exhausted, I fell in and out of sleep as the *Ghent* pitched wildly. The waves pounded against the porthole. I thought they would never stop.

The ordeal ended when we reached the shelter of the Scheldt. Since the sixteenth century this river had been used by the fleets of the world. The noises of the wind and the sea died away. I went on deck as soon as I could get myself together. The dawn was pale, grey and cold; lights flickered at the mouth of the river; a pilot came aboard. The shore loomed like a shadow; low clouds roiled across the land. Our prow divided the water into two curved sheets. Our engines beat more confidently now that the sea had been left behind.

Fifty miles later I caught a glimpse of the spire of Antwerp Cathedral soaring above the city. Its bells rang across the land. The *Ghent* shut off steam and glided to its berth. Ropes plopped into the water and were made fast; the shuddering stopped. We'd arrived. Moored ships and tall warehouses stretched as far as the eye could see. With a protesting creak the gangplank was lowered.

Feeling that it would be spurious to thank anyone for such a dreadful voyage, and reluctant to meet the captain again, I gathered my belongings, cleared customs with a Belgian official who came aboard, and staggered on to the quayside. The stamping of my passport restored my self-esteem. I had become an important person whose movements uniformed foreign officials took seriously.

I found a small dockside café and took a seat. For the first time in my life, I was on foreign soil. What a difference the crossing of a strip of water made. People looked different, talked another language, and drove on the wrong side of the road.

I ordered a strong cup of coffee. The proprietor detected the smell of onion soup. 'S'il vous plait, Monsieur . . .' (beyond that I understood not one word). Using his hands he wafted me to a little white-painted iron table outside. A parrot perched on a ring by the door screeched as I passed. To my surprise he squawked in French. I wondered what 'Merde! Merde!' meant.

Everything on the quayside was wet from the storm. I pulled my clothes tight around me in the freezing morning air as I drank my coffee and ate a miserable piece of flaking pastry called a croissant. No wonder we British believed that everything at the other side of the Channel was inferior. I was much too exhausted to take delight in having reached another world.

Chapter IX

Spreading My Wings

After another cup of coffee, I began to take an interest in my surroundings. Gulls wheeled overhead, sea water slapped and sucked against the quayside. The deep bass sounds of a foghorn filled my ears. The overhead cranes were busy swinging freight ashore.

After breakfast, I took a tram to the railway station. The train to Brussels departed with a feminine shriek. We slid across pasture land intersected by canals; parks, sleepy villages, cows and lumbering carts, all wrapped in the mist, slipped by. Later the sun broke through.

In Brussels I made my way to the youth hostel of the Jeunesse Ouvrièr Chrétien (Young Christian Workers) on Boulevard Poincaré. A lively young man, who introduced himself as Jean Doeraene, welcomed me. He was the secretary of Abbé Joseph Cardijn. He was delighted to have the opportunity to speak English. I was given a sleeping cubicle, open to all and sundry, and had a shower. While helping me to wash the onion-soup stains from my clothes, he told me that the Jocistes (whose aim was to bring the Christian gospel into working-class life) had played a militant role in capital-labour relations since the French sit-down strikes in 1936.

Later that morning, Doeraene took me on a whirlwind tour of the city. I have a dim recollection of churches, palaces, parks and triumphal arches – enough to last a lifetime. The pace was killing. I tried to say in French, 'Let us sit down under the trees and rest.' He probably didn't understand a word. Desperate, I looked up the word for hangover: I wanted to tell him I had a hangover and that I needed to go a little slower. The dictionary said *gueule de bois*. I decided to skip that one. Instead I raced after him. By lunchtime, the con-ducted tour had become a blur.

Our tour ended at the Luxembourg Gardens among flower beds that stretched for acres. We were lost in admiration of the roses when a young couple stopped arm in arm along-side us. Without one word of 'by your leave', the young man took out his penis and watered the roses. It caught us both by surprise. I was all for the workers of the world uniting, but not to piss on the roses.

―――――◇―――――

The following afternoon, I took the train to Louvain. After a good deal of hunting I reached the Ecole Sociale, where I was met by the director, Pater Perquay. To my embarrass-ment he kissed me on both cheeks.

Pater Perquay was a tall, white-haired Dominican priest in his late fifties, who spoke English in a deep Flemish voice. He was the soul of hospitality. He was quick to tell me that I had come to what at one time was the outstanding university of Western Europe. We drank a cup of coffee together, after which he insisted on showing me the college. I almost had my hand shaken off by the students to whom I was introduced.

Later, he took me to my room – a spacious, airy study on the ground floor that looked directly on to a canal with water lilies. Beyond were vegetable gardens and fields. A wood crowned the horizon. Although I still had to learn about the swarms of mosquitoes that would descend upon me at night and the pungent smell of 'night soil', which would greet me each morning, the arrangement seemed admirable. Through the open windows I could hear a carillon.

I sat next to Pater Perquay at dinner that night. While nuns, wearing white, starched headdresses, served us, he told me about the destruction of the university and the town in the Great War. Belgium had endured four years of German occupation. I was more concerned with the fact that I was eating horsemeat for the first time. As I was the only Englishman, the other students looked upon my arrival as a heaven-sent opportunity to try out their English. I had to fight every step of the way to speak French. After dinner we sat about in the common room. There were about twenty students there. Their greatest worry was the growing threat of war. Most of them had done military service, and were subject to immediate recall. At Oxford, war was a subject of conjecture; at Louvain it stared you in the face.

The next day, interspersed with endless cups of coffee, a couple of students showed me the university. The library had a soaring tower with a famous carillon. I saw the statue of Erasmus who had taught here; also a treasured copy of Thomas More's *Utopia*. Later, I was taken to classes. I learned little, but it gave me the chance to see Louvain's famous lecturers in action.

A couple of weeks after my arrival, our tour began. Our bus, when it arrived, did not inspire confidence, nor did Denis the driver. With a cigarette clenched between his yellow teeth, he looked a sad gnome.

Our journey took us south-west to Mons on the largest coalfield in Belgium. Every town we passed through had its memorial to those who had fallen in the Great War. From Mons through a flat countryside, we went eastward to Charleroi, centre of the Belgian iron industry.

As I stood among the showers of sparks and watched the workers toil, I couldn't help wondering how a 'sand rat' could sweat his guts out and be paid very little for it; whereas if you studied workers – as I was doing – you did very well. The farther one got away from working with one's hands – the work that made the wealth of nations, that gave us our daily bread – the better off one was. I had been brought up to believe that hard manual work paid – it didn't. None of the men I was looking at would come to be known individually; they'd play almost no role in forming the opinion of their age; yet without them our world could not continue.

From Charleroi we rattled eastward to the Liège-Seraing area on the banks of the Meuse, the heartland of Belgian industry. Here the night sky was lit by the eerie glow of blast furnaces, and coal and iron dust filled the air.

Ominous preparations for war met us wherever we went. In Liège we saw a machine that produced a rifle a minute. The finished rifles came off a moving belt faster than they could be handled. Production went on round the clock. Paradoxically, at one Belgian plant they were busy shipping crude iron to Germany by the trainload to make more weapons, to make . . .

On the wharf at Seraing, I came across a bronze statue of John Cockerill, son of the Oxford student William Cockerill, the English mechanic who had helped to turn Belgium into one of the workshops of the world, and on whose ship I had sailed from Britain.

Wherever we went, reinforced steel and concrete mounds and dragon's teeth tank traps scarred the countryside. I had never seen fortifications like that in England. Our defences were at sea, or built in somebody else's land.

The irony of studying the means of killing people during the week, and the treasures of Western art at weekends was not lost on me. We were the heirs of a very strange world.

———— ◇ ————

The racket of our engine echoing through the hills, we bounced through the narrow wooded valleys of the Ardennes. With nerve-racking regularity, Denis would halt the bus on the hills and struggle to find a lower gear. We would all breathe a sigh of relief when, amid the howls of the clutch, we were jerked forwards again.

We finally reached the city of Luxembourg perched on a rocky plateau. We stayed for several days and visited towns with unforgettable names such as Dudelange, Differdange, Rudange and Dommeldange. In 1937 Luxembourg was benefiting from rearmament and was considered an economic miracle. There was only one man unemployed there, or so they said. He was dusted off and brought before us when we visited the Minister of Labour. He was a jolly fellow in his fifties who enjoyed the role he was playing.

<hr/>

One day we lunched close to the German border. Through binoculars, we could see the frontier post at the top of a white-gravelled road. I took on a wild bet with the Belgian students that I could sprint to the German village of Roth, buy some German beer and sprint back again before the bus moved on. Bets placed, I left to a cheering start.

Once started, I began to have second thoughts. The road was steeper than I had thought, and I could not get a grip on the stones. Except for the buzz of insects and my own heavy breathing, no sound broke the withering heat. Knowing that my progress was being watched from above and below, I refused to turn back.

By the time I reached the checkpoint, my face was burning and I was drenched with sweat. The border guards concealed their thoughts with a curt 'Heil Hitler.'

'Good day,' I choked.

'Wo wollen Sie hin?' one of them said, as he studied my passport.

'I want to go to Roth to buy two bottles of beer.'

'Warum?' they demanded, eyebrows raised.

'I want German beer.'

They looked suspicious.

'Wo ist Ihr Gepäck?'

'I don't need any bags, only beer.'

While one of them consulted the regulations, the other fixed me with an unblinking stare. I sensed that he thought me a dangerous idiot.

Slamming the book shut, the first one took up his stamp and struck my passport a powerful blow. 'Gehen Sie,' he ordered, pointing to the door.

Gladly, I ran down a long hill to Roth. Using sign language, I purchased two large bottles of beer from a startled shopkeeper, then, clutching the bottles, I ran back to the two Germans at the top of the hill.

With a wooden stare, they told me that the beer could not be exported to Luxembourg without paying duty. But I had spent my German marks. One of them read out something in German. He was strangely serious, as if he was dealing with a smuggled bomb rather than smuggled beer.

'Basta,' he ended.

For a moment I was flummoxed. Did I have to surrender the beer? Had I run through all that heat for nothing? I could hear the Belgians laughing. The Germans looked as if they might laugh too.

Excusing myself, I left the hut and sat down among the wildflowers outside. With the two men watching, I drained both bottles. There was no regulation against that.

A little unsteadily I got to my feet and asked them to stamp my passport again. They looked at me angrily.

Clutching my passport and the two empty bottles, I stumbled down the hill to the bus and amid whoops and cheers I clambered aboard. Concealing his impatience, Pater Perquay studied the empty bottles. 'Holy Mother of God!' he said.

My passport and the empty bottles were passed from hand to hand. I revelled in my triumph. Although I had not returned with the beer in the manner intended, I had won the wager;

my slightly drunken state confirmed that. 'Sauvage anglais,' said Denis, starting the bus.

———<◇>———

Before leaving Luxembourg, Pater Perquay spoke to us about Germany and the 'new order' that governed it. He talked about the use of cameras, of guarding our tongues and not going off on our own. He left us in no doubt about his own disquiet. Nazism, he feared, threatened to create a godless state: slowly but surely the Nazis were divorcing the Church from the people, the children from their parents, and the nation from God. For evil men to triumph it only remains for good men to stay silent. For refusing to compromise their conscience and their soul, many Germans were now languishing in concentration camps. A few months earlier in March 1937 the encyclical *Mit brennender Sorge* (With Deep Anxiety) had been smuggled into Germany and read from every Catholic pulpit. In the encyclical the Pope denounced the Nazi doctrine of race and blood.

After the Roth incident, I think Perquay worried about me. 'You English,' he warned, 'are a happy-go-lucky people with a sense of humour; the Germans are not, especially when they are in uniform. You have a lot to learn, my child, be prudent.'

Perquay would never know the effect his few words of caution had upon me. In a flash I realised what Father D'Arcy had been talking about in his lectures on moral philosophy. 'What is the Good?' 'What is the true end of man?' he had asked, and it had all gone over my head. Now I realised that there had to be a Good – a right and a wrong way – independent of the exigency of the moment, independent of the political regime in power, independent of time. Man is a moral being and he has to make choices. D'Arcy had not been in the clouds after all. I had. He had been dealing with a real problem; a problem that was now costing people their lives and their liberty. I spent much of the rest of that day turning

183

these things over in my mind. It was like catching a fever.

From the moment we reached Trier with its Roman ruins, we were conscious of having reached a different country. The impression grew as we drove along the Mosel to Koblenz, where I first caught sight of the Rhine.

The countryside was so beautiful that I took time off to send coloured postcards of ancient towns and castles to family and friends. (My sister Brenda's reply awaited me when I returned to Louvain. It read: 'Have you robbed a bank?')

Compared with Britain and Belgium the atmosphere in Germany was almost euphoric. There was a brightness and a vibrancy about everything: a feeling of strength and pride. The post-war anarchy and humiliation of Germany were a thing of the past. The note of exhilaration conflicted with Perquay's grim warnings.

The Ruhr Valley throbbed with industrial power. There was a bitter smell of iron dust in the air; sombre clouds of smoke and steam hung over the region like a fog; blast furnaces glowed at night. A depressed area in 1933 when the Nazis came to power, the region now worked round the clock. The Belgian students were awestruck; it did nothing to lessen their fears.

The ugliness of the towns was deceiving. Alongside the smog and dirt were parks and forests, and lakes where we swam. We often sat in beer gardens eating sauerkraut and a vast variety of sausages and black bread. We learned to sing, 'Trink, trink, Brüderlein trink.' Some of the towns were renowned for their choirs, orchestras and museums. The Gothic towers of ancient churches rivalled the factory chimneys. Moats and ramparts were there to prove that there was hardly a town that hadn't been beleaguered at some time or other. The houses huddled together behind the walls like sheep. The only walled cities I knew in England were Chester and York, and that was because of the Romans.

For a week and a half, we visited industrial plants in Dortmund, Bochum, Wuppertal and Duisburg. People did everything they could to make our visit a happy one. Our arrival at Krupps coincided with that of the company's directors. They got out of their limousines wearing long black frock coats and tall silk hats; it looked like a meeting of funeral directors. Our bus was shunted aside until they had entered the building. I thought it fitting that such a group of sombre crows should direct one of the largest armament plants in the world.

The first thing I noticed on entering Krupps' main building were poster-size photographs of Hitler and other Nazi leaders on a visit to the plant. Armament manufacturers, like bankers, have to be humoured. A senior official formally welcomed us, clicking his heels and bowing. He reminded us that Krupps had been occupied by French and Belgian troops (emphasis on the Belgian) between 1923 and 1925.

On our last evening in Essen, we were addressed by a gently spoken party functionary who came to our lodgings to extend the best wishes of the state. Starting with 'Heil Hitler,' he stressed the need for cooperation between the youth of all nations. He went on to extol Germany's strength, pride, virtue and invincibility. Under Adolf Hitler the Germans had realised their age-old dream: the creation of a unified state. Their only wish now was to live in peace. In coming to power, Hitler had placed the peaceful cooperation of nations above all other aims. He reminded us of the pledge given by the Führer on the Fallen Warriors' Day in 1936 that he would never sacrifice the flower of the German nation in war. 'It is not for you to *die* for your country,' Hitler had declared, 'but to *live* in a country worthy of your love.' The speaker ended with a plea for peace.

I'm convinced he honestly believed every word. No questions were invited; none were asked. After a hush, Pater Perquay thanked him on our behalf.

The next morning we heard that Japan, with whom Germany was cementing relations, had begun an undeclared, all-out war against China.

185

And then our trip was over and we were back in the rattling, wheezing bus headed for Aachen on the frontier. The visit had made a deep impression on us. Nobody on the bus criticised the German people who had been so generous; nobody denied the exhilarating feeling that we'd felt throughout our tour; nobody doubted that Germany was a most civilised country. What we feared was the brutality of the regime. The persecution of minorities and opponents could not be talked away.

Our thoughts were best summed up by one of the students: 'We are Athenians,' he said, 'returning from a visit to Sparta.' There was little humour in Sparta and even less tolerance.

The debate about Germany continued after we returned to Louvain. Each of us had his own version of how the future would reveal itself. The hope of the rule of law prevailing in international relations was being shattered daily in Spain, Ethiopia, and now in China. Crude power was taking over the world.

During the remainder of my stay in Belgium I visited the homes of students across the country – from the flax fields of Flanders to the valley of the Meuse. Always I was asked the same question: 'Will there be war?'

Meanwhile, I did my best to study the books I had brought with me. Staring at the fields beyond the canal outside my window, I also tried to improve my French with the help of a Hugo *Teach Yourself* book. Occasionally, I'd continue to work at my open window until the long, graceful shadows had yielded to darkness and a pale and mystic moon.

At the beginning of September I met up with Jean Doeraene, the young man I had met in Brussels. Together we went on a two-week cycling tour of the Ardennes. We took a train from Louvain Station late one morning on a fine summer's day. Our destination was a low, blue ridge on the horizon. Hour after hour, our train creaked its way into the hills. The higher we went, the colder it got; we finally wrapped ourselves in our blankets. Steam misted the windowpanes. We were still rattling along when the sun set behind us among blood-red rays.

We finished up hours late, half-dead, in the pitch-dark, on the platform of an abandoned railway halt called Quarreux. The station was the nearest point to the Jociste youth hostel we were headed for and trains stopped on request. We watched the dwindling red light of the departing train rocking into the gloom. Its whistle sounded lonely and sad.

We didn't know where we were, or how we could get to the youth hostel. The platform was covered with nettles; the building – abandoned for the wind to batter and the rain to beat – was collapsing from lack of repair. All around us was a dense forest with a strong resinous smell; somewhere below us a river rushed by; a low mist lay among the trees; there was no moon. We gazed at our bleak surroundings and bedded down where we stood.

'This will test les Anglais,' Jean said, as he took out his groundsheet and blanket. Reluctantly, I followed suit.

Half an hour later the cold forced us to get up. We stamped about to restore circulation. Desperate, we removed the hasp from the waiting-room door and lay down on the benches inside. We'd hardly put our lights out when we heard a pattering of little feet. Warily, we stared into the darkness.

I woke to rats rustling among my kit. Light filtered through the dirty windows and the cracks in the walls. We got our things together and, guessing at the route, entered the forest. The land was hushed and grey. My spirits were a little better than they had been the night before. As we pushed our bikes, sometimes climbing over fallen trunks, the greyness changed to green.

We eventually located the youth hostel by its smoke. It was a remote cabin, buried in a wood of silver birches and pines. It had about it an air of wanting to remain hidden. Breakfast was being cooked; we were given a warm welcome.

It is amazing what a hot drink and food can do to make the world seem a better place.

The hostel contained a bench, a table made from local pine, a Dutch tiled stove with logs stacked against it, and several cots. The table had been scrubbed so often that it was milky-white. Candles and paraffin lamps were the only light. Everyone helped with housekeeping and log splitting. The pervading smell was one of wood smoke and bodies.

When the sun had gone down and the hills had risen huge and dark, we sat around a crackling campfire – the light flickering on our faces, the smoke sometimes blowing in our eyes – singing and telling tales, disregarding time. For the hardy, there was a homemade swimming pool filled with ice-cold water. The less hardy could share a tin bath with water heated on the stove. Except for those who washed first, the colour of the water went from grey to black.

If the weather was good, Jean and I cycled along narrow winding roads to isolated villages. En route, I was given a lecture on the Ardennes, most of which I promptly forgot. Sometimes we'd have to push our bikes up the long, silent grades. Exhausted, we would lie on our backs in the velvet grass against the sun-warmed earth, listening to the hum of insects. We picnicked by gurgling streams, feasting on bread, cheese, onions and apples. One day we stood and watched a solitary hedgehog crossing a lonely country lane. We'd sit in bright sunshine on a stone bridge and lose ourselves in the water's flow. With a hawk hovering almost motionless overhead, a partridge leaped from the grass with a startled whir. With the shadows becoming night and darkness creeping through the hills, we'd return to the hostel, mosquitoes singing in our ears, our handkerchiefs full of mushrooms

Gritty porridge and mushrooms were the staple diet. We boiled the mushrooms and ate them with salt and pepper, or cut them to bits and fried them in butter with garlic and onions. Everyone except me seemed to know where to find them, and how to distinguish the poisonous from the wholesome, the tasty from the bitter. Jean was a connoisseur. There was always speckled trout. At the end of the day our bodies ached with weariness. I seldom had time to study the knot-filled ceiling above my cot before falling asleep. You don't notice mosquitoes when you're worn out.

I usually rose early to watch the dawn – my senses have always been most aware of beauty at first light. The morning dew gleamed on the trees like pearls. I revelled in the cloudless sky, the sun touching the hills, the pine-scented air, and a lark making its tireless chant. I was entranced by the countryside in its summer garb: I watched the hills changing colour in the different light, the river hurtling and foaming, and the trees bending in the breeze. I caught a glimpse of red deer bolting for cover.

At day's end, pools of shadows and the sun's rays faded among the trees. A long twilight and a reddened sky gave way to a hushed blackness. The nightingales sang. Occasionally, planes flashed across the sky reminding us of another, more urgent world.

On our last night around the campfire, with an improbably large yellow moon rising over the hills and a ring of young faces turned to the flames, we talked about the coming war in which we probably would have to fight. It was a still night with the hills settled into silence. Before turning in, somebody began a lullaby; the rest of us took it up:

Ferme tes jolis yeux	Close your pretty eyes
Car les heures sont brèves	For the hours are brief
Au pays merveilleux	In the wonderful country
Au beau pays du rêve.	In the beautiful country of dreams
Ferme tes jolis yeux	Close your pretty eyes
Car tout n'est que mensonge	For everything is but an illusion
Le bonheur est un songe	Happiness is but a dream
Ferme tes jolis yeux.	Close your pretty eyes.

After singing it several times Jean and I said goodbye to the others. I left the fireside lost in thought. While I was moved by the singing, I rejected the idea that the whole adventure of life was false and that only in sleep was there relief.

'What do you think?' I asked Jean.

He shrugged. 'Leave it to God,' he said, turning away.

We rose at dawn to catch the only train halting at Quarreux that day, silently creeping out of the hut before the last star had faded. Around us the world was hushed. Capped by the morning mist, the brown hills slept. We took a short cut across a field to the station, leaving a track of black footprints. We climbed from a cold platform into an even colder train.

Our train creaked its way downhill through fields of marigolds and cowslips. We returned to the plains with our senses sharpened, our eyes and ears keener, and our range of feelings widened. We were bursting with good health. As the day wore on and the cold mist melted from the land, we ate the blackberries we had picked the day before. We had come across great thickets of them and had pulled them down and gobbled them hungrily by the handful until the juice ran from our chins.

From Brussels I went with Jean to his home in the village of Bois d'Haine for a weekend visit. The countryside was tinted with autumn colours. Jean's fiancée Julienne Olivier, a petite, attractive girl wearing a Brussels university cap, met us at the station. She called me Guillaume. She was accompanied by her aunt; chaperoning was *de rigueur*. Whenever we went for a walk in the countryside, the aunt always trailed us.

On Sunday morning we went to church and returned for a midday feast to Julienne's sprawling family farm outside

190

the village. It was the first time in my life that I had been treated as the guest of honour, and I found the warmth of it overwhelming. Relatives had come from miles around.

When Jean and I arrived, we were greeted by a jolly, noisy gathering. A long dining table and benches ran down the room; a selection of wines lay on the table in wicker baskets. After introductions, we were offered an apéritif and were soon jostling and shouting with the rest. At one end of the room women were cooking among a cloud of steam. Julienne and her mother constantly ran from guests to ovens. Close to the entrance, a man played a fiddle. All the windows were open and the shutters were thrown back.

Before the feast, Monsieur le Curé said grace. After a delicious vegetable soup the real eating and drinking began. Just when I thought the meal was done, we started all over again – each dish greeted with a cheer. We ate shellfish and duck and veal and vegetables and puddings and savouries and blackberry tarts and cheeses and nuts and fruits and goodness-knows-what else. You either met the challenge of the next dish or felt the shame. Everyone gave the impression that they intended to sit there eating and drinking for days.

As course followed course, talk and laughter became more excited; faces reddened. Between drinks, the fiddler played. Like the others, I loosened my tie and unbuttoned my jacket. I was intrigued by the way the men would light up their pipes between courses, or chat with each other at the open windows, or even wander off and come back again. It was like going to a long play at the theatre where one was allowed to go out at the interval to recover. The women chatted to each other, trying to exchange years of gossip in a single afternoon. The children ran about uninhibitedly; the infants were passed around the room.

At the end of the meal, Jean suggested that I should offer a toast of thanks. I responded as best I could in halting French. Either the company had ceased to be discerning, or my eloquence had improved with wine; whichever, my toast brought prolonged applause and a whole stream of other toasts. Jean got up to toast my health and obtained from me a pledge that I would return to Flanders. For each toast it was compulsory for me, as the guest of honour, to consume twice the amount that other people were drinking. At least that is what happened. I began to wonder when all the conviviality would end – I knew I couldn't keep up much longer.

After the guests had gone, Jean and I staggered out of the house and threw ourselves down under the branches of an apple tree, where we slept until the shadows fell.

By now the two of us had become firm friends. It was hard for me to say goodbye to him in Bois d'Haine and make my way back to Louvain.

———— ⟨◇⟩ ————

At the beginning of October, with the earth a little cooler and the summer fragrance gone, I parted from my friends in Louvain with the greatest regret. They gave me a send-off by taking me out on a drinking spree, and as a parting gift they gave me a German bicycle lock I had admired. It was far superior to anything we had in Britain. Fixed to the frame of the bike, it threw a bolt across the spokes; it was extremely effective in putting off bike thieves. Later on I could always identify my bike with it.

'My child, I think war will come,' Pater Perquay said as he hugged and kissed me farewell. 'I shall pray for your safety. I think Hitler will drag the German people and us into the pit. I don't believe the League of Nations will make the difference. What is everybody's business is nobody's business.'

Once more I travelled from Antwerp on a Cockerill vessel down the Scheldt. We went slowly in the evening light, trailing smoke, the silver river ruffled by a breeze, the water whispering at the bow. For the moment I was conscious of a shining, sensuous world. I remained on deck as we passed through the shadowed dunes, the sun-tipped spire of the cathedral receding behind us. Westward the sky glowed red.

The echoing notes of the carillon could be heard long after Antwerp had disappeared into the night. With each peal of the bells the hush of night deepened; there was goodness in the moment. The world was at peace; heaven was on earth and we were at its centre. Time was suspended.

The captain of this ship could not have been more hospitable. With much yarning and laughter, we drank our way to Tilbury. For one night, I forgot all about the threat of war.

I reached Oxford at the beginning of Michaelmas Term, with some ice-cream money still in my pocket. I was glad to be back, and aware of the great debt I owed O'Hea, Perquay, the Cockerill shipping line and Wall's ice cream. My north-of-England conscience reminded me that while my fellow students at the hostel had been working, I'd been having the time of my life. I felt a touch of guilt. I wondered if I should salve my conscience by returning the unspent money to the ice-cream company.

I returned with greater self-confidence and a much broader outlook than I had had when I set out. Above all, I recognised the universal nature of Christianity. A Mass in Germany or Belgium was the same as a Mass in Oxford. Going abroad had enlarged my imagination and my knowledge of French and German. I came home to England's odd-shaped fields and winding roads realising how lucky Britain was to be an island. How peaceful it was compared with the continent. Yet I no longer saw it – as I had done since childhood – as the strongest country on earth. While Germany was self-assured, officious and bold, Britain seemed to be faltering. Germany couldn't find sufficient labour to do all the jobs it had to do; millions of people in Britain were still out of work.

My travels had played havoc with my pacifism. What I had seen and heard had convinced me that the Nazis were bent on aggression; and the same could be said for the

Japanese who were now pillaging China. How much longer, I asked myself, could I afford to be a pacifist?

But I returned to an Oxford untroubled by the threats of war. People like me, who came hurrying back from Germany with a note of alarm in their voice, were called prophets of doom. My companions had no time to discuss that clown Hitler.

Chapter X

An Old Hand

Oxford, when I had set eyes on it a year ago, had been love at first sight; now it was love enduring. The fears I'd felt then had long since passed. Superior voices and Oxford airs still jarred me, but I no longer felt my separateness, or had to clench my teeth or watch my temper. When I heard the endless peals of Big Tom, I knew I had come home.

Foggerty and I were glad to see each other. We had a beer to celebrate. We now occupied the other large bedroom at the front of the hostel – why we should have occupied the best rooms for two years was something we didn't enquire into.

While I had been enjoying myself on the continent, Jim had been mining coal. 'I've never known anything else,' he said.

Thanks to O'Hea and Rodger, I was directed to all the right tutors. By now Rodger had become my mentor and I was careful to follow his advice. He had a way of smoothing out bumps without fussing. I settled down once more at a desk in the Camera, did my tutorials, and attended the lectures I wanted to hear.

After Louvain, with its stuffy afternoons spent in smoke-filled cafés and students' rooms, I was happy to get back to football, swimming and canoeing. The work-hard, play-hard Oxford regime suited me better, and I got more work done. While the soft autumn air continued, Foggerty, Thiel and I would sometimes cycle to the low-beamed parlour at the Trout at Godstow and have a bite of food and a drink, which is what people had been doing there since the twelfth century. While the water rushed over the weir, we talked about life and its tangled human relations.

The threat of war was never far from our talks. Although my hope for peace was beginning to fade, it had not faded enough for me to join the Officers Training Corps. Those who did would be commissioned on the outbreak of war. I was too much of a pacifist to take their advice. Hans and I stayed out because we were anti-military; Jim stayed out because mining was a reserved occupation. We'd been brought up in an age that was appalled by the staggering losses of Ypres, the Somme, Verdun and Passchendaele. Our fathers' generation had been fooled and betrayed. A great many of us believed that the military had botched the Great War, and that the politicians had botched the peace. If we didn't watch out, the old men would sacrifice us next. We didn't agree with Winston Churchill that war with Germany was inevitable. With his scaremonger views, he was in the wilderness, isolated and unpopular. But as time passed, the odds of war grew. 'Our frontier,' said Lord Baldwin, 'is on the Rhine.' Many of us wondered whether we would have time to finish our studies.

———<o>———

I kept the growing tensions in international relations from interfering with my life by indulging in a good deal of outside reading. I didn't respect the dictum: 'You should read what you're told to read, and keep your nose out of books that don't concern you.' With Thiel pointing the way, I discovered Thucydides and Herodotus, Livy and Tacitus. I found the Bible, the Koran and the Bhagavad Gita. I also read the Jewish Book of Psalms. With the exception of the twenty-third Psalm, 'The Lord is my shepherd . . .' I was appalled by them. 'Why are they so full of horror and violence and vindictiveness?' I asked Thiel.

'To remind us of terrible times.'

I bought used books at a shilling a time, and consumed the works of Swift, the Brontës, Hardy, Ruskin, Wells, Shaw, one after the other. They greatly enriched my life. Rodger encouraged me to read Macaulay, Green, Gibbon and Hume. Gibbon I found ironical; Hume was too dour. I couldn't swallow the idea that we could never prove something to be valuable or right. I thought that reason guided emotions and not the other way round. Everything Rodger recommended stirred my imagination, which is what he intended. The appeal of history, he kept saying, is imaginative. Perhaps that's why I loved history. A manual worker has an inborn antipathy to theories – as I discovered when doing economic theory – but shows no reluctance to use his imagination.

I have to thank Thiel for introducing me to the Old Vic. 'Come with me, Woody, you lack sophistication; can't let studies interfere with a renaissance in the theatre.' The West End plays were a long way from the 'penny readings' I had heard as a child. If I had any reservation, it was that too few of them dealt with the problems of the masses.

———◦———

In November 1937, my old East End friend Peter Levine paid me a visit. Invalided out of the Republican Army in Spain, reality for him was that he no longer had a right hand. I'd already been told about it and I couldn't help wondering what might have happened to me had I gone with him.

He got out of the train full of life and greeted me warmly.

Neither of us mentioned the missing hand, but for a moment it made our meeting awkward. Although the weather was mild, Peter was wearing heavy clothing. His face, which looked older and thinner, still showed its customary pain of commitment. He wore a Trotsky-like beard and a coarse cap; his spectacles were of the cheapest kind. I thought that something abstruse had crept into his face since I last saw him: it had hardened. As he gripped my shoulder with his good hand, I caught a glimpse of the old fanatical fire in his eyes. He could have been a member of the Soviet Politburo.

I introduced him to O'Hea, whom he had once called 'dark and sinister'. Talking about old times, we wandered about the town, eating and drinking as we went. I remembered the day in Poplar when he had invited me to join the Communist Party; I wondered if he was about to try again.

Without a word being said, I could see that the beauty of the university was lost on him. His mind and his feelings were elsewhere. He spoke with great passion, as he always had done, of the uselessness of intellectualism. He regarded Oxford as a citadel of class privilege aimed at perpetuating a social order that benefited the rich. 'Vacuous, feeble people,' he said viciously, 'too tired to lead. It's this herd that is bringing the country to its knees.' He didn't give a damn if he was over-heard. I listened to his bitterness with impatience. I'd never known him quite so censorious.

After a year at the university I was willing to adapt traditional institutions to a new setting. Why sweep away a centre of learning that expressed so well the ideals of order, harmony, proportion and beauty? I couldn't help thinking that with Peter as vice-chancellor the university would be a bleak place.

That afternoon Peter spoke before the Labour Club; communism was respectable at 'Red Oxford'. The club had been infiltrated by the Communist Party and the Young Communist League, especially since the outbreak of the Spanish Civil War. The talk was a Peter performance, full of sacred fire. He described the heroic resistance of the Loyalist troops in Madrid. 'But for Russian tanks, Franco would have entered Madrid in October 1936.' He didn't hesitate to tell his audience that almost all of the British volunteers of the International Brigade were working class.

'Spain is the dress rehearsal for a worldwide conflict between socialism and fascism. The British labour movement should stand up and demand "Arms for Spain". Labour's opposition to conscription is utter madness. Sooner or later you'll all have to fight. Pacifism means abandoning the world to tyranny. Weapons are the crucial factor in the saving of the world.' Krupps would have agreed with him.

He finished to great applause. The students were on Peter's side – this fellow, we thought, is talking about the war he's fought. Yet Peter had his critics. One student accused him of depicting the war as part of a contest between good and evil. Another complained that Peter had led us to believe that the Republicans were united, which they weren't. They were killing each other. Someone else thought that the Soviet Union was being painted in too good a light. Its intrigues and growing influence in Madrid had provided Franco with an excuse to intervene. Peter was so spiritually exalted with his crusade against Franco that he was not open to argument. In answer to a question, he accepted the murderous purging by Stalin of leading Russian communists as completely above board. He refused to believe reports of atrocities committed by the socialist republican government of Spain.

The meeting was an eye-opener for me. I didn't realise that there were so many ifs and buts about the conflict. I saw the Spanish Civil War, as Peter still saw it, as black and white; right and wrong. I don't suppose Peter would have gone off and lost his hand had he not seen it like that. He had risked his life because he had had a vision.

We went for a beer after the meeting. Making no allowance that Peter was a guest, Thiel went after him hammer and tongs. It was an experience for Foggerty and me to listen to two brilliant people arguing from different sides of the barricade.

'Communism is not out to save the working class,' Thiel argued, 'it's out to use them. Your loyalty does not lie with the British working class but with the Communist International and Russia.'

The two became so heated that they did not even take time off to drink their beer. 'What is the difference,' Thiel asked finally, 'between a Nazi and a communist tyranny? They are both tyrannies.'

Peter was not slow in answering. 'One tyranny, if you must call it that, represents the masses, the Nazi tyranny represents the few.'

'Those two spoiled my beer,' Foggerty later complained.

Peter and I met again the next day. No matter how hard I tried to avoid it, we started arguing with each other. 'The nobs have captured you,' he interrupted me, as he strode restlessly about my room. 'They'll turn you into a bourgeois intellectual, you'll see; you're going to be as effete and ineffective as the rest. You're no longer one of us.' He stopped his pacing to look out of the window as if he were expecting someone. Then he was off again.

'You don't know what you are talking about,' I shouted. 'You won't listen. I can't stand it any longer.' What I wanted to say was: 'You frighten me, Peter. You have become so concerned with the struggle that you have lost sight of the ideal with which you and I set out. You've stopped talking about people, except to say that the people must not rule; the revolutionary minority must rule, of which you leave me in no doubt you are one. When you imply that inhumanity can be excused on the grounds of class war, we must go our separate ways.'

I learned later that Peter returned to Spain as a political advisor. In 1939 I spoke with someone who swore he had seen him in Moscow; he had had no difficulty in identifying a fellow without a hand. After that there was silence; no subsequent inquiry succeeded in finding him. He must have been liquidated in one of the communist purges by someone more dedicated and ruthless than he.

Peter's certainty about a coming world tragedy haunted me after he'd gone. A nice pickle I'd be in if he was right: I'd either have to go to jail as a conscientious objector, or I'd be sent to the front. Either way, it would be the end of Oxford for me. He'd been so cocksure that I expected a declaration of war to appear on the newspaper placards every time I went out. It was a relief when leaving the Camera at night to read that 'Lightning wins Aintree at 20 to 1', or that Jean Batten had flown from Australia to London in five days, eighteen hours. As long as the horses kept running and Jean Batten kept flying, I felt safe.

I don't know what Peter would have said had he seen me a week later. To my surprise, the girl who sat opposite me in the Camera slipped a note across the desk, inviting me to dinner.

I spiffed myself up and, clutching a bunch of flowers, climbed the staircase to her rooms at the appointed time. Everything went well: the meal, the drinks, the conversation and the candlelight. The room was pleasantly warm. What more could I ask, I wondered?

I soon found out. Dinner done, the girl opened the window 'for a breath of fresh air'. Up went the window, out went the candles. The room was plunged into darkness.

'I say,' a voice reached me from the dark, 'isn't this all too jolly?'

There followed a tense silence during which I did not come up to scratch. I behaved miserably – I struck a match.

Since then I've never seen candles blown out with one puff without thinking of that wonderful girl.

In mid term I had a visit from Ma and Emily Hargreaves. They came off the train carrying umbrellas and handbags.

Their hair was curled, they wore floral dresses, loose jackets, large straw hats and fancy shoes. I don't know how much robbery had gone on to turn them out like that. Mum's cameo of a swan was pinned to the centre of her bodice. I hugged them both. They hadn't changed a scrap.

'How are you, Mum?'

'I've still got me 'elth an' strenf.'

'You talks like a nob, Billy,' said Emily.

I made an impressive start by taking them by taxi to the lodgings I had rented for them.

Their reaction to Oxford was like my own a year earlier – they thought it unreal. They couldn't get over the beautiful buildings, the empty streets, and the colour people had in their cheeks.

The first night we dined at the Mitre, where I'd reserved a table for three with candles. The second night we dined with O'Hea at the hostel. He liked to fuss over people from the East End.

He talked with Ma Hargreaves about her work. He scolded her for opposing the building of air-raid shelters in Poplar.

'Only encourages war,' she argued.

'But if you're wrong?'

'Well, we'll sing "Hain't it grand to be bloomin' well dead".'

Later that night, she talked to me about the Hargreaves family. 'Clem an' Chris are still at the Poplar 'Ospital. If war comes, they'll go to an 'ospital in Cambridge. Clem 'as made sure that if 'e 'as to jump 'e'll be given a good place to jump to. Carol is still in 'er old clerical job.'

I asked about Miranda.

'She's 'avin' a stormy affair with Milton. Much better if it 'ad been you. I'd always 'oped it might be. Miranda's dad 'as died. It was the wallop that dun 'im in. They 'ad trouble getting 'is coffin out of the 'ouse. Bernie too 'as died. The TB did it. 'E was the family clown till the end.'

Alex – my old night school mate – had married a widow and lived in a penthouse in the West End. He was prospering in some shady financial business. He'd done what he'd set out to do: he'd left the working class behind.

I worried about Ma Hargreaves after she'd gone. Like Lansbury, she seemed so fixed in her views about pacifism. She was ignoring the growing menace of the fascist powers. In her daily life she was down to earth; in politics she could be in the clouds.

———◇———

To my intense surprise I came home one night to find Miranda sitting in my room. She had come uninvited and unannounced. She could not have come at a worse time. She was provocatively wide-eyed and beautiful. She wore a yellow jacket and skirt, silk stockings, high heels and a wide-brimmed straw hat. Her hair straggled out in an enchanting way; around her neck was an imitation gold chain. Anticipating problems with the principal (female guests did not go upstairs), I immediately found a room for her in Walton Street.

I soon discovered why Miranda had come. She'd hardly got settled than she reached for me and snuggled her head against mine.

'I think we should get married,' she said. She kissed me gently and looked deep into my eyes.

It took several moments for me to get hold of myself. I was too confused, I'd thought that my going to Oxford had made a clean break between us. Common sense told me that marrying Miranda would be a disaster.

She bit her red lips as she awaited my answer. The street noises faded away. There was a great quiet between us. Only our eyes were joined.

'Miranda, it would be wrong of me to marry you. We are good friends, we've meant a lot to each other, but we are not life partners. If I married you it would end up in my making you unhappy.' I dared not say that the university atmosphere would choke her to death.

Tears filled her eyes. 'I wish you knew 'ow much I love you. Don't you love me just a little?' She put her head on my shoulder and held me close. Passion and pity nearly did me in.

'Of course I love you Miranda, but that's different from marrying you. Try to understand me. We love each other but we live in different worlds; it would be a lie to think anything else.'

'You only see your own world, you do. You think I'm set in my ways, but I'm not. I've got a good 'eart, I 'ave.'

'Of course you have. I don't want to try to change you. Be yourself. Stay as you are.'

'What you're saying is that I'm no longer good enough. You've become a nob, Billy. You've no time for a working girl like me. I can understand you wanting to get rid of me.' She burst into tears.

'Miranda, I'm not a nob and never shall be. My being at Oxford has nothing to do with my liking you or not. Let's not hate each other whatever happens.'

'Why don't you just say I'm not good enough, and 'ave done with it. I'd understand that; it would be 'onest.'

I tried to console her, but she shook me off, exclaiming, 'You're a no-good nob.' Tears ran down her face; her make-up became a dreadful sight. I felt guilty, it was terrible to see her like that.

The next two days were spent sorting out our relations. My work had to go to the wall. It was an exhausting experience during which I had to struggle repeatedly not to be unkind. I wanted to smooth away all anger and hurt, but no words fitted. The more we talked, the less we understood each other. Eventually we saw the futility of it all and lapsed into silence – what was there to talk about? We were both in a daze.

Miranda left on the morning of the third day. She had seen almost nothing of the university. It was a strain to look at each other, so awkward were our feelings. I thought it cruel that our friendship should end this way. It was hard for both of us until the train pulled out. I must confess that as I watched it disappear, I felt relief.

———◇———

It was shortly after Miranda's visit that German refugees began to arrive at the hostel. They talked with O'Hea in his office. I noticed that he shut his door. They were always hungry, always downcast and always in transit – an hour or two and they were gone with their worldly possessions under their arm. Apart from introducing us to the visitors, O'Hea was tight-lipped about them. He had strong connections with the German labour movement and was saddened at the refugees' plight. 'Heads will roll, heads will roll. For some, vengeance is sweet,' were his only comments.

As 1937 gave way to 1938 the drumbeats of war grew louder. From this point on there was no stopping Hitler. On 4 February 1938 he assumed sole command of the German armed forces; on 12 March, while the French government was in complete disarray, German troops entered Austria. By uniting Germany and Austria, Hitler had violated the Treaty of Versailles. Britain and France breathed fire and smoke; the League condemned the Anschluss, but nothing was done. What could be done? Ninety per cent of Germans and Austrians were cheering. Another nail had been driven into Europe's hope for peace.

Two days after the Anschluss, Winston Churchill rose in the House of Commons to warn Britain of Hitler's aggressive plans. Terrifying forecasts had been made about the overwhelming superiority of the Luftwaffe. Anthony Eden, also critical of Chamberlain's policy, resigned his post as foreign secretary and joined Churchill in the wilderness. 'We are heading,' he said, 'for a universal tragedy that will engulf us all.'

———◇———

I offset my growing worries about the worsening world scene by playing cricket in the Parks. Although I hadn't played cricket before, I took to it at once. War or no war, I bought white trousers and white boots. My sister Brenda knitted a pullover of the right colours and away I went. There must have been something about cricket that suited me because I excelled at it. It thrilled me to clout the ball with all my strength. Yet it was a nob's game, played low-key.

I loved bowling most of all. What a thrill to get the feel of the ball while rolling up your sleeves and taking stock of the batsman and the field. What joy to run up to the wicket with the right pace, skip and a jump. How wonderful on reaching the stumps to throw your body right back, point your left shoulder at the batsman, shoot out the left arm to the full, and then come through with the right arm, hurling the ball with enough strength to blow the batter and the wicket away.

What peace later on to lounge about in the sunshine in the outer field, while chewing on a stalk of grass and waiting for a catch or the last over. What fun to listen to the spectators calling, 'Run, run man. Make a single . . . Oh I say, well stopped . . . lovely!' Cricket taught me a great deal about the adaptability of my fellow countrymen. It also tested my courage. Anyone who can face a fast ball on a bumpy pitch with the sun in his eyes can face anything.

———<o>———

I cannot refer to the Parks without feeling embarrassed. A terrible thing happened to me there one day. Coming out of a crowded lecture at Keble, I saw a young cleric jump on my bike and pedal away. My bike was old – I'd bought it for ten shillings – but it was my only transport. While all Oxford bicycles were old and looked alike, I knew it was mine because I recognised the German lock that my Belgian friends had given me. It was the only bike in Oxford with a lock like that.

'Excuse me!' I shouted after the cleric as he passed through Keble's gates. 'Excuse me! You've taken my bike!'

He pedalled away harder than ever.

I ran after him. 'I say,' I called as I caught up, 'you've made a mistake!'

He gave me a frightened look.

I either had to let him go or do something drastic. I chose to do something drastic. Almost out of breath, I gave him a hard push that sent him and the bike flying into the gutter. Wheels spun around, books and papers littered the street.

It is hard for anyone to appreciate how I felt when I discovered that the bike was *not* mine. I didn't know where to look, or how to begin to apologise. No words fitted my predicament.

Uttering a string of 'terribly sorrys', I helped the poor fellow to his feet and dusted him down. He stifled a groan. I recovered his possessions, while he watched me with injured, fearful eyes. I knew he was looking upon me as a dangerous lunatic.

I pointed to the lock on his bike. 'I thought I was the only one in Oxford with such a lock.'

'I bought it on a visit to G . . . G . . . Germany,' he stammered.

The wonder is I wasn't sued.

During the Easter vacation of 1938 I kept the promise I'd made to Jean Doeraene and went on a cycling tour of Flanders. I wanted to see the places my father had talked about, such as 'Wipers' (Ypres), Dixmude, Poperinge, Menin and Passchendaele – places where countless British soldiers had died in the Great War. That war was like a cloud above my head when I was young. There was no escaping it. My father had gone to war out of idealism and adventure, and had come home cynical and disgusted.

I took the train to Tilbury, where I crossed to Antwerp.

My passage to the continent was provided by the Cockerill Line, my pocket money by my friends in the ice-cream business, Tom Wall's.

Everybody said that April was the wrong time to cycle in Flanders, but I went anyway. I didn't worry about the weather – after cramming books for eight weeks, I needed to get out in the open air, my energies needed release. I didn't give a thought to where I would sleep, or what I would eat.

I spent the first night with Jean Doeraene and his parents in Bois d'Haine. He'd offered me the use of his bike. The next day I packed my belongings on to his old-fashioned machine and cycled back to Antwerp via Malines. It was a bad start; it rained all day and I was wearing all the waterproof garments I had brought.

I saw the unfinished spire of Maline's thirteenth-century cathedral through the drifting rain long before I got there. I arrived alongside busloads of chattering school children. I had come because Jean had insisted that I should see Van Dyke's famous *Crucifixion*. Standing before it, I was as spellbound as the wide-eyed children whispering at my side. I saw the pierced feet and hands, the sorrowful face and the blood-besprinkled head beneath its crown of thorns. I forgot Thiel's criticism of Van Dyke: 'Lacks vigour and authenticity. Your time will be better spent with Rubens.' This was not just another Crucifixion. It was *the* Crucifixion. It caused something embedded in my soul to come alive. That was the moment in my life when I decided that more important than form or design or colour in art was mystery. Van Dyke conveyed to me Christ's pain, agony, suffering and death as I'd never felt them before. I also felt Christ's victory over evil. I stared for a long time at the Cross, which I knew was the symbol of my civilisation, and I came away moved by the painting's timeless, universal appeal.

From Malines I cycled across a land veiled in a thick mist. By the time I reached Antwerp again it was night. I found the youth hostel and was glad to eat and sleep.

The next day, to the sound of cooing pigeons, I climbed

the endless, narrow staircase, past enormous bells, to the top of the cathedral tower. I watched the birds coming and going from their nests in the stonework; I looked down on clustered roofs, the docks, the harbour, and the shimmering Scheldt stretching away in the sunlit distance to the sea. 'God made man, the Scheldt made all else,' was the local saying. I was not deceived by the calmness of the scene. I knew that the city had endured the ravages of the Dutch, the Spaniards, the French and the Germans. Time and again, violence and death had swept past the cathedral's doors.

A favourable wind blew me out of Antwerp and set me on the road to Ghent. Rain stood on the horizon like smoke. It was good to be in the open countryside again. On lonely roads, I made my way through village after village, past cottages covered with budding apple trees with lime-washed trunks, past gardens with the first crocuses and tulips, past fields planted with flax, and along poplar-lined canals, where twittering swallows dipped merrily. In the fields lambs played, in the hedges hawthorn bloomed. All breathed the new life of gentle spring. Here and there I came across linen mills. In earlier times migrant Flemish weavers had enriched England.

There were potholes and puddles all the way, which I bumped in and out of in the best of spirits. Without the tools and spare inner tubes Jean had given me, my travels would have come to a halt. In the villages, I feasted off bread and honey or bread and apple jelly, or bread and poached eggs. I ate one of the best omelettes I have ever eaten in a village post office.

Sometimes I'd stop at an inn. I made myself understood by body language, or English, or broken French. At one place I met a craggy little fellow, who wore a frock coat and a sailor's cap. I had to shout to make him hear. He not only insisted on paying for my drink, despite the hubbub in the inn, he insisted on singing 'It's a Long Way to Tipperary'. His face shone as Caruso's might have done. I clapped – I didn't dare say that I hadn't recognised one word. The peasants nodded their round heads and grunted their approval – they thought me daring for having crossed the Channel. From the inn I went to the church across the way, where a cold still-ness prevailed. I found a knight and his lady resting in stone. Outside, old moss-covered gravestones leaned against the wall or nodded together in the long grass.

I enjoyed cycling alone. That way I was free to go where I would. The rhythmic pedalling encouraged me to sing. The flatness of the land was in my favour. The rain was part of the grey landscape and there were moments when it would pretend to let up. The birds didn't mind it, nor did I. Indeed, once I was wet to the skin I took a reckless delight in getting wetter.

The people on the road were invariably kind. In asking directions of peasants who knew no English – for I often got lost in a tangle of lanes – I became expert at matching my facial expressions and gestures with theirs. People would shake my hand in a country lane and jabber as if I were a local youth. They'd drop what they were doing to show me the way.

One day, while the bells pealed joyfully, I followed a strag-gling, sombre-clothed procession into a church. I sat in a back pew and listened to hymns. The next morning, my curiosity to know what was going on in another village church trapped me in a christening ceremony. Before I could extricate myself, I was shaking hands with relatives who indulged in a plethora of kisses, which the cold English find so hard to bear. Henceforth I kept my curiosity in check.

The next day I ran into a village fair with its wheezing hurdy-gurdy. The roundabout was mounted on a cart and rotated by hand. It brought great joy to the children. I dallied to watch a wrestling match. As night fell a bonfire was lit to commem-orate some poor wretch who had been burned for witchcraft four hundred years before; there was a metal plate in the square to prove it. Her crime, they said, was to have consorted with the devil. Amid showers of sparks and the crackle and roar of the fire, we held hands and solemnly moved round the pyre. I thought it a bit odd that someone who had been a witch should have become a martyr.

I came to Ghent on a fine morning with the sun shining on its roofs. As I arrived, a carillon was playing Bach's 'Jesu, Joy of Man's Desiring'. In contrast to the grey countryside, the town was full of flowers; begonias were cultivated there by the million. That night I joined a dance on the square; I had no choice – everybody joined in with gusto. I didn't know the movements, but it didn't seem to matter. Across the square, mocking our jollity, was a moated castle with a most dreadful collection of instruments of torture which I had seen earlier.

I left Ghent early on a fresh spring morning, with the dawn's pale light shining through the wayside trees. A brisk wind blew me along the road. It was late and quite dark when I passed through one of the gates into Bruges. Attracted by noise in the square, I became entangled in a torch-light procession headed by the local firemen, their brass hats flashing light, their faces red with wine. Everyone found my predicament humorous.

Bruges was a friendly, medieval town. The river and the canals mirrored old houses, bridges and windmills. Chimes rang out from the twelfth-century belfry. I visited the Gothic town hall. In one of the churches I saw a miraculous relic of drops of blood of the Saviour; it had been brought back from the Holy Land in the twelfth century. People came from near and far to worship.

I was given shelter for two nights in a church. An unfriendly housekeeper served dinner in a cold, whitewashed room behind the altar. On the second night, a young farm labourer joined me. His face was as rough as his hands and his smock. He couldn't believe that I had nothing else to do but cycle about for pleasure, stopping and starting as the mood took me.

We were given a small dented enamel pot containing what I presumed was coffee. My meal was just sufficient to get me through the night. My companion ate several slices of bread with a little margarine: it was all he could afford. I tried to share my food with him, but he would not hear of it. We slept in a draughty room where the window rattled all night.

The next morning I left early for Ostend. Having dawdled en route, I reached its line of broken dunes in the late afternoon. I met an elderly couple and asked directions to the youth hostel. When they heard that I was an Oxford student, they adopted me on the spot. Against my protests, my bike and I were almost carried back to their house, where I was offered a feast. Piling food on my plate, they said they were paying back a war debt to Britain. During dinner they described the Germans' attempt to reach the Channel ports in 1914. To halt the Germans, the marshlands of Belgium had been deliberately flooded. Indescribable suffering had taken place; Ostend had become a large mortuary. Their own lives had been in peril.

'Will the nightmare of those years be repeated?' they asked. Not wanting to spoil a wonderful evening, I painted the most optimistic picture of the future I could and I'm afraid they believed every word.

The next morning they protested when I proposed going on to Ypres. I had to agree to stay another day, in which they took me by car along the coast to Zeebrugge and to Dunkirk in France. The next day, by which time I had stopped protesting, we went on a picnic.

After three days we walked out together to the Dixmude road and said goodbye. If I had listened to them I'd have let them take me by car on a conducted tour of the battlefields. I looked back to see those two lovely old people standing by the side of the road waving. I was to see them once more, in the summer of 1939.

I cycled across a countryside that was completely laid to waste during the Great War. On reaching Dixmude I was struck by a cloudburst so fierce that I fled to the nearest farmhouse for shelter. Battered by the slashing rain, my wheels swishing through the deluge, I reached the door amid dreadful thunder and lightning. As there was no answer to my frantic knocking, and no cover above my head, I tried the latch. The door opened with a loud creak on to a dark hallway; I stepped inside and called out. To my horror a mastiff, the size of a small donkey, sprang at me with bared teeth. I fell back, slammed the door behind me and overwhelmed by fear, leaped on to my saddle and cycled away frenziedly through the deluge . . . regardless.

From Ypres I visited the various battlefields. Between 1914 and 1918 the whole area had been bitterly contested. All the towns had been reduced to rubble. After twenty years life had returned; the villages and the towns had been rebuilt; bells were heard across the countryside again. The repairs to the cathedral and the Cloth Hall in Ypres were almost completed. Soon the scars of war would be effaced. What could not be effaced were the war cemeteries containing the remains of thousands upon thousands of husbands, sons and brothers – all of them, including the enemy, comrades in death. The pitiful, serried ranks of white crosses spoke of the desolation of war.

Flanders is a land haunted by past hatreds and tragedies. My father had struggled in the mud here before being gassed in the third battle of Ypres. Nick Hargreaves, whose picture hung in the basement in Bow, had died here. The sea of graves was an overwhelming sight. There was nothing like this in England. Had the dead risen and joined in a deafening scream, I could not have been more overwrought; nothing expressed so poignantly the madness of war. These men had been the best that Europe had to offer. Our entire civilisation had been impoverished and permanently impaired; reverence for life had never been the same. If 'little men' led us after 1918, it was because bigger and better men were buried here. I began to understand the phrase 'the Lost Generation'.

On my first night in Ypres I went out to the British War Memorial at the Menin Gate. The rain fell in sheets at either end of the tunnel-like building. There was not another person in sight. A hundred feet above my head was an arched roof. Mist filled the air. I stood my bike against the kerb. Inscribed on the lighted walls were the names of more than 58,000 men: 'Here are recorded names of officers and men who fell in the Ypres salient but to whom the fortune of war denied the known and honoured burial given to their comrades in death.' I thought of Bunyan: 'So they passed over and all the trumpets sounded for them at the other side.'

What I wanted to express was inexpressible. I followed the names down the street, gazing at an endless tragedy. For a moment I felt that there were thousands and thousands of eyes looking down at me, asking me why they had had to die and what I was going to do about it. My mind did not respond. I felt intense sadness. How horrible, I thought, for life to end with a little name on an endless wall in an empty, mist-filled street.

I was just about to leave when two muffled-up civilians rode up on bicycles. Standing their bikes next to mine, they took out their bugles, removed their caps, and on the stroke of nine sounded the Last Post. The sad notes, echoing against the high vault and the cold stonewalls, contained all the sorrow that mankind had suffered since the beginning of time. In two minutes the buglers had come and gone, leaving me alone with the dead. No longer conscious of the rain, I cycled back to my lodgings across the Ypres salient, past endless cemeteries, wondering how such madness could have occurred.

On leaving Ypres the next day, I came across a stone marker: 'Here the invader was brought to a standstill.' The cost was a staggering million lives. No wonder that so many of my generation were pacifists. As I stood there among the fields of dead, I thought there had to be another way. I recalled the words:

> Take up our quarrel with the foe:
> To you, from failing hands we throw
> The torch; be yours to hold it high.
> If ye break faith with us who die
> We shall not sleep, though poppies grow
> In Flanders fields.*

* *In Flanders Fields*, Lieutenant Colonel John McCrae (1872–1918).

I took shelter from a downpour against a barn in Courtrai. All around were wet, ploughed fields. Hearing a rattling above my head, I looked up to see a macabre collection of rusted helmets, rifles, bayonets, shellcases and gun parts all hanging on wire and blowing about restlessly in the wind. German tin hats were mixed with British. They had been dug up by the farmer.

Before leaving Courtrai, I saw a plaque in a Flemish church which read:

Leven is weven   Life is weaving
En sterven   And dying
Is zijn stuk   is to give your work
Aan God afgeven   to God

After three weeks I returned Jean's bicycle to him at Bois d'Haine. How wonderful it was to have his family's hospitality showered upon me: for a couple of days I was thoroughly spoiled.

———⟨◇⟩———

I returned to Oxford from my solitary tour knowing myself a little better. My travels had brought home to me the great richness as well as the periodic insanity of Western civilisation. Flanders was my first lesson in art. It was also my introduction to death on an unimaginable scale.

Flanders taught me something about the turbulent nature of religious faith and heresy, and the extent to which they had helped to shape the past. The effect of the Reformation in England was not to be compared with its effect in Flanders. To my generation all things were possible to science; in an earlier age all things had been possible to faith. I now appreciated to what extent the Cross had been the symbol of an age when nothing mattered as much as the saving of a soul.

———⟨◇⟩———

Back at Oxford, Flanders quickly faded before the threat of final examinations for the university diploma in economics and political science. I worried if Trinity Term would be my last. My two years were up, yet I desperately wanted to stay. Life was rich, it had meaning. 'Let's see how you come out of "Schools",' Rodger said, 'then we'll talk.' Thiel was his usual calm self, but he had more options. I needed to excel and was determined to do so.

The only way I could affect the future was to work. Apart from an early morning swim, I sacrificed everything to study. I became antisocial. For the first time I had emotional highs and lows. I did not answer mail. Even though there was trouble brewing in Czechoslovakia, I spent little time reading newspapers.

I was not the only one to become antisocial at the hostel. Nothing concentrated our attention as 'Schools' did. The tension grew as the dreadful days approached. After I'd put out my light and gone to bed, Fog was still hunched over his books. He ended his day on his knees at the side of his bed. His silent prayers conveyed a feeling of rare purity. I felt my inadequacy. Yet there were times when I could almost touch the God he was worshipping.

In the end my orderly planning of revision came to nothing. I discovered that time before 'Schools' is not ordinary time: sometimes the day was gone before it had begun.

The madness ended one morning with Fog and I cycling to 'Schools', dressed in dark suits, wearing the mandatory white shirt and white bow tie. Given a tall hat, Fog could have passed for a duke.

With sixty to seventy others, we finally faced neatly tied bundles containing writing paper and examination questions. Each candidate was identified only by a number. At a given signal we untied our bundles, looked at the paper and began to write. To the merriment of the room, one student stood up and slowly swallowed his string. I envied his light-heartedness.

I slogged away for most of that week and part of the next.

One after another, the papers in economic theory, modern economic organisation, the economic history of England, political science, political history and organisation, and labour movements came and went. I didn't think any paper was easy, and there were times when I wondered what on earth I was writing. At night I sometimes regretted what I had written. Fog and I supported each other, coming and going together, having a couple of beers at the end of the day, getting ready for the next bout, and doing our best to forget the errors we had made. Even in my sleep I kept answering questions.

And then the last day came and the last paper was done. We looked at each other meaningfully as we left the 'Schools', took our bikes out of the racks and quietly pedalled away. In a week's time we would know the results.

———◇———

With O'Hea's blessing, Fog and I had decided that instead of sitting about waiting for the results, we would spend our last week running wild up the river. We both had the right shoulders for prolonged canoeing. We had no set plans. We might get as far as Lechlade, even Cricklade, near Thameshead, the disputed source of the Thames. We'd see. We carried a small tent. There was always food available at the locks, or at the occasional pub. At worst, there were plenty of fish in the river to keep us alive.

The day after exams we were paddling my canoe *Ruby* towards Godstow Lock. It was June and the weather was warm. We had been under strain for so long that it was a relief to escape into the open air, especially to escape on to the river, which conveyed a sense of adventure. A faint mist was rising; the rippling water sparkled in the sun; a gentle breeze ruffled the reedy, flowered banks; a lark high above Port Meadow heralded a new day. Rhythmically we paddled through lakes of light, with fish leaping and nervous moorhens trotting briskly on the water.

Finding our pace we paddled through Port Meadow, dotted with pasturing animals, to the ruins of the Godstow Nunnery at Wolvercote, 'built by Editha ye Prioress in the year 1138 and dedicated in honour of ye Virgin Mary and St John ye Baptist'. On our left were the Wytham hills.

Sometime during the morning I realised we had company in the canoe. Every now and again a field mouse would appear from nowhere, run across our feet, examine the baggage, squeak and disappear again. While I had been doing examinations the mouse had made a home in the lining of my boat.

Enticed by peanuts, the mouse adopted us; it enjoyed the voyage every bit as much as we did. Often it sat and preened itself on the baggage until drowsiness overcame it and it took shelter in one of my shoes, which I had kicked off. At night it used the ropes to scramble ashore. Often we glimpsed the glitter of its eyes in the firelight. We thought we might lose it to the land, but it would appear in the canoe the next day. Fog and I became very fond of it. We called it Midge.

For the next three days we steered through endless water meadows, the water reflecting the sky, the sunlight catching our paddles. Our course was generally westward, but the river's twists and turns meant that we pointed in every direction. Each minute brought a fresh view. Each night we searched for a bank, not too high, not too low, and tied up against a willow tree. Having pitched our tent and fastened it down, we stuffed ferns or dry grass under our ground sheets to level the ground and make it softer. We hung the kettle above the fire, and fried the day's catch of fish. The stars shone, the bats flitted about, the river glittered in the moonlight. After eating and talking lazily, we bedded down in our tent on the sweet, clover-smelling earth. Around us the trees and bushes huddled together and slept as soundly as we.

Each day we woke to the crowing of cocks and the barking of dogs. From the woods a cuckoo called; a chorus of birdsong greeted the new day. The fish rose, the rabbits played outside their burrows on the gravelled bank, long-legged herons stalked along the water's edge. A light mist rose above the long wet grass.

Some afternoons during those endless summer days we tired of paddling and our rambling conversation, and threw ourselves down in the shade in a drowsy world to sleep. On waking we'd silently and dreamily listen to the voice of the river and watch the odd sluggish cloud drift by. It was enough just to stare at the ever-moving water and wonder. Around us were peaceful meadows with daisies, buttercups and poppies, flitting butterflies and glassy-winged dragonflies. Wild ducks flying low cut the water with their feet. To me it was joyful. To Jim, who spent so much of his life digging deep into the earth, it was heaven.

In the locks, the gushing, roaring water lifted *Ruby* up the shining walls. To rise in a lock on a summer's day is a magic ritual, which carries you into another world.

With the meadowlarks singing and the river heavy in the heat and insects flying about, we paddled on. Cows studied our passing with drowsy eyes; we greeted fishermen cast in stone; a distant grey church tower rose out of the tall grass. Between the dipping of our paddles, we exchanged a smile with lovers on the bank, answered the wave of a hand from a passing boat, and followed the course of a barge horse straining on a taut rope dripping rain. We met barges bright and barges dingy. Occasionally, we heard the hiss of a haughty swan, the slow majestic flapping of a heron's wings, ducks squawking by shaded banks and the mellow call of the thrush. At night there was the sound of laughter and music on water, and pub talk between darts and draughts about 'Itler and Czechoslovakia.

On Sunday morning we stepped from the sunlit river into the dark interior of a moss-covered village church to hear Mass. Corn sheaves stood in a corner, the relics of a harvest festival.

We turned around at Lechlade; beyond, the river was too shallow. To reach the bank we had to walk the canoe up the current through a mass of vegetation. We had our last swim there, the reeds clinging to our arms and legs. Lechlade's church steeple stayed with us long after we had left.

A strong headwind slowed our homeward pace. The water hissed against us like a cold rain; small waves lapped our prow. We were thoroughly tired by the time we reached Godstow's high arched bridge. Arriving a day late, we docked our boat as the sun's last rays were flickering across Port Meadow. We also brought Midge back home.

The first thing we asked for at the hostel were the examination results. Yes, they had them. Fog and Thiel had passed. I had been awarded distinction. Speechless, we grasped each other's hands. I felt an indescribable satisfaction. I had set my heart on doing well. The results ended any self-doubts I may have had. Yet all things considered, Fog's was the better performance; he had spent half his time working down a mine. O'Hea was tight-lipped, but I could tell he was pleased.

That night a crowd of us met on Port Meadow to drink and sing songs to the moon. Thiel joined us, with the detailed results of our examinations. We were puzzled how he got them, but nothing ever stumped Hans. In the early hours the police escorted us back to our colleges, but not before we had held hands with them and sung 'Auld Lang Syne'.

In the next day or two the hostel emptied. For Fog and I the time for parting had come. 'I shall always pray that you may remain in the safekeeping of God, Billy,' were his last words. It was wonderful to have known such a man; though there were times during our two years together when I had longed for him to fly off the handle. He taught me serenity, and that man has a soul that gives life to the body, and that the soul, unlike the body, is immortal. He taught me to give as well as to take. I don't know what I'd have done without him.

On the last day, we all pitched in to buy Mrs Padmanabha a new handbag. The Catholic Church will never know how much they owed to that wonderful Protestant matron.

Having no job to go to, I found temporary shelter at a house in Walton Street where I'd rented rooms for visitors before. I wrote thank-you notes to all who had helped me during the past two years. In response to my note Rodger invited me to tea at his home. He asked me what I intended to do. I told him that the only thing I really wanted to do was to enter the university and graduate in the School of Modern Greats: Philosophy, Politics and Economics. 'You're on a fairly straight course, Woodruff,' he said. 'Take Modern Greats, go to the Bar in London, become a barrister, and I predict you will make a fortune in labour litigation. You have the ability to grasp quickly the essential features of matters quite strange to you. You are a natural for labour.' So that I might do all these things he offered to write a letter to Mr E. M. Rich, the chief education officer at the London County Council.

That night I telephoned Ma Hargreaves and gave her my examination results and told her that I wanted to stay on to take a degree. I also told her that Rodger was writing to Rich, whom she knew. I didn't ask her to pull any strings at the LCC. I knew she would do that without asking.

Not long afterwards I was surprised to receive a note from Mr Rich himself. There was an impressive seal on the stationery. He asked me to call his secretary for an appointment. I did. A few days later I was standing outside County Hall in the heart of London. The size of the building intimidated me. The entrance was overrun with people. I told one of the clerks that I had come to see Mr Rich. 'Oh you 'ave, 'ave you?' he said huffily, as if I'd asked to see the Pope.

'This young gint's come to see Rich,' the clerk said turning to one of his superiors.

''E 'as, 'as 'e?' The senior approached me. 'U got han appointment?'

'Yes,' I answered, producing Rich's personal note. 'My appointment is at eleven.'

'Oops-a-daisy, so you 'ave. Wonders never cease. George, take Mr Woodruff to Mr Rich's office at once, get a move on.'

After that it was, 'Yes, sir, no, sir, three bags full, sir.' George whisked me to the office of the great man and I found myself sitting at a long table facing Mr Rich. His secretary sat next to me.

Mr Rich was a courteous man with piercing grey eyes. 'I've heard so much about you, Mr Woodruff, that I wanted to see you for myself.' He took a moment to congratulate me on my examination results. 'What do you hope to do next?' Resting his hands on the table, he waited for my reply. I repeated what I had said to Rodger. Gracefully, yet always to the point, he questioned me about my background and my studies. I had the uncomfortable feeling that he was reading my mind. The two men began to exchange notes across the table. I wondered why they didn't speak up. I was tempted to look over my neighbour's shoulder to see what he was writing.

The exchange of notes eventually ceased. 'Mr Woodruff,' Mr Rich said, turning to me, 'I'm afraid that there is no major London County Council scholarship to Oxford for which a person like you can apply.'

My heart stopped.

'However, provided the university will allow you to matriculate, I think I can persuade my committee to meet your special needs.'

My heart started again.

'We need to create an adult scholarship – a senior adult county scholarship for people like you.' Somewhere in the room I could hear Rich's voice. 'If you will let me have Oxford's acceptance, I shall convey the committee's decision to you as soon as I can.'

He asked if there was anything else I wished to discuss. I said I thought not. We shook hands. I made for the door.

'Mr Woodruff,' he called as I was about to leave. 'If in due course you graduate and are looking for a job, I hope you will come and see me again.'

I said I appreciated his kindness and I certainly would return.

'Good luck!'

Once out of the building, I stood for a moment on the embankment trying to get my breath back. I was so happy, I could have somersaulted down the pavement or jumped into the Thames. I looked across the river at the House of Commons. Everything was going the right way, all I needed now was acceptance by the university. I walked away as if striding on air.

I had to rush back to Oxford after my interview, but I called Emily Hargreaves the next day and asked her to tell her mother all that had gone on at County Hall.

Following Rodger's advice, I applied to the university to be accepted as a candidate for the degree in Modern Greats. I also petitioned to be excused Responsions (the entrance examination) and Pass Moderations (the examination at the end of the first year). I wanted to bypass the school work I had not had.

The outcome of my petitions was a compromise: the university accepted me as a student and waived Responsions. Beyond that they were not prepared to go. A custom that had been built up over hundreds of years was not going to be changed because a queer frog had jumped into their pond. Fit in or fall out was the gist of the ruling. I had no choice. Somehow I'd have to get through Pass Mods. 'Half victory, half defeat, Woodruff,' Rodger said with pursed lips. 'Stability has become rigidity.'

I informed Rich of the university's decision. I was on tenterhooks now to know if I was going to get a scholarship. No good the university accepting me if I was broke. A week or so later I received a letter from County Hall telling me that I had been awarded an LCC Senior Adult County Scholarship for the year 1938–39. Its renewal depended upon my performance. I'd got myself so worked up about the scholarship that all I could do was to collapse in a chair and keep reading the letter. I simply couldn't believe it.

With money in the bank, I turned to finding a college. I should have consulted Rodger. He would have found a place for me at Balliol. But from here on I felt obliged to look after myself. After consulting Thiel, I joined St Catherine's Society in St Aldates. Its great advantage was that although I was required to eat dinners in Hall, I could live out.

I was interviewed by the Dean of St Catherine's, W. G. Kendrew, and by the Censor, the Reverend J. V. K. Brook. There was an incredulous look on the Dean's face when, having intoned 'Education,' I answered, 'Elementary school, sir, some night school, and the Diploma in Economics and Political Science with distinction.'

'Do you know any Latin or Greek?'

'No.'

'Do you speak any modern language?'

'A little German and French. I spent the summer in Belgium and Germany.'

He rested his chin on his fist and studied me. 'And you propose to take Pass Moderations in one year?'

'I hope to.'

'Well,' he sighed, 'you've got a cheek, I'll say that for you.' There was a strained pause. 'No one to my knowledge has ever done it without having had a secondary education, but I see no reason why you shouldn't try. I look forward to hearing what the Censor says.'

After climbing the narrow spiral staircase, I entered the office of the Reverend John Victor Knight Brook, and sat before him on the edge of a chair. 'Woodruff, Woodruff,' he kept saying as he ploughed through a stack of papers. He'd been interviewing students all morning and his face was beginning to show the strain. His collar was digging into his neck.

Having read my application, he placed his spectacles on the desk, drew his lips together and fixed me with a stare. His eyes were kind; I felt I was in the clear. But there was a long, uncomfortable pause during which he continued to eye me. I felt my colour rising.

'You know, Woodruff,' he said, picking up my application form, 'I can't for the life of me understand why people like you want to come here.'

I was devastated. I must have looked crushed. It was the only time at Oxford that anyone had really hurt my feelings. We looked at each other. Neither spoke. There was a cold stillness. Had I deluded myself in getting mixed up with the toffs, I wondered. Surely, he couldn't believe that I should be excluded from the university because I was working class! Didn't he understand that it was lack of knowledge that had always kept us back?

Eventually I stammered some kind of reply.

'Oh well,' he said rising, 'we'll see how you get on.' He reached across, offering his hand. I touched his fingers for a moment and left. I never spoke to the Reverend Brook again. It was a cold reception, but I knew that I had been admitted.

To console myself, I went out and bought an undergraduate cap and gown.

Chapter XI

To Germany Again

T hat afternoon I burst into O'Hea's office with the news that I had been accepted by the university. If he was pleased, he didn't show it. Instead, he picked up a letter lying before him.

'I was thinking about you,' he said. 'Are you interested in returning to Germany? I've just received this letter from friends of mine, the Wolfrath family. I'm sure they will put you up for the rest of the summer if you want to go. They have a son about your age.'

For a moment, his change of topic knocked me off balance. I tried to show interest.

'Professor Zimmern has a very close friend at Bonn, Erwin Fritsch, professor of international relations. Why don't you audit his seminar. Zimmern will arrange it for you.'

At O'Hea's suggestion I went and talked to him. A week later, on a calm sea, I sailed from Tilbury to Hamburg; from there I took a train to Bonn.

Using what German I possessed, I asked my way to the

Wolfrath's house. I rang the bell; a woman opened the door a crack and peered at me. While I was spluttering out in German who I was, she continued to stare. I wondered if I'd come to the wrong house. I was so confused that I forgot to bow. After some moments she opened the door. 'We were expecting you,' she said in a subdued tone. On arrival in Louvain a year earlier I'd been hugged and kissed on both cheeks. Not here in Bonn. Not until I had been received formally by Herr and Frau Wolfrath, and we had sat down to coffee, did our relations thaw. He was a small, rounded, thick-necked man, who worked at the Rathaus. She looked and dressed as if there had been a death in the family. They were both in their early fifties.

I met their son Ludwig several days later when he came home on leave from the Arbeitsdienst (Labour Service). He was in uniform. He was a little younger than I, tall, thin and as intense as his mother. He had a beaked nose, an olive skin, brown eyes and curly hair, of which he was inordinately proud. Educated in England, he spoke perfect English; until the Nazis abolished dual nationality, he had travelled back and forth on his British passport. I thought him a complex character and was ill at ease with him.

He introduced me to Professor Fritsch, a small, middle-aged scholar with the sharpest eyes. After talking about Zimmern, he mentioned that he had lectured at Oxford in 1937. It's as well that Ludwig was with me that day because Fritsch spoke so quickly that I could hardly follow him. I worried about what I would get from his seminar. I did not see Ludwig again during the rest of my stay.

Once a week I went to Fritsch's seminar, which was completely over my head. I would have drowned but for the help of the other students. Yet my German improved by the day.

The students were a light-hearted lot – despite the fact that two-and-a-half years of their time had been taken up with military and labour service. I joined them in outings to Bad Godesberg, or to picnics in the countryside. We also canoed on the Rhine. I was amazed at the risks they took canoeing among the large ships. There was always a drink and a song when the day's paddling was done. Indeed, there were times that summer when life could not have been better.

The crisis over Czechoslovakia in the summer of 1938 ended all that. I walked into the student cafeteria one day to get my breakfast to be told by a couple of English students that Britain had put all its defence forces on twenty-four hour alert. France, Germany, Poland and Czechoslovakia followed suit. All men under the age of sixty-five were forbidden to leave Germany; food supplies and transport facilities were conscripted by the government. The threat of war played havoc with our studies. Anxiously, we stood around discussing our options.

The Czech crisis was the point where we young people lost our innocence; it ended the carefree outlook of our youth. I began to question whether my idealism was adequate enough to deal with the realities of the deteriorating world situation.

As the news worsened, the atmosphere at the Wolfraths grew more intense. Whenever we talked politics we first closed the windows. We avoided talking seriously in the presence of the maid. Frau Wolfrath was always cautioning me. 'Vorsichtig sein, Wilhelm,' she would say, finger on lips. To relieve her worries, she would sometimes sing at the piano. Her shrill voice unnerved me, but I always applauded when she'd finished. It was expected.

Herr Wolfrath began to put on a double act. In one act he was a member of the old guard, admirer of the Kaiser, survivor of the battles of the Somme and the Marne, and enemy of the Nazis. In the other he was a 'good party man', the district collector of scrap metal, the maker of speeches, the admirer of the 'Führer', the one who never forgot to give the right salute. 'Heil Hitler,' he would call to a departing guest, 'and don't forget to shut the gate.' As a civil servant he had to buy *Der Stürmer* whether he liked it or not. Frau Wolfrath despised the Nazi paper and used to destroy it the moment it came into the house. 'It is incautious to do that,' somebody warned her, and thereafter the paper was prominently displayed in a neat pile for visitors to notice.

I once had occasion to meet Herr Wolfrath in his office in the town hall. 'Make sure you give the Hitler salute when we meet,' he warned me. 'People will be suspicious if you don't.' I really didn't have much choice – above the town hall entrance was an enormous sign: 'Hier grüßt man nur Heil Hitler.'

As I got to know Frau Wolfrath better, I came to appreciate her unease. I learned that on the death of her first husband in London, where she had lived for years, she had returned to Germany with her son and married again. In 1933, the year of her second wedding, Hitler had come to power. Since then she had known nothing but trouble. Under the Nazi racial laws, her son Ludwig, born in London of a Jewish father, had been debarred from studying medicine. 'I never dreamed that a son of mine would be persecuted in Germany for his blood,' she told me.

The local dentist and his family, the Bettermans, whom I got to know through the Wolfraths, shared their fear of the Nazis with me. Willi Betterman was a huge, moon-faced sceptic. He was called 'der dicke Mann'[*]. He spoke German slowly, which helped me. If we got stuck, his English was passable. Sometimes, when he was talking about things better not heard, he would cover his mouth with his hand, which gave a furtive expression to what he was saying. We used to eat at his club and talk in a corner. Every speck of uneaten food was taken home. 'Self-sufficiency in Germany is a dream,' he said.

More serious conversations we exchanged on a bench in his garden.

'How do you explain Hitler's popularity?' I asked him one day.

'Look at what preceded him,' he answered. 'The Germans brought him to power because they were sick of street fights, sick of labour unrest, sick of having no job, sick of a useless

---

[*] the fat man

234

currency, sick of hunger, sick of profiteers, sick of communists, sick of corruption, sick of democracy that didn't work,
and sick of being trodden on by France and Britain. They
thought Hitler couldn't make matters worse. At the outset he
didn't, he made things better. He put an end to hyperinflation,
unemployment and the destitution of the post-war years.
Street fighting was stopped; law and order were restored. He
also denounced Versailles – a treaty that had accused
Germany of sole guilt for the war and burdened us with a
tribute that we couldn't possibly pay. This boosted Hitler's
popularity. He reoccupied the Rhineland because the
Rhineland was German. He brought German-speaking
Austria into the Reich, because that's where it wanted to be.
Believe me, Hitler's record is a success story. No one is going
to throw out a winner. For most Germans, he is a hero, a
man of action, the wished-for Führer sent by Providence.
Who knows what lies ahead?'

There was a long silence between us.

'The price of all this,' Herr Betterman went on, 'is tyranny.
Anyone who opposes Hitler is silenced; all sense of justice is
lost sight of in the Nazis' determination to stamp out opposition. Every item of news here is doctored: the only items
you can rely on are those the Nazis denounce. You don't dare
raise your voice: the Jews and anyone who raises his voice
are deprived of their legal and social rights. The number of
people to whom I can speak openly has become less and less.'

'None of this is known in England.'

At the end of September, while I was still in Germany,
Hitler, Chamberlain, Mussolini and Daladier signed the
Munich Agreement. Czechoslovakia was stripped of its
Sudeten territories – Hitler's last territorial claim in Europe
had been met, or at least we thought so. Chamberlain vouched
for it.

I was back in London on 1 October 1938 when
Chamberlain returned from Munich. The Western world had
marched to the brink of war and had marched back again.
Sanity had prevailed. Mr Chamberlain's statement on his

return to London: 'I believe it is peace for our time . . . peace with honour,' left us drunk with relief. 'Peace for our time,' we called to each other in the streets. The crowds cheered and sang. No. 10 Downing Street was mobbed. A lot of us forgot our previous opinion that Chamberlain was a blinkered old fool. The war that every country in Europe feared had been avoided.

With other students, I got on top of a London bus and sang my way through the streets. Where the bus was going didn't matter – we'd won a respite. Next day all the churches thanked God for our deliverance; in Westminster Abbey the crowded congregation sang, 'Now Thank We All Our God'. 'Never has the power of prayer been more obviously and gloriously vindicated before our eyes,' proclaimed the Dean of Westminster.

In time, Chamberlain would be blamed for the Munich Agreement. It became known as appeasement. The truth is we were all responsible; we were prepared to agree to anything to allay our fears. Everybody except Churchill and a few others wanted a peaceful solution as much as Chamberlain did. We cheered him when, in our name, he had avoided war. Only later, when the Munich Agreement turned sour, did we accuse him of betraying our trust.

Chapter XII

War Clouds Gather

I returned to Oxford for my third academic year in October 1938. At long last, I stood with other students in cap and gown before the Vice-Chancellor at the matriculation ceremony. It was a sombre affair. He addressed us in Latin, telling us that we were now members of the university. As our names were called, amid the doffing and donning of caps, we each stepped forward to receive our certificate.

> Oxoniae, Termino Michaelis AD 1938,
> Die XXII, Mensis Oct.
> Quo die comparsit corum me
> William Woodruff

If only Grandmother Bridget had been there.

I had found rooms with the Tates family on Botley Road, close to Wytham Wood. The university regulations required me to rent a sitting room and a bedroom. Fortunately, I could now afford it. The Tates were a wonderful family, consisting of Mr Reg, Mrs Minnie, a son Reg Jr and a daughter Charlene. The only problem was Minnie's endearing habit of tidying up after me – I could never find a thing.

My day began at seven-fifteen when Reg brought me a cup of tea. He was such a happy man that I was convinced he would live to be a hundred. With the tea came the headlines from the BBC, which he had just heard downstairs. Then came the gossip: Reg worked at a store in town and always lingered to share the previous day's catch, his laughter shaking the room.

Breakfast was at seven-thirty; it was the only time we were together. I preferred eating with the family to eating alone. Minnie shuffled about the dining room in her dressing gown and curlers serving gargantuan portions of eggs and bacon, toast and marmalade. I think it was her ambition to increase our individual weight to the 250 pounds she carried.

By eight-thirty, except for Minnie, we'd all gone off to our different jobs. To get to the university I rode my bike. I ate lunch with student friends; dinner I had in Hall at St Catherine's. Each night I looked down the rows of fresh-faced youths sitting at long, polished tables; I saw the play of light on cutlery and glassware; I heard the nightly grace: 'Benedictus . . .' The ritual was so secure, so certain, so civilised. If Oxford taught me anything it taught me to respect tradition. 'Tradition is the dead hand of the past,' I had shouted from soapboxes, without knowing what I was talking about.

What struck me most when I first began dining in Hall was the waste of food. It came as a shock. These people were not only eating without having worked for it; they were wasting what was put in front of them – food was often pecked at. At the workers' hostel meals had always ended with polished plates.

My belief that I could catch up on seven years' secondary school work in one was plain arrogance. I soon found out that preparing for Pass Mods was formidable. They seemed like a barrier to ensure that I couldn't graduate. Yet I had to respond to the challenge or leave. 'Security is mortals' chiefest enemy,' said Shakespeare.

The support I got made all the difference. Dean Kendrick found the best tutors for me and planned my strategy. He advised me to take French and Political Economy in Hilary Term, and Latin and Constitutional Law and History in Trinity. Wilfred Kendrew at St Catherine's was my tutor in Latin. He was first class. If he thought that it was impossible for me to learn Latin in so short a time, he never said so. The 'set' book was *Agricola et Germania* by Tacitus; I was also required to do translations from 'unseen' texts, usually drawn from Livy, Caesar, Ovid and Vergil.

Kendrew knew what was going on in my head. 'You are not wasting time, Woodruff, in trying to meet some ridiculous requirement of the university. You are being given a chance – nay, the privilege – to learn about a civilisation whose achievements were unrivalled in the history of the West.' Having let that sink in he went on: 'Rome is the base on which you are standing. If you want to know about lasting greatness in thought and deed, you must study Rome. Latin provided the Catholic Church with a universal language. It's also the language of medicine. When you speak Latin you speak to the world. It is not a dead language.'

With Kendrew's words ringing in my ears, I got down to work. Every morning as I shaved, I learned the verbs and nouns I had pasted on to my bathroom mirror. In cycling to the university I would recite: 'I'm a bo, I'm a bis, I'm a bat,' or something else I needed to memorise. Kendrew poured Latin grammar into me until I choked. The experiment of trying to make a Latin scholar out of a foundry worker fascinated him.

Studying Latin was the toughest mental assignment I had faced until then. There was no other subject that I started out hating and finished up being grateful for having had the chance to study.

Help with French came from Miss Hugo, a friend of O'Hea's. She was sixty-ish, almost blind, and read with a large magnifying glass. She lived in a rambling house beyond Magdalen Bridge with her brother, a devoted churchgoer, whom she regarded as 'un peu malade de la tête'. As a teacher she was devastating. 'Dites après moi: un, deux, trois . . . Again. Encore une fois. Encore. Encore. Encore . . .' After an hour's mental pummelling, I didn't know where I was. 'That's enough for today,' she would end.

She expected me to study French and only French, twenty-four hours a day. Responding to my ignorance with true Gallic élan, she instilled in me a love of the language. The great thing about Miss Hugo was that she believed in me. She got so excited about my growing ability to translate the 'set' book, Alexis de Tocqueville's *L'Ancien Régime*, that she often rewarded me with a cup of tea. Whenever I asked her or O'Hea who was paying for my lessons, they would reply, 'It has been arranged.'

Certain things I refused to sacrifice to the daily madness. I continued to play football and cricket and go canoeing in my precious *Ruby*. Time lost to sport during the day I'd make up by working late at night. On Thiel's insistence I regularly went with him to the theatre. 'We'll make a gentleman of you yet, Woody.' We had an understanding: I'd take time off for the theatre if he helped me with French and Latin.

I was able to work hard and play hard because I was blessed with abundant energy and excellent health. Vitality was the key to my success, and I was in love with life. Without tiring, I worked longer and longer hours as my first examinations approached. When they arrived in March 1939 I sailed through the papers with ease. Thanks to Miss Hugo, I did so well in French that I found myself outside 'Schools'

242

going over the 'unseen' paper with a group of students who had been studying it since they were thirteen. The paper was about a French circus, it was full of Gallic humour. Later that day I went over the paper with Miss Hugo, who clapped her hands repeatedly. 'Merveilleux! Merveilleux!' The 'set' book I'd almost memorised, so that gave me no trouble. Thank goodness for my memory.

Arriving one morning a few minutes late for my tutorial with Rodger, I found the student who usually preceded me still sitting there. The week before, we'd exchanged glances as we passed each other at his door. Rodger thought her very bright. She was one of his favourite pupils. I thought her darkly enchanting, but a little mysterious. Now, she looked pale.

'Be a good fellow,' Rodger boomed as I entered his study, 'and take Miss Bradington for coffee. She needs cheering up.' The request must have caused me to raise my eyebrows. 'You'll fill the bill, my boy, don't worry.' There was a rattling of coins. 'I'll make up the hour later.' Miss Bradington's gentle protests were ignored.

I must have stared at him strangely. Not like Rodger to turn his students pale, I thought. 'Nothing to do with me, my dear boy,' he shrugged. 'We all feel off colour at one time or another.' With Miss Bradington still protesting, he ushered us through the door.

There was an embarrassed silence between us as we crossed the quad.

'Well,' I said, 'it's typical of Rodge, I must say.'

'He was only trying to be kind. I'm perfectly well now and I hope you will not bother about me any more.'

'What do you mean, "not bother", I've got to bother. You know Rodge as well as I. Next time I see him he's going to ask me how many lumps of sugar you took.' She laughed.

We went to one of the cafés in the Cornmarket. I did my best to be social, as I'm sure she did, but our conversation fell flat. To make matters worse, she was a pebble-in-the-mouth type – beautiful manners but no warmth. Grudgingly, I noticed her flawless features, her rose-pink lips and her excellent taste in clothing.

After she insisted on paying, I walked her back to Somerville. I left her at the entrance, where she thanked me formally. I said I hoped she would soon be well and turned away, ready to forget her.

After that I seemed to be bumping into Margaret Bradington every time I went out. I saw her as she left her tutorial with Rodger; she smiled at me across the room at lectures. One day we walked across Port Meadow; on the way back we were holding hands.

She'd turn up in her car when I was playing football and haul me to my lodgings with my bike strapped on the back. She was ever considerate, supremely unpretentious. Her car was a Sunbeam deluxe, all polish, leather seats and real oak panelling. She couldn't believe that I'd never sat in such a car. Later, we saw the Cotswolds together. As the weather warmed, we went up the river. She handled a canoe as well as I. We swam in the weirs with the joy of two wild otters. The lock keeper kept up his shouts: 'You'll break your bloody necks, you will.' She was a real tomboy, and that's how I treated her. I used to come up through the water beneath her and topple her over with my back – she loved it. She shared my intense love of life; as long as we were two boys having a rip-roaring time, everything was fine.

Gradually a bond of affection grew up between us. It seemed that we'd both found the person we'd been looking for: despite our different upbringing, we had so much in common. She couldn't get enough of my tales of Lancashire and east London; poverty was something she studied. She became my tutor in English and continental literature.

Everybody expected us to get engaged. We didn't for the simple reason that deep down Margaret Bradington didn't want to get married. There was a strange spirituality about her that went beyond her devout Catholicism. Although she was wonderfully affectionate to me, she had a vocation – an inward vision – to give herself to more than me. Having spent some years with her family in India, she had what I called the 'Indian bug'. Perhaps because of Gandhi, she'd always wanted to return to help the poor of India. Why not the poor of Britain, I asked. My question was pointless; India drew her like a magnet. In going to India Margaret sought self-realisation. I owed it to her to stay silent.

One day she took me to tea with her family who were staying at the Randolph. I met a group of aristocrats who outwardly could not have been more gracious. Margaret introduced me to her father, who had the bearing of a retired general, regular army, Indian-frontier type. He was affability itself. 'My dear boy, my dear boy,' he said as he took my hands, 'Margaret has told me all about you . . . Interesting, most interesting.' He kept saying this to himself, while studying me with a keen eye. I was not deceived – however warm his grasp, his half smiling eyes said, 'What on earth are *you* doing here?' I turned to Lady Bradington. She had Margo's slender build, the same sweet face. She received me kindly, but gave the impression of being confused. Only our fingers touched. 'Charmed, charmed,' she murmured, but her eyes betrayed her: 'My God,' they said, 'there's a Hottentot on my lawn.' Margaret looked on sympathetically.

I had enough common sense to realise that to marry into the Bradingtons would have been like going over to the enemy. The importance of class was written on their faces. They belonged to the class who owned; I belonged to the class who worked. The barriers separating us were too wide. Had I joined this family of delightful snobs, I would have died from suffocation in the first three months.

In any event, I was too proud to think of marrying Margaret. I couldn't imagine living on her money. It hurt enough that she would never let me pay for anything. 'For me it makes no difference,' she would say. She was the only person in my life to whom money did not matter. One of the first things she bought me was a silk dressing gown for which

I had no use. I learned that a private income can give self-assurance and self-respect.

Margaret Bradington graduated in the summer of 1939. Shortly afterwards she made plans to leave for India.

We spent our last evening together, as Margaret had planned, at Bourton-on-the-Water in the Cotswolds. She drove across the peaceful countryside at great speed, with the warm night air rushing in through the open windows. With the light fading, we came to a hotel in a small park, where she told me her family often came. From the moment we entered, it was all bows and scrapes. Our table was ready against a window that looked out on to a river and trees. The water was the colour of dull silver, the trees were charcoal black, not a breath moved the leaves. Patches of hair-like mist rested on the banks. The muted notes of a piano came from an adjoining room. Margaret wore a long, low-necked, deep-blue dress of moiré silk with puffed sleeves; across her shoulders hung a white mohair shawl. Her silky hair was held back by a blue velvet ribbon. I thought she looked very beautiful.

She had arranged the meal before we arrived. It was exquisitely prepared and served. We had trout washed down with hock, followed by a steak grilled over a charcoal fire. The meat, she said, required burgundy, so we had burgundy. We ended the feast with fruit and pastries, cheese, coffee and brandy. I was allowed to smoke my pipe. By now we were a little red in the face and I wondered how we were going to get back. She had imbibed a bit much, I couldn't drive – despite all her efforts to teach me.

Margaret paid the bill without flinching. I'd have had to work for several months to pay it. We drove back to Oxford across a moonlit landscape. The countryside was wrapped in sleep; the first bats had begun to flicker. I thought it a magically beautiful night. This time she drove slowly, lost in thought. Although we'd chattered all the way there and through dinner, it didn't seem right to chatter all the way back. There are times when silence is the tie that binds. I knew better than to talk about India.

She dropped me off at my lodgings on Botley Road at about midnight. 'A topping evening,' she said. I promised to give her a hand in getting away the following morning.

By eleven o'clock the next day we'd got all her bits and pieces out of her rooms into her car. After paying her bills and handing in her keys she joined me outside. She was wearing a velvet hat, a leather jacket, which went with her dark features, and a blue skirt. Her people were expecting her for lunch, after which she was taking a train to Liverpool. We gripped each other's shoulders as she made to get into the car. I had a feeling that there was nothing real about what we were doing – it was a play I'd seen at the theatre. Whatever it was, it brought us both close to tears.

'God keep you, William,' she whispered through the open window. She always called me William. 'And thanks for the wonderful times we've had together.'

'God keep you too, Margo.' We kissed, her face touching mine tenderly. There was a wave of the hand as she moved off down St Giles. I stood waving back, and thinking of the first time I had taken her to coffee and why I hadn't made a last try to keep her. Then I climbed on to my bike and pedalled away aimlessly. Our joy had become pain.

I heard from Margaret after her arrival in Calcutta where she was working with a group of nuns ministering to the poor. It was a long letter in which she described the immense beauty and the overwhelming poverty and ugliness of the city. For the first time she was living life intensely. She sounded very happy and, much as I missed her, I was glad for her sake.

———— ◇ ————

Meanwhile the June examinations had come and gone. I got by with Latin because of the coaching I had received. Also by then I had grown to love the language and had worked hard on it. I think I could have stood up in the examination room and recited great gobs of the 'set' book.

In passing Pass Mods, Dean Kendrick thought I might have

created a precedent. 'I say, Woodruff, you surprise me. I honestly thought you'd come a cropper. Well done, very well done.'

'Knew you'd do it,' Rodger said. 'Sensible fellow, Woodruff. Now it's on to the degree. No more roadblocks. Nothing to stop you.' O'Hea gave me a silent, pensive look over his spectacles. Thiel and I drank too much that night. Reg Tates had a hard job waking me the next morning.

A few days later the LCC renewed my scholarship for the coming academic year 1939–40.

While I had been going out with Margo and studying to get through Pass Mods, the world had been falling down about our ears. Japan continued its conquest of China. There were clashes between the Japanese and the Russians in Manchuria. There were growing threats to Western empires in the East. The situation in Palestine and Northern Ireland was worsening – IRA bombs exploded in many parts of Britain. In March 1939, while I was struggling with examinations, Hitler had seized the rest of Czechoslovakia. Nothing changed Britain's attitude to Hitler as much as this did. He had broken his word to both Britain and France – you could feel the sudden growth of anti-Hitler sentiment in the streets and in the pubs. The British were conscience-stricken. Public anger exploded; our faith in Chamberlain was reversed.

No matter what reasons Hitler gave, after March 1939 he was disbelieved. Any hope of reconciliation between Britain and Germany died. There was a sea change in the country's attitude toward pacifism and conscription: students no longer debated whether they should fight for King and Country, but whether they would have to fight this year or next. Rearmament was no longer a dirty word.

Hitler had gone on to denounce the Anglo-German Naval Treaty and the German-Polish Non-Aggression Treaty. No day went by without Hitler rattling the sabre at Poland. The bone of contention was the Polish Corridor (created by the Versailles Treaty in 1919) that separated Germany's West from Germany's East Prussia. Also in dispute was the ancient German town of Danzig – now under League of Nations control. From Spain came an announcement that General Franco's victorious government would join the Axis Anti-Comintern Pact, which meant in effect that Spain had allied itself with Germany, Italy and Japan. 'Are there not signs of a return to the Dark Ages?' the Archbishop of Canterbury asked. The changes came so quickly, one after the other, that I was left confused. Whatever hopes for peace had been raised at Munich the year before were now dashed.

Forced by public anger, in April 1939 Chamberlain's government made it specifically clear to Hitler that if he went to war with Poland he would find himself at war with Britain. This time there was no prevaricating. The power that had dragged down Napoleon and the Kaiser now prepared itself to confront Hitler. Britain even held talks with the Russians, about whom the British had the greatest suspicion. Physically and mentally the United States was too far away to be of any consequence.

Meanwhile the distant rumble of war grew louder; the movement of soldiers and military equipment filled the highways of Britain. While I was doing the final day of 'Schools' in June 1939 a mile-long military convoy rumbled up the High. Step by step, Britain moved towards the brink; with inexorable momentum we were being drawn into war. Appeals for peace were made by Washington and the Vatican. Unlike Thiel, I still clung to the belief that we would be spared. No one, I figured, would be evil enough, or mad enough to start another world war.

Despite the darkening scene, I had already made plans to return to Bonn in the summer of 1939. O'Hea knew about it. A week before I was due to go, I had a call to come and see him. He asked if I would deliver an envelope to the Wolfrath family. It contained a British passport for Ludwig, who was in hiding – a fugitive from the law. 'There is no danger in delivering the envelope,' he said, 'but you might wish to think about it.'

I knew enough English history to know that the Jesuits were not good at cloak-and-dagger tactics. In the English Reformation Jesuit spies had come to England from the continent seemingly to become martyrs. Many a doomed missionary, confined to the priest holes of England, had ended up being burned alive at Smithfield. I was not seeking martyrdom.

'What about customs and passport control?' I asked.

'That depends. Normally the train you get on at the Hook will take you straight to Cologne. My information is that you might have to change trains and go through immigration and customs at Kaldenkirchen on the frontier.' He pointed to a map. 'If that happens you will be met by a porter who will take your suitcase and your coat containing the envelope.'

'How will I know him?'

'He will approach you as soon as you arrive. He will wear a metal disk on his blouse with a No. 6 on it.'

'How will he know me? What if he is not there?'

'He will know you and he will be there. That is all I can tell you. He will see you through all the formalities and will put you and your baggage on the train to Cologne. By then the envelope will have been returned to your coat.'

'And what do I do if I don't get the envelope back?'

'Simply forget it and continue.'

Studying timetables, we discussed the undertaking. I didn't think it dangerous. Entering and leaving Germany had always been plain sailing. I agreed to collect the envelope immediately before my departure. To me it was a chance to help someone O'Hea thought ought to be helped. I knew better than to discuss with Thiel what had occurred, he thought me mad for going back to Germany anyway. As I cycled to my lodgings, it occurred to me how O'Hea could be so sure that the German porter would recognise me. He had recently taken an end-of-term photograph of me in the garden behind the hostel. I wondered at the time why he was taking it. I'd been most uncooperative.

The next day I continued my preparations to leave. This time I didn't bother the Cockerill Line or Tom Wall's. I could afford to pay my way.

The last thing I did was to take some flowers to Miss Hugo and thank her for her pains. She wasn't used to being given a bouquet and received it awkwardly. I think she wondered why on earth I was going to Germany instead of France. 'Quel dommage!' she murmured.

I embarked at Harwich on the day that the British call-up of conscripts began. The ship had few passengers. Early the next morning I disembarked in Holland and took the train to Germany. Very few British people accompanied me. As O'Hea had feared, the train stopped at Kaldenkirchen and we were asked to alight. Surrounded by other passengers and their luggage, I had not gone far before I was met by a middle-aged porter plainly marked with a No. 6. The way he came up to me left me in no doubt it was the right man. Taking my valise and coat, he led me through customs and passport control. The whole thing only took a few minutes and was too quick for worrying. I crossed the platform and found a seat on a train to Cologne. The porter put my luggage on the rack, my coat on the seat beside me, took his tip, touched the neb of his cap and left.

I felt inside my coat pocket. The envelope was there. How foolish of me to have got myself worked up over nothing. I resisted the urge to break open the envelope and study the passport. O'Hea had said that it was an English passport prepared with great care. I presumed it was made out in the name of Ludwig's father, Steiner. It certainly couldn't have been made out in the name of Ludwig Wolfrath – deserter.

As the train pulled out, I settled down to read some newspapers I had brought with me. Eventually the compartment emptied. The last to leave was a brewer who knew a little

English. The worse for a few drinks, he talked about the German sky, the German landscape and the German sun – he couldn't say enough about the wonders of his fatherland.

On approaching Cologne, I heard the door slide back. From behind my newspaper I assumed that someone was entering the compartment and went on reading. But the door did not close; the air from the corridor continued to blow about my legs. Curious, I peeped over the top of *The Times* and looked directly into the bespectacled eyes of a uniformed member of the Sicherheitsdienst. I knew I was in serious trouble.

'Engländer?' the man challenged me, his cold eyes holding my stare.

'Ja,' I murmured, doing my best to feign indifference.

'Wo fahren Sie hin?'

'Bonn.'

I thought of the envelope in the coat lying beside me. My mouth went dry; I became frozen to the seat. O'Hea and I had not rehearsed this scene.

I waited for him to make the next move. The train rocked gently from side to side, the officer blocked the door. The silence was unbearable.

After a long, wringing pause, he stepped into the compartment. My heart jumped. I thought he was going to arrest me. Instead he reached for my newspapers.

'Geben Sie mir die Zeitungen,' he commanded.

I couldn't give him the newspapers fast enough.

Having gathered the last sheet, he stepped into the corridor, gave me a sardonic look and went off with the papers under his arm. I sat back exhausted. I felt he might return, or that I would be taken into custody in Cologne. Nothing of the sort happened; on leaving the train there was no sign of the security police.

Even so, my heart pounded until I reached the Wolfraths. Frau Wolfrath opened the door before I had time to ring. Unlike my first visit, there was no stiffness between us. With great concealed relief, I handed over the envelope. I didn't tell her how glad I was to be rid of it. She thanked me. I told her about the Sicherheitsdienst officer on the train and she became worried that I might have been followed.

The three of us sat down to supper. Inevitably, there was a Kartoffelsalat: everything was becoming pinched, they said, but potatoes were plentiful. They both looked under strain. They told me that Ludwig had gone underground. While marching along a country road with a platoon of the Arbeitsdienst, Ludwig had made a joke about Hitler. Without a moment's hesitation the fellow behind him had brought his spade down on Ludwig's head and knocked him unconscious. In fear of his life, Ludwig had fled his unit.

I spent most of my time that summer in Bonn. I had a room in a house in Ermichelstrasse, close to the university. I attended Professor Fritsch's seminar again, but I never succeeded in piercing his worried exterior. There was no familiarity, no invitation for me to visit his home.

I was allowed to come and go at the Wolfraths as I pleased, but my visits were rare and always brief. Ludwig was not there, nor was he mentioned. Whoever came to the house looking for him was given the same answer: they didn't know where he was. Frau Wolfrath spent long periods staring out of the window as if she expected her son to suddenly appear at the gate. On occasions she'd burst into tears for no reason at all. During one of my visits I was told that the police had been to the house demanding a list of visitors – of whom I was one. The news left me uneasy. To get your name on lists was not advisable.

The general atmosphere of uncertainty and fear got on my nerves. I didn't need Frau Wolfrath's constant warnings to keep out of trouble. I became doubly careful to whom I spoke and what I said. Like everybody else, I became adept at dodging and weaving in conversation. I learned what to say to whom; I took seriously the idea that somebody was listening. Letters coming from England, or from Margaret in India, always had a tape across them saying that they had been opened by the censor. From my going into Germany almost to my coming out I avoided writing letters. O'Hea had told me not to. After Margaret's first letter from Calcutta, I asked her to write to my college.

During the summer I visited the old cynic Willi Betterman again. He had acquired a Nazi party badge, which he wore in his coat lapel. He took me several times to dine at his club. He told me that some weeks earlier a group of drunken Nazis had marched in, stamped about as if they owned the club, and drowned out everybody else by bawling the 'Horst Wessel Lied'. Some members had collided with each other getting through the doors; others had refused to panic.

He told me that he no longer went to the Netherlands. He had been a courier, illegally carrying German currency in his rectum. On his last trip someone on the train had warned him to turn back. He did. It saved his life: he had watched someone less fortunate being seized and dragged away.

One day he led me up a long staircase at the club. He walked slowly as if he was about to reveal a mystery. At the top he threw open a door and stood back. I looked in. Directly opposite was an impressive portrait of the Kaiser with the inscription: 'Hoch lebe der Kaiser'. He shut the door and shuffled downstairs again.

'What are the odds on peace?' I asked him.

'I've given up hope. The stage is set for war. It only needs one more confrontation between Hitler and the French–British alliance to bring the European house down. Hitler is intent on war, especially against Poland. Armes Deutschland!' he muttered. 'Sometimes I think the Germans are a fated people. We triumph only to fail.'

Despite growing tensions, there were times that summer when I could not have been happier. I fell in with the same wonderful group of students that I'd known the year before. Full of high spirits, we forgot the Nazis; we shut our minds to the persecution of dissidents and to the possibility of war. Instead, we talked and sang and drank and cycled and forgot the Polish Corridor. Whatever was reprehensible about Germany didn't concern us. It concerned those others, whoever they were. We didn't arrange our lives according to someone's desperate predictions. We didn't even hear the warnings. We wanted to believe that all was well.

And so the band played on and on and the Führer was in charge and it was a wonderful summer. There was merry-making at the university and in the town. There was a week of festivals with fireworks and searchlights playing on the river and the fountains, and dancing and boat parties and *Gemütlichkeit* with delightful companions. But the silly talk about atrocities against Germans in Poland, which screamed from the newspaper headlines every day, refused to go away. I found it impossible to close my ears to the growing rumours of war – not least because the possibility of war kept intruding.

I became friendly with a young married couple, the Müllers. Richard Müller was a gifted young scientist who was not good at clicking his heels. I was visiting them one day when they were preserving beans: they put beans and salt in a barrel and then we took turns treading them down with washed feet, rather like pressing grapes. As I took my turn, I thought they were preserving an incredible amount for one winter – they already had a barrel of sauerkraut. 'Might be a long war,' Richard said. While I was in the cellar I could not help noticing box after box of spark plugs. The cellar was full of them. I could not imagine what he wanted them for. He had no car. 'We'll barter them for bread.'

After we'd finished with the beans, we went to his mother's house for 'Kaffee und Kuchen'. While the others were in the garden, the white-haired old lady showed me her bankbook. 'As you are an Engländer,' she said hesitatingly, 'perhaps you'll be able to tell me what has happened to the savings which Herr Müller and I had in the bank. All they can tell me is that they have vanished. But how can so much money saved over so many years disappear? Herr Müller never understood; I think it killed him.'

Embarrassed, I looked at the book. It recorded a fortune in marks saved before the Great War. There was no mystery about what had happened to it: like so many others, the Müllers had lost their savings in the hyperinflation of the 1920s. I was too shocked to explain to Frau Müller what her family must have tried to do many times. I was relieved when the young Müllers returned from the garden and the woman squirrelled the book away. I wondered if she hadn't lost her mind.

A couple of days later a young priest with whom I had become friendly visited me in my lodgings. We had often met to discuss politics. 'Will there be peace,' I asked him as he was leaving, 'now that the Czech problem has been resolved?'

'No, Hitler is bent on conquest in Poland. He's determined to bring war down on our heads.'

When I met the priest again he asked me if I would come to talk at a meeting that a friend of his, a professor of philosophy, was arranging. Only students who could be trusted would be there. I accepted the invitation without thinking.

On reaching the meeting I was introduced. I had seen the professor before, but had never spoken to him. I recognised some of the students who were scattered about the room; they sat silently with watchful eyes. A lamp in the corner was lit, the curtains were drawn. Frau Wolfrath's 'Vorsichtig sein, Wilhelm' echoed in my head. I could see her finger on her lips. 'Psst! Maul halten Wilhelm.'

I thought I was the one to speak, but to my surprise the professor preceded me. He talked mainly about Germany's woes. 'What a scapegoat Germany has been,' he ended. 'The world press, controlled by international Jewry, has maligned the Third Reich. The Jews would not be persecuted had they not brought their troubles upon themselves. They insisted on a separate identity which created a state within a state. Their power in the media, finance, business and the professions was out of all proportion to their numbers.' He went on and on with me standing there.

The first thing I said when it came my turn to speak was that the British no longer trusted Hitler. 'He gave his word that he neither wished nor intended to annex Austria: he broke it. He gave his word after Munich that he had no further territorial claims: he broke it. Britain will declare war if Germany attempts to conquer Poland.'

As the night wore on the professor and I reached an impasse. Tempers flared. His taut face and indignant eyes made me regret ever having come. Both of us – whether in English or German – kept using the same phrases: 'That is not the point,' 'That is not what I said.' I thought it pathetic that a sincere German and an equally sincere Englishman, both of whom hated war, were unable to find the means to avoid it. I could tell from his face that it was purposeless to prolong the debate any longer and I said so. In a choked voice, his hand emphasising and beating time to his words, he ended: 'If war comes, my sons will be proud to fight and die for Germany.' Curiously, not once did either of us mention America.

The meeting ended with the priest thanking us both. I shook hands with the professor and left. Only in the corridor were the students prepared to talk.

I decided finally that war was imminent at a mass rally in Düsseldorf where Hermann Göring was to speak. I'd become friendly with the university barber and he invited me to go with him. Once more I ignored Frau Wolfrath's warning not to get mixed up in Nazi meetings.

When we reached Düsseldorf the railway station was filled with a wildly excited crowd. Special trains and buses had brought people in from all over the Rhineland. The streets were packed with a heaving, pushing human mass. With the barber's son riding his father's shoulders, we made our way to the town square. Every window overlooking the square was occupied; every roof had its bands of Hitler youth. Hysteria swept through the crowd like electricity – you could hear it crackle. Long black, white and red swastika flags draped every building; hundreds of lighted torches blazed. My friend and I eventually found a place on the far side of the square encircled by a forest of flags. The podium was too far away to see clearly. We saw bodies moving about, we could hear Göring's heavy voice on the loudspeakers, but for all we saw of him, he might as well have been in Berlin.

Göring's approach was direct and brutal. His appeal was emotional. It was as if he was sending out flashes of lightning and the audience was the lightning rod. Every declaration was followed by delirious, thunderous: 'Sieg Heil! Sieg Heil! Sieg Heil!' In a voice that rang with conviction, he declared that Germany's hour of trial had come.

As the speech continued, Göring introduced a strident note that threw the audience in all directions. On and on he went, his voice getting heavier and heavier, his pace quickening to a crescendo.

An hour later he reached his peroration. He became more and more heated. He appealed to patriotism. A certain rough eloquence possessed him. And then, quite suddenly he stopped. His last words were greeted with half a million people shouting: 'Sieg Heil! Sieg Heil! Sieg Heil!' Pandemonium reigned. I was shaken; I'd just heard the most emotional harangue of my life.

The din continued until the sinister rattle of kettledrums broke across the square. A hush fell on the crowd, thousands of arms rose. 'Hand hoch, Wilhelm,' my companion whispered, a note of anxiety in his voice. I raised my right arm. I hate to think what would have happened had I not done so. I looked up at the barber's infant son on his father's shoulders. His tiny arm was raised like mine. There followed the 'Horst Wessel Lied' and 'Deutschland, Deutschland über alles'. The singing must have been heard for miles.

The dignitaries gone, we found ourselves inextricably locked in a swaying, surging sea of humanity, which had no thought of going home. We were swept out of the square by this great human tide. Once more I feared that I might be separated from the barber. The whole thing had become scary.

We remained part of the cheering, turbulent mob for at least another hour; only when the great wave had spent itself were we able to extricate ourselves and make for the railway station. We took turns carrying the child who had long since fallen asleep. And as I walked down the street with the infant on my back, I noticed the moon had emerged from the clouds. Through all the turbulence, it had remained serene and unaffected.

The meeting in Düsseldorf banished any doubts I had about a coming war. Back in Bonn, I wrote to my parents telling them to buy food.

A week later, we were shaken by the news of the non-aggression pact between the Russians and the Germans. Hitler had seized the initiative again; mortal enemies had become allies. In Bonn most Germans thought the pact would ensure peace – Poland would have to capitulate.

I asked the young priest what he thought of it. As always he was dangerously outspoken. 'Why shouldn't Russia and Germany make a pact?' he answered. 'Both countries were outlawed in 1919 and drew together; both are without principles except naked power; both are led by tyrants; both are militaristic and intolerant. They think that the Western democracies are rotten.' He paused and studied his hands. 'They will take us into the dark night, but they will not prevail.' Such talk would have brought imprisonment had he been overheard. I feared for him.

Not long after the signing of the Moscow–Berlin pact, I received an urgent message from the Wolfraths to come at once. I went and was told that Ludwig was going to try to flee to Britain the next day. Despite their denials, the Wolfraths had hidden and hung on to their son as long as they dared. They were now concerned to get him out of the country before it was too late. The idea was that I should take him to O'Hea, who had promised to help him. Ludwig was expected to arrive before dawn.

'Pack and return at once,' Frau Wolfrath said. 'Leave the travel arrangements to us.'

Their note of urgency did not surprise me. I'd already ignored three warnings sent by the British Consul in Cologne telling me to leave. Other foreign students had long since gone. Only that morning my landlord in Bonn had pleaded with me to go: 'Es macht mir Ärger daß Sie noch hier sind. Wenn Sie noch einen Tag länger bleiben werden mir die Fenster eingeschlagen. Man hat mich gewarnt.'* I didn't want to be around when his windows were broken. I had already felt a coolness towards me by certain students; some were becoming hostile. I didn't need persuading.

In a mad scramble, I went back to the university, packed up, paid my bills, said goodbye, and rejoined the Wolfraths that afternoon. I didn't go out of my way to take my leave of Professor Fritsch, I thought it might embarrass him.

While Frau Wolfrath busied herself preparing her son's luggage – suitcase and contents all English – I cycled to a neighbouring village to tell the maid not to come the next day. I had delivered similar messages before. I was told to say that the Wolfraths had decided to visit friends. When I reached the village I called at the post office to mail cards to England.

'Sind Sie Engländer?' the man asked as he studied my cards. 'Ja.'

'Gibt es Krieg?' He regarded me earnestly. How many times had I been asked, will there be war?

'Ja,' I answered. Ting-a-ling went the doorbell as another customer entered. Not another word was said.

---

* 'I'm in trouble because you're still here. If you stay another day they'll smash my windows. I've been warned.'

As I continued my ride I couldn't help noticing a stillness lying across the land: a note of expectation was in the air. Was it the hush before the coming storm?

The maid was not at home but her brother was. I'd met him before and thought him a crank. I was always repelled by his swaggering. He was a Nazi and had a blind hatred of all things foreign. He detested the English. He was startled when he opened the door, especially when I didn't respond to his 'Heil Hitler.' He suddenly grasped me by the collar.

'Was machen Sie noch in Deutschland, Engländer? Ich werde Sie anzeigen.' I wasn't afraid of him calling the police. His dull face was contorted by anger. There was danger in his eyes.

'Mach das,' I said brusquely. With all my pacifism, I was conscious of a desire to bash him on his silly head. Thank God I didn't. Eyes blazing, his face grim and iron-hard, he went on about English spies. Feldmarschall von Brauchitsch was to make an important speech on the radio that night; war would follow. The way he gripped my neck and kept making accusing wags of his head at me seemed to imply that I was responsible for the whole thing.

Having delivered my message, I struggled to escape his grasp. He was holding both lapels of my jacket and would not let go. I had a horrible dread that he was going to hang on to me until war was declared. I could see him dragging me to the police station.

Eventually I broke his grip and fled on my bicycle. He spat after me. I couldn't help thinking how stupid it was of Frau Wolfrath to have sent me there. Perhaps it was an excuse to get me out of the way while they discussed things they didn't want me to hear. When I got back, she didn't show any fear that the fellow might raise a hue and cry. 'Danger does not come from those who fly into a rage,' she said. 'It's the silent and the meek you have to watch.'

The rest of the day and night was unbearable. None of us went to bed, instead we sat and worried whether Ludwig would come home in time. We could only hope that he would not be trailed, and that the house was not being watched. Frau Wolfrath rarely left her seat by the window.

Towards dawn a tired, worried-looking Ludwig arrived. He made us all jump with his scratching on the windowpane. He didn't say where he'd come from, or how he'd got there. I thought he'd aged since I saw him last. There were emotional scenes; Frau Wolfrath wept. Ludwig thanked me for the passport. 'Don't forget that I am now called Steiner.' I knew that to help a fugitive was to share his crime, and that the penalty for desertion was death. Yet I felt no peril. No one could trace the passport back to me, and I knew that the Wolfraths would not betray me.

After breakfast, it was decided that Ludwig, his mother and I would take different routes to the railway station. I was the first to leave, at about noon. I shook the hands of Herr and Frau Wolfrath and of Ludwig. 'Auf Wiedersehen,' they said. I wondered when that would be. For a moment there was a painful stillness between us, then I picked up my valise and climbed into a taxi.

Our movements had been worked out to the last detail. I was not to recognise Frau Wolfrath or Ludwig again until we reached the Netherlands sometime that afternoon. It was a grey day; the town was going about its business. The people I saw looked subdued. I stopped en route to buy my father a pipe with a coloured tassel and a removable grate for the ashes.

'Gibt es Krieg?' I was asked once more.

'Ja,' I answered, collecting my change.

Shortly after I reached the station, Ludwig's mother arrived. After her came Ludwig. We all sat apart. In the distance a radio was playing military marches. Endlessly long troop trains slowly made their way past us going westward. The trains must have travelled through the night because the soldiers were lying in heaps, asleep.

At Cologne we sat and waited for the train to Kaldenkirchen and the Netherlands. The time for departure came and went. No train. After an hour Ludwig began pacing the platform, his open English coat hanging limply on his narrow shoulders. From time to time he glanced at his English gold watch; Frau Wolfrath looked as though she was about to cry. Other passengers became equally tense.

'Try the ticket office,' Ludwig whispered as he passed me, watch in hand.

I went and asked. 'Das weiß ich nicht,' the ticket man said, snapping the window back into place. Obviously, I wasn't the first to ask.

'No one knows,' I whispered to Ludwig.

'Try the man in the signal box, he's sure to know.'

So I went to the end of the platform and climbed a narrow iron ladder leading to a little door. The troop trains rumbled below.

'Entschuldigen Sie bitte,' I said as I entered the box, 'wann kommt der Zug nach Holland?'

The man turned his back on me and rubbed some grease on a switch lever. I tried again, raising my voice against the clatter of the trains. 'Entschuldigen Sie, kommt der Zug nach Kaldenkirchen und Venlo?' The man continued to grease the lever. I got the message and left.

'He won't answer,' I told Ludwig who was anxiously peering up the line.

Ten minutes later the train arrived and the few passengers got aboard. There was only one open coach. Foreigners had long since been ordered out by their governments; Germans no longer had the freedom to cross frontiers. We sat apart, complete strangers. The atmosphere was tense.

After a further delay the guard blew his whistle. Our journey had begun. We overtook a packed troop train lumbering along on a parallel line, then our train was shunted into a siding to allow other military trains to pass.

Two hours later, we threaded our way out of the siding and headed for the border. I watched Frau Wolfrath and Ludwig out of the corner of my eye. No turning back now. Through the windows I saw weekend allotment gardens; Nazi flags flew defiantly above the roofs of the tiny cabins.

The train came to a halt at Kaldenkirchen. There were more officials on the platform than there were passengers on the train. Frau Wolfrath left the train with several others. She muttered something in a choked voice as she passed her son. Someone entered the coach to announce that passengers for the Netherlands should remain seated. All formalities would be completed on the train. We sat still in embarrassed silence.

Through a curtain of steam, I watched Frau Wolfrath as she crossed the platform and sat down on a bench with her back to a wall. Now and again she fished into her bag for a handkerchief to wipe her eyes.

After a few minutes German frontier officials came aboard working their way from one passenger to the next. I took out my papers and waited my turn.

'What have you been doing in Germany?' an official asked me, thumbing through my passport.

'Having a good time.' He knew that I had been a visiting student at Bonn. He was just about to say something else when we were startled by a distraught-looking man in his fifties, who bolted past us and ran through the open carriage door. We watched silently as he fled across the railway sidings with policemen and dogs after him.

With furtive glances at the door, my interrogator took up his questions where he had left off.

'Why didn't you leave earlier? The British consulate in Cologne told you three times to leave.' He stopped talking and squinted at me.

He was right. It surprised me that they should have assembled such detail.

'I was enjoying myself too much.'

The official didn't reply. He thumbed through my papers. After the longest pause, he stamped my passport. 'Gute Reise,' he said stiffly, with what might have been a smile. He moved on to the next passenger. There were other officials who questioned me about currency and baggage, but I knew I'd survived the crucial test.

Without making it obvious, I now turned my attention to

Ludwig. He seemed to be producing all kinds of papers from his wallet. All I could hear was a rumble of voices speaking in English. Two Sicherheitsdienst officials were working on him. They were also going through his luggage, which they had not done with mine. Outside, Frau Wolfrath, hands clutching her bag, watched every move. She didn't look as if her heart was in her mouth, but it must have been.

The questioning of Ludwig went on and on. I worried if the name of Steiner would hold up. I wondered if the passport and the papers – which were being handed from one official to another – would survive their scrutiny. Every moment I thought that they were about to escort him off the train.

I gave a great inward sigh of relief when the officials finally stamped Ludwig's papers and left. My respect for Ludwig rose. I had obviously underestimated him: one had to be very smart to get past that hawk-eyed crowd.

For the next half-hour we sat in the empty station. I pretended to read a German newspaper, but my eyes would not follow the print – I was too nervous. The mournful howl of a dog in the distance didn't help. What is going on? I wondered. Are they checking up on Ludwig by phone? Except for Frau Wolfrath, the platform was empty and quiet. I knew that neither of us was safe until we had crossed the river Maas and reached Venlo. I did not look in Ludwig's direction. I'm sure he was feeling worse than I.

After what seemed like an eternity, the coach suddenly lurched forwards, jolting as it passed over the points. I heard the clank of the couplings. Puffs of steam flurried over our window. I could have cheered. Frau Wolfrath did not wave; nor did her son. They both sat quite still.

A few minutes later the border came into view. Tortoise-like, giving haphazard jerks, the train trundled across the bridge into the Netherlands.

Ludwig was the first to get off. Falling on his knees, he kissed the ground. Then he hoisted me into the air. He was radiant with joy.

Before boarding another train for the Hook of Holland we stood and watched the German train jerk its way back towards the frontier. It would be a long time before a train passed that way again.

At the Hook we boarded a crowded ship. Lights shone on the masts of other vessels at the quay. The radio told us of the appeals for peace made by the British government and the Pope: 'Once again a critical hour strikes for the great human family . . .' President Roosevelt had appealed to the King of Italy to mediate. I stayed on deck until the shore gang cast off, severing the last links with the continent. The ropes hit the water with a burst of spray. A bell rang; the engines started. A flutter in the bowels of the ship told me that we were under way; the water stirred into slow ripples at the stern. To the sound of gongs and shouted orders, with the water moving past us quietly in long, swelling waves, we slid away from the lights of the land to the encompassing darkness of the sea.

It was a rough crossing. Ludwig found some friends in the first class who were also fleeing Germany and abandoned me. His leaving me on deck was not appropriate, but I didn't mind. I had the company of three pretty English girls who'd been wandering across Europe together, and hadn't the slightest idea that war was imminent. They'd never stayed in one place long enough to hear from a British consul. They'd been wakened the previous night by police in their hotel in Nürnberg and unceremoniously escorted to a train, which rushed them across Germany into the Netherlands. The only thing they regretted was that the mad flight to safety had not been done on horseback. As far as they were concerned, it had all been 'terribly ripping'.

I was disturbed during the night by a ship's siren that silenced all other sounds. It had a sinister note. I rushed to the rail to see a German steamer sailing directly ahead of us towards the English coast. Minutes later, the ship broke course and turned back in the direction of Hamburg. Not a good sign, I thought. I didn't sleep much more that night.

At four-forty-five on the morning of Friday 1 September, while we were approaching Harwich, Germany attacked Poland. World War II had begun. As our ship sidled up to the dock and made fast and the vibrations and movements in the water stopped, I noticed that the buildings along the quayside had been camouflaged. The town was still wrapped in the darkness of night, still unaware that war had come.

I dropped Ludwig off at the hostel. O'Hea didn't think there was anything remarkable about our both being there. I hesitated to mention the trouble I'd had with the Sicherheitsdienst officer on the Cologne train, for fear that he might ask why I hadn't brought the fellow back with me.

In the early hours of 3 September I took a fast train from Oxford to my parents in Derby. The government had already begun to exercise emergency powers. School children were being evacuated from London. The blackout of Britain had begun. England had girded for war.

Chapter XIII

The Enemy at the Gate

I arrived at my parents' house shortly after eleven on the morning of Sunday 3 September 1939. My mother came to the door, her eyes frightened. 'Chamberlain is declaring war against Germany,' she said. That the events of 1914–18 were to be repeated was too much for her.

I reached the radio in time to hear Chamberlain's closing words: 'It is the evil things that we shall be fighting against – brute force, bad faith, injustice, oppression and persecution – and against them I am certain that the right will prevail.'

Angered at Czechoslovakia's fate and Germany's brutal attempt to conquer Poland, the British could hardly have done anything else but declare war. Many wanted it: they were tired of Hitler; they were glad that the deceit had ended and the life-and-death struggle had begun. Month by month our country had slid down the slippery slope that led to war, while we acclaimed each new calamity as a step towards lasting peace. Now reality had intervened. My friends in Germany had become my deadly enemies.

Later that day King George VI spoke to Britain and the Empire: '. . . For the second time in the lives of most of us we are at war. Over and over again we have tried to find a peaceful way out of the differences between ourselves and those who are now our enemies. But it has been in vain . . . We can only do the right as we see the right, and reverently commit our cause to God.' Because of his stammer, it was as much of an effort for us to listen to him as it was for him to speak.

That night I heard the wailing of British air-raid sirens for the first time. I listened for the bombs and the anti-aircraft batteries. We'd been led to believe that with the declaration of war the bombing would begin, but it was a false alarm. When the all-clear had sounded, I tossed and turned in bed deciding what I should do. For hours I lay there, first on my back, then on my side, wide awake, listening to the night sounds. Should I stick to pacifism, or take up arms in defence of my country? My feelings towards Nazism had hardened: Hitler was a fanatic who had no real concern for peace, truth or sincerity; he was leading the German people and us into the abyss. He obviously intended to go on using force until somebody stopped him. I felt that he ought to be stopped, even if the heavens fell.

By dawn my mind was made up. I looked out of the window on to a grey day. To fight was the lesser of two evils. I would arrange my Oxford affairs and join up.

In a night I had grown from youth to man. I understood myself better than I had in a long time. Patriotism had become more important to me than pacifism. I was not eager to be a soldier – I was concerned with resisting aggression – but to fight in self-defence I thought justified. The idea of justice – of doing the right thing – possessed me. I had a cause.

I went down to breakfast. Mother never mentioned the war.

'Did you sleep well?'

'Of course.'

While I ate, she told me what was happening to the rest of the family. Other than mother, all my family was now on war work. I was afraid that she would ask me what I intended to do, but she didn't. She asked me silently with her eyes instead.

Before leaving, I told her that I had business to do in Oxford and that I'd be back soon. She shrugged her shoulders as if to say, 'You don't have to tell me. I know what you're about to do.' I knew that my father had told her something similar when he'd gone to join up in 1914. I think she was too sad to cry.

I returned to the railway station through the silent rain. The people in Derby were as subdued as the people in Bonn had been: the same worried look, no flag-waving, no hysteria.

At the station, I bought a newspaper. It had a banner headline: BRITAIN AT WAR. A liner had been torpedoed off the Hebrides; theatres and cinemas were to close; car lights were to be dimmed; factory sirens silenced; cars were to be immobilised at night; machine-gun emplacements had been set up at Buckingham Palace gates; the French Army was preparing to invade Germany.

The ticket office window was taped with strips of brown paper against blast; sandbags were stacked against the wall. A large new sign greeted me: IS YOUR JOURNEY REALLY NECESSARY? I thought it was. I walked past a military guard who had been posted in the night.

The train was packed. The atmosphere in the compartment was as heavy as that of a funeral cortège – everyone sitting in their private worry. In hours, the tone and moral climate of Britain had changed. The talk in the train was dreary. It was all about the blackout, air-raid precautions, anti-aircraft balloons, guns and scrap iron. Trenches were being dug in the parks, gas masks were being distributed. People were volunteering for Red Cross work and fire service.

Mother had given me a letter from Harold Watkins. He'd joined the RAF. Back in Oxford I went to their office in New Inn Hall Street. Disorder reigned. I was not the only one wanting to join the air force. I volunteered for Bomber Command; I wanted to be a rear gunner in a Wellington bomber, and I hoped I might be with Harold.

'We don't have the planes,' they said. 'We'll call you when we do.'

Later, under a university scheme, I switched to the army, which deferred my call-up until after my examinations in June 1940.

Following my visit to New Inn Hall Street I ran into Harold Wilson on the steps of University College.

'I've just volunteered,' I said. 'What are you going to do?' His reply startled me. 'I've been called to higher things.'

I suppose I jumped to conclusions, but his eyes were upraised, he did have a hand on his heart, and his face expressed pain.

'I didn't know you had trouble with your heart, Harold.'

'Nothing wrong with my heart, Woody, I've decided to join Bill Beveridge.' (Sir William Beveridge was head of University College.)

'Doing what?'

'Studying the five giant evils: war, sickness, ignorance, hunger and unemployment.'

I was perplexed; perhaps he was pulling my leg. I thought of Harold during the war. He had joined the economic section of the war cabinet. In 1945 he became a member of Attlee's government and later Prime Minister.

<hr />

After talking with Harold Wilson I collected my mail from St Catherine's. I was excited to see a letter from Calcutta, though I thought it odd that the writing was not in Margo's hand. I opened the letter in the street outside the college. It told me that Margaret Bradington had died from typhoid fever a month earlier. The news left me stunned. For a moment I didn't see or feel or hear anything: there was a giant hush. When I came to, I was leaning against the college wall, holding the letter. All I could think of was Margo diving off the weir gate, arms outstretched.

Separated by class, by money, by vocation and by distance, we were now separated by death. What was the rhyme and reason of it all? For a long time I simply refused to believe that she was dead. Nothing mattered any more. I remembered the lullaby I'd sung at Quarreux three years earlier: that happiness is a mirage, life an absurdity.

I conveyed my condolences to her family but received no reply.

Oxford in wartime was Oxford in disarray. The old, steady, peaceful place I had loved so much was no more. Tutors had gone to war, or were preparing to do so; Rodger was in air force uniform. Fellow students were getting ready to go to France. By 12 September 1939 the first British contingent had crossed the Channel. Ruskin College and the Catholic Workers' College had been requisitioned for war use.

On the steps of St Catherine's I ran into a student I knew. He had just been commissioned as a second lieutenant. For a moment I didn't recognise him, he looked a different man. As he turned round for inspection, his peaked officer's cap and his shining belt, brasses and insignia dazzled me; so too did his large revolver. His chest was wider, his face glowed with pride. 'No more exams for me, Woody,' he said. He called the little stick under his arm his swagger-cane.

I was so struck that I stood and watched him as he swaggered up St Aldate's on his way to France and God knows where. He went with the excitement of a child going to the seaside.

Thiel thought my volunteering an act of madness. 'You're impatient to get yourself killed.'

I took refuge studying in the Camera, coming out at night to creep about in the blackout, which lasted from sunset to sunrise. Only the odd flashlight pierced the gloom.

At the outset of the war the massive bombing of Britain did not take place. Instead, Poland was overrun by Germany and Russia in a month, after which there was a lull. The expected attack of Germany on the Western front did not materialise; except at sea, war seemed suspended. Until April

1940 we called this the 'Phony War'. Britain and France waited for Hitler to make the next move. Meanwhile, we bombed Germany with propaganda leaflets and sang 'We're gonna hang out the washing on the Siegfried Line'. Many of the evacuees from London and other major cities took advantage of the lull to go home again. From Oxford, those without the train or bus fare walked for three days along the Thames' towpath until they reached Westminster.

Gradually the university adjusted to the changed conditions. Students who were excused military service until June 1940 were given the option of taking a shorter war degree. I opted for this.

I took the army's physical examination. 'Put out your tongue, say "Ahhh" . . . Take a deep breath . . . Any serious illnesses? . . . None . . . You'll do.'

I tried to get down to work, but I didn't have my heart in my studies any more. My determination to excel had gone. I realised that having joined up I might never see Oxford again. I kept busy by force of habit, but I was limping and shuffling instead of striding. I didn't go up the river, after Margo's death, it didn't seem right.

Every day brought new disasters at sea. In September 1939 the aircraft carrier *Courageous* was torpedoed. In October the battleship *Royal Oak* was sunk in Scapa Flow. Hitler offered his peace terms and was rebuffed by both Britain and France. In November the losses of British merchant shipping were becoming insupportable. The USSR, having conquered half of Poland, attacked and defeated Finland. In December the German battleship *Graf Spee* was scuttled at the mouth of the Rio de la Plata.

One day I was sitting with Rodger in his study when I happened to see a list of names above his head on the wall. Below it were the words 'Dulce et decorum est pro patria mori'. Students I'd known were already dead, the college's first casualties. I was shocked – one of them I'd known really well. He'd joined the navy; he'd been one of the toffs with whom I'd been so ill at ease when I first came to Oxford.

A troubled Christmas, which I shared with my parents, came and went. They were silent about my joining up. Now that I was committed, both kept their thoughts to themselves. The war was the recurrence of a bad dream.

George VI made his first halting Christmas broadcast to the nation:

And I said to the man who stood at the gate of the year:
'Give me light that I may tread safely into the unknown.'
And he replied: 'Go out into the darkness and put your
hand into the hand of God. That shall be to you better
than light and safer than a known way.'

All of us felt helpless in the face of the unknown.

———◇———

Shortly after Christmas 1939 I cycled the eighty miles from Oxford to Cambridge to visit Ma Hargreaves who, with Emily, Clem and Chris, had been evacuated from Bow. I found them living like country squires in a large requisitioned house in the countryside. Clem's foresight had paid off. I think he had traded on his mother-in-law's prestige. In a world at war, he felt entitled to all he could get. I thought the house was ideal: all conveniences including heating. There was a good pub within easy walking distance, a flourishing village institute, a district nurse, and a bus to take them into Cambridge. Clem thought me mad for having joined the army. 'You're supposed to be the one with a "loaf of bread" [head].' The way that Mum and Emily looked at me, I knew they thought I was about to share the fate of Nick Hargreaves.

Mum was the only one who still called herself a pacifist. I thought her a tragic figure. All that she had secretly feared had come to pass. She didn't know what to do; and now that Lansbury was ill and her husband dead, where to turn. She had been on tiptoe to see the coming Jerusalem, instead of which she was witnessing a new hell.

The news they gave me from the East End was sad. London was being bombed. Old friends in Bow had been killed; youths we had known had been mobilised; families had been broken up. We talked about Alex. 'He's belly-up,' said Mum. 'Lost 'is own and 'is wife's money. She stood behind 'im until the end, but 'e treated 'er badly. Fought with 'er until the day 'e left. Chased by creditors, 'e's gone into 'iding with the army in the Middle East. Miranda 'as walked out on Milton and taken 'er baby with 'er. 'Er life 'as become a bit of a mess. Milton 'as gone back on the bottle. Carol is still at Poplar Town 'all. She 'as grey 'air loik a woman twenty years older, and refuses to dye it.'

It wasn't a pleasant visit and I was glad to begin the journey back. Mum's eyes filled with tears when she gave me a final hug.

I fell in with another cyclist on the way back to Oxford, but the current spy scare reduced our conversation to a stale patter.

The 'Phony War' ended in April 1940 when Germany invaded Denmark and Norway. Britain fought briefly in Norway, but retreated at the end of that month.

One day, about this time, I was going to a tutorial in Christ Church when I happened to look up at the girl who was coming down the wide oak staircase. My heart stopped. The girl approaching looked like Betty Weatherby – an older Betty, but unless I was mistaken, it was her.

'Excuse me,' I stammered, as she made to pass me. 'Are you Betty Weatherby?'

She flicked the prettiest brown eyes at me and smiled. 'I'm afraid not. I'm Kay Wright.' The flash of her teeth added to her charm. I detected a northern accent.

'Look,' I dared, 'I'm sorry to stop you like this, but I thought you were a girl I knew years ago in Blackburn.'

She gave me a long, friendly, wordless stare. I could see

she was blushing. 'I hope you're not disappointed.' Her voice was sweet, her eyes merry. 'I come from a village north of Blackburn in Westmorland.'

'Well, we have something in common. Can I take you for coffee?'

'But what about your work?'

'It can wait, I hope.' She thought that was very funny.

—◇—

We sat over coffee as we told each other what we were doing in life. Wisps of silky brown hair protruded from beneath the scarf knotted under her chin. All her features formed a harmonious whole. I thought her beautiful. There was not a shadow of affectation in her. I told her that I was taking Modern Greats. She told me she had recently graduated from Glasgow University, and was now in her first job at the Oxford County Agricultural Board. She had been consulting with an agricultural scientist in Christ Church.

Neither of us could conceal our joy at having met. We both talked at once, interrupting each other. I could have sat there all day gazing into her smiling eyes.

After ages of talk, we rode our bikes along St Giles and Woodstock Road to Kay's lodgings in Warnborough Road. I was introduced to her two dolls, one a rag doll called 'Joy', the other a colourful clown called 'Sorrow'. Having got there, Kay couldn't think of any reason why we should be there, so we got on our bikes again and cycled to the Botanic Garden. We forgot what we should have been doing. I had never seen the garden so beautiful, or felt the air so fragrant. Why hadn't I noticed it before? There must have been other people there but I cannot remember seeing a soul. Come to think, there was no one in the street either, I saw only Kay's happy face.

Late in the afternoon we went to her office near Carfax where she handed in some kind of report. We went somewhere for dinner; it didn't seem to matter where we ate or what we ate as long as we were together. After dinner I took

Kay back to her lodgings. I sensed how nervous we both were on entering her rooms. We suddenly became tongue-tied. She opened her mouth to say something but there was no sound. For a moment we did nothing but stare into each other's eyes. We had fallen in love. I don't know how long we stood clinging to each other – long enough for me to tell her that I loved her. I didn't dare tell her that I was about to go to war.

I cycled back to my lodgings in Botley Road late that night and thought only of Kay. Something had happened in our lives with aptness and finality – something I knew was wholly right, so right that I was prepared to believe that it was intended.

We spent the whole of the next day canoeing on the river. We felt utterly free. Our love was like nothing else on earth, everything willed it: the river, the trees, the clouds. Everything shared it: the people we met, the gardens we sat in, the birds that sang. Our love had made everything complete and one; it brought to us beauty and meaning. If only the music we heard would last for ever. That night we saw *The Wizard of Oz*. On our way back to Warnborough Road, we lightheartedly skipped to the tune of 'The Yellow Brick Road' along St Giles. The world's worries were far away; we were wild and childish, with all thought driven from our heads.

Henceforth we were rarely apart. The university didn't exist; the Agricultural Board didn't exist either; only the two of us existed in our dream world, and in our love the two of us were united. On May Day 1940, long before six o'clock, I woke Kay by throwing stones at her bedroom window. Muffled up against the cold, we climbed the steps of Magdalen Tower. There, while the bells pealed, we greeted the sunrise by chanting a Latin hymn into the wind. We breakfasted in a punt on the Cherwell. We sang together in the boat:

> Bliss was it in that dawn to be alive
> But to be young was very heaven.

That night I told Kay that we would have to part in June.

Our dreamtime ended nine days later, on 10 May. I was lying in bed at the Tates, staring at the apple blossom pressing against the window. In Wytham Wood a cuckoo called. I found myself humming the tune Kay and I had sung the day before:

> Sumer is icumen in, Lhude sing cuccu!
> Groweth sed, and bloweth med,
> And springth the wude nu.

There was a bang on the door. Reg appeared. 'Get up,' he said. 'The King wants you.' For the first time he wasn't smiling. There was no tea.

I was shocked. 'What is it Reg?'

He handed me the newspaper. The Germans had invaded Luxembourg and Belgium and were racing towards the Channel ports. The British Expeditionary Force (BEF) had left France and entered Belgium to halt the German advance; the continent was aflame.

I jumped up, had a little breakfast, collected Kay, and together we went to Thiel. We found him glued to his short-wave radio tuned to the Netherlands. We heard the Dutch stations tracking the German planes bombing Rotterdam. Fighter planes were strafing the streets of The Hague. The air was full of wild voices. This was the real thing; people were getting killed. It was the only time I'd ever seen Thiel's eyes large with tears – the clockwork man wound up for life had become very human. I'd often wondered what went on behind those eyes. I knew his family had been scattered. With the bombing of the Netherlands, the dam had burst; the care-free period of his exile had ended.

Later that day Churchill became Prime Minister. Only Churchill could meet the hour and the peril. MacDonald, Baldwin and Chamberlain had gone. Five days later the Dutch surrendered.

Thenceforth, hour-by-hour, blow-by-blow, Britain, France

and Belgium tried to stem the German tide. To no avail – lines of defence were pierced one after another. In ten days the Germans were at Abbeville, Calais and Boulogne. I wondered what was happening to Jean Doeraene and the students I'd met at Louvain and Quarreux.

On 26 May a service of intercession was held in all the churches for our troops across the Channel. We hadn't the vaguest idea what was happening to them, but we could at least pray for them.

Kay and I were coming down the river in *Ruby* one peaceful Sunday morning at the end of May when we saw what looked like a sea of human beings – thousands of them – pouring on to Port Meadow. As we drew closer, we were told that they were survivors from Dunkirk, who'd been brought from Dover by train. It was in all the newspapers and on the radio. Saved by a miracle – the sea had remained calm throughout the evacuation – the major portion of Britain's fleeing army had been brought home.

We moved among the bedraggled and exhausted survivors listening to their tales. The ordeal through which they had passed was reflected on their faces, some of them were unspeakably weary. The speed of the German attack had overwhelmed them. Some had been rescued from the sea several times. Their uniforms were torn and dirty, their boots cracked; their eyes were hollow from lack of sleep; two weeks' growth of beard was on their chins; they were hungry and thirsty. They were a brave but sorry-looking lot.

A week or two later Paris fell. The invasion of Britain was imminent. Not since the Norman invasion of 1066 had Britain faced the prospect of fighting an aggressor on its own soil. Our change of fortune left us dazed. Hitler called upon Britain to surrender. 'We shall never surrender,' answered Churchill. There would be no surrender, no appeasement, no panic. Never had Britain rallied to a leader's words more than it did during those dark days. For a brief moment in our history, oratory closed our ranks. In June, Mussolini ('that Jackal' said Churchill) entered the war on Hitler's side.

The crisis revealed us to ourselves. In the white heat of those perilous days our resolution, our sense of goodness, hope, commitment, patriotism and service intensified. With the enemy at the gate, any wound of class and national divisiveness was healed. Britain spoke with one voice; indecision was replaced by certainty and action: Britain would fight on. We were proud to be standing alone, and we were not going to be licked by Hitler or anybody else.

Kay and I dashed about as if everything was normal. We didn't express our fears and doubts. Having found each other, our only concern was to get married before we were parted.

While all this was going on, early one morning in June 1940 I went across to Thiel's place to have breakfast with him. The breakfast was on the table; his lodgings looked as if he'd just stepped out. There was the usual disarray: newspapers and books stacked to the ceiling, jazz records on the floor, clothes on the bed. His landlady didn't know where he'd gone. I sat and waited. Eventually I left.

Unknown to any of us Hans had been taken into custody early that morning and interned as an 'enemy alien'. I found out only by chance. Ferdie Smith, the college secretary at Ruskin had bumped into Hans and his escort on a crowded London railway station. It was a shock to lose him that way. No goodbyes.

While this nightmare was unfolding, I was trying to prepare for 'Schools': whatever happened, I was not going to leave Oxford shabbily. The morning of 'Schools' came. I did the best I could, and well enough. (It would be six years before I could return to graduate.)

---◇---

The days before my leaving Oxford weighed heavily upon me. Kay knew I had to go. But with the sword of parting above our heads, we kept on pretending it was not so. Yet the days passed and then the hours and then it was time to say goodbye. The last night we spent together in

Warnborough Road – a candle flickering, the breeze moving the creeper against the open window. We tried to forget tomorrow, it was all a bad dream that would pass in the night. Perhaps an earthquake or something dreadful would happen. There might be peace. I said silly things such as not to worry, and that it wasn't the end of everything, and that I'd see her soon, and that the odds were that we'd remain together for ever. We were young; we were determined to have nothing to do with reality. We buried our heads in each other's shoulders and cried silently with joy. We swore no one would part us. Outside, the nightingales sang.

But then the dawn came and with it reality. It crept through the window and told us to get up. We dressed and went into the street. A column of army ambulances was making its way through the town. Heavy of heart, we passed Worcester College, whose walls now seemed grey and streaked with damp, and made our way to the railway station and on to the crowded platform. Trains came and went. Everybody, it seemed, was either going to war or coming from it. We weren't the only couple saying a sad farewell; tears were plentiful. When my overcrowded train arrived it hissed clouds of steam. Kay stood outside the carriage window with glistening eyes. With everybody pushing and shoving, and people running backwards, and forwards, on the platform shouting about seats, I asked stupid questions such as, 'How will you get back to Warnborough Road?' She remained silent, not trusting her tongue. Our clasped hands remained firm until the engine broke our grip. As the train slid away I looked back to see a small, lonely figure waving to me. The wind was blowing her dress, and her soft, brown hair.

It's said that if you live with beauty you fail to appreciate it. I appreciated Oxford and Kay until the last moment – until the waving figure and Oxford were no more.

Chapter XIV

The Years the Locusts Ate

That night I slept in a bell tent with eleven other recruits at a barracks at Devizes in the west of England. With our feet against the tent pole, we were like sardines in a can. I wore drab denims; my head had been shaved. Supporting my makeshift pillow were the heaviest boots I'd worn in years. Feeling like a parson who'd strayed into the village pub, I talked about Oxford and my reluctance to join the OTC.

'Ox, mite? Aren't you on the wrong bus? Ox nobs are officers. Does yer mean to say, mite, that yer passed up a bleedin' bed and a batman to live in a tent wiv us?'

'Look,' I answered, 'forget everything I said. I'm here because I dipped into somebody's petty cash box.'

That seemed to satisfy them and they never questioned my credentials again. 'Yer all right, mite. Yer one of us. We'll 'elp yer go strite.' The irony of having to be specious to get back into the working class was not lost on me.

Henceforth I was one of them, laughing my heart out,

nodding my head, closing my eyes and ears to what I found hard to bear – especially the foul language.

They had every reason to be curious about me. Out of a thousand recruits there were only two university men, myself and Edward King, a Cambridge classics student, who had also neglected to join the OTC. He was a bright fellow with a mad glint in his eye. The hard conditions, the tempers of the drill sergeants and the intellectual poverty of army dialogue gnawed at him. Wisely, he hid his feelings behind grins and silence. He and I used to wonder how we had got ourselves into such a pickle where education didn't matter one jot.

The trouble was that we had read too many books and heard too many lectures, especially ones extolling Western civilisation's vital contribution to the widening of individual freedom. In the army you did what you were told; to think was to ask for trouble. We were in fact prisoners of thought. While we discussed the finer points of Nazism and fascism, or Greek or Roman history, the other soldiers were content to scrub their mess tins, polish their brasses and make sure they'd got the drill right. They had a feeling of duty and sober resolution, which, despite all our education, we lacked. I envied their unselfish, simple outlook. It moved me when they practised marching and counter-marching outside the tents at night.

Before the summer of 1940 was out the Battle of Britain was well under way. Bombs fell on London almost daily. Havoc struck the East End. Recruits from Cockneyland came back from leave mourning their dead. They told dreadful stories of monstrous fires that had engulfed everything and set the Thames alight. Often when news of relatives' deaths arrived, a soldier would throw himself down on to the grass and weep. Everybody was sympathetic, knowing that it might be his turn next.

Edward King and I felt that we'd both been short-changed by the military. I suspect my fate had been decided during the interview with the Oxford University Joint Recruiting

Board. I should have kept my mouth shut about my pacifism. But with A. D. Lindsay, Master of Balliol, in the chair,
I felt I had nothing to fear in speaking out. I'd been taught
to speak out. I thought that I would be sent to an Officers
Training Unit. At least I thought they would make use of my
knowledge of German and Germany.

Time proved me wrong, I was taken down a peg. His
Majesty the King sent me a postal money order for seven
shillings and sixpence so that I could get to boot camp. Once
there, it was too late to protest.

After four weeks of boot camp, I was promoted to corporal. I held my rank for seven days. While walking down a
street one day, I heard 'Corporal! Corporal!' I looked round
and saw an officer threshing the air with his swagger-cane.
I crossed the street hurriedly and gave him one of my best
salutes.

'Have you stopped saluting officers?' he spluttered.

'No, sir.'

'Then why didn't you salute me?'

'I didn't see you, sir.'

'Are you without eyes?'

A knot of people was collecting.

'I've saluted so many officers today . . . I was bound to
miss one.'

An old lady tittered: 'Take no notice of him, luv, he's just
showing off.'

Embarrassed that he was becoming an object of ridicule,
the subaltern took my name and hurried off to do as much
harm as he could. I lost my rank.

How Edward King laughed as I picked the stripes and the
threads out of my tunic sleeves.

The separation from Kay gnawed at me so much that I climbed the camp wall before dawn one Sunday morning to go to Oxford. Edward King covered for me. A car soon picked me up; those who still had cars were glad to help a lone soldier. The real danger was running into the military police, they were out in force. The country was awaiting invasion, and all leave had been cancelled.

When I arrived at Kay's lodgings, the landlady, being a romantic type, insisted that I should take Kay's breakfast upstairs. Having knocked like a maid on her bedroom door, I entered, juggling a tray with breakfast for two, a tin hat, a gas mask and a rifle. We had a whole day before us that we might never have shared. We were overwhelmed by our richness.

I returned to the camp by the same route in the dead of night, careful to avoid the trigger-happy guards who occasionally took potshots at nonexistent Germans coming over the wall.

Every Sunday after that I disappeared to go to Oxford. Only once did my scheme falter. I was tramping along an empty country road back to camp late at night, when a car pulled up. 'Want a lift to Devizes?' the driver shouted. I quickly jumped in. Only when I had slammed the door shut did I realise that I was sitting next to a drill-sergeant from the camp. Of all the stupid things I might have done, this was the worst. I'd managed to get myself caught red-handed. I could either throw myself out of the car or be arrested at the barrack gates. I sweated at the choice.

The sergeant's amiable conversation only added to my discomfort. He was ten years my senior and a civilian recruit like myself. He lived halfway between Oxford and Devizes. By the looks he gave me now and again, he must have thought me strangely tongue-tied. My mind was on other things.

Before we reached the camp, I decided to confess. 'Sarge, I don't have a pass. I came out over the wall.'

I expected the car to stop with a sharp jolt, but it kept going.

'Why would you want to do a daft thing like that? Could land you in clink.'

290

'My girl's in Oxford.'

He didn't reply for some time. The engine knocked away. 'Look,' he said eventually, 'I haven't heard a thing you said. I'll drop you off before the barracks. If you get your bloody head blown off going over the wall, that's your business.'

'Thanks, Sarge.' I blew out my cheeks and sat back. There was a long pause.

'Listen,' he said as he dropped me off. 'If you're as mad next Sunday, come to my house before ten and I'll bring you back. I need to flee too.'

His help was important, his sympathy even more so.

———————

At the beginning of July, while the Germans were bombing London, my unit was doing manoeuvres on Salisbury Plain. One day the 'enemy' made inroads into our positions; the next day we flung him back. It was all done in the best of spirits, though it was largely a waste of time.

After several days my interest had fallen to zero. How much better everything would be, I thought, if I were with my own true love in Oxford. It wouldn't do for everybody to think like that – there'd be no manoeuvres – but then not everybody was in love. Whether I stayed or took to my heels would not make the slightest difference to the outcome of the 'battle'. Chaos was so widespread that I wouldn't even be missed. While I was wondering how best to get away, I met a motorcycle dispatch rider who was willing to swap roles with me for the day. He didn't mind riding backwards and forwards all day in the back of a truck.

Of course there was a risk about my madcap scheme: the military police were always looking for fools like me. But that was a risk I'd have to take.

The next morning I was on a motorcycle tearing down country lanes, past mile-long military convoys. With crash helmet, goggles, gloves, dispatch bag and the motorcyclist's long coat, I looked the real thing. In two or three hours, I thought, I'll be in Oxford. The faster I went the more the army urged me on. At the speed I was going, they presumed that I was carrying top-secret dispatches upon which the fate of the 'battle' turned. The military police gave me the right of way. It's just as well they didn't know that all that was in my bag was a bread and cheese sandwich.

Oblivious of fate, I pushed on with greater speed. Everything went well until I began to overtake a column of tanks on a narrow road alongside a river. Suddenly the road swerved sharply to the right across a high-arched stone bridge. There was a tank in the middle. As I struggled with the brakes, I caught a glimpse of the narrow gap between the tank and the stone parapet. There was a dull thud as I slammed into the gap. I was thrown on to the stones and heard a muffled voice calling down a long tunnel: 'Don't touch him! Don't touch him! Leave him alone!'

I woke up in St Hilda's College, which had become a hospital for head injuries. Ironically, Kay lived in the next street. One of the first things I recognised when I came to was a crushed helmet lying with my possessions on the floor. My head was bandaged, as were my left leg and arm.

I spent most of that day with doctors, nurses and X-ray technicians. They told me that the helmet had saved my life and I had been spared from broken bones. Except for a few bruises and cuts and a slight dizziness, I thought myself in the best of health, and said so.

It was eventually decided that I was fit enough to be returned to my unit. My appeals to be allowed to visit Kay in the next street were not heard. 'Let's go!' my officer escort said, pointing to a car at the kerb. 'Don't you know there's a war on?' I looked in the direction of Kay's lodgings and sighed. Did I know there was a war on!

Edward King had a wicked grin when I told him what had happened. 'Pure Aeschylus,' he said. 'In Greek drama there is a law of inevitable justice whereby every wrong brings its own punishment; one's sins are always found out.'

Nobody bothered about me, or the bike, or the accident

again. But American photographers had been taking pictures of the tanks crossing the bridge at the moment that I made my spectacular entry. My flying through the air was grist to their mill and photos of me landing on my head on the cobbles were distributed by Movietone News throughout Britain and America. They used a dreadful caption, something like 'Rider lays down life in defence of Britain'. An odd way, I thought, of describing my going courting.

—◦◦◦—

Later that summer I returned one Sunday night from Oxford, where I had been on forty-eight hours of leave (this time legitimate), to find that my entire unit had vanished. As I approached the entrance to the disused factory where we had been billeted, I waited for the usual harsh cry of: 'Halt, who goes there?' Instead silence reigned. Bewildered, I wandered into the empty building. Only one feeble light burned; there was not a soul about. Except for the scratching and squealing of rats, there was no sound. Hanging from the ceiling of the long, empty barracks was a solitary duffel bag – mine. The men I'd known might never have existed.

I went out and stared at the moon and wondered what on earth had happened. With my duffel bag over my shoulder, I reported to a neighbouring barracks. They knew as much as I did about where the others had gone.

[In 1948 I met a man on the London underground who recognised me and told me what had happened to my comrades years before. While I had been in Oxford my unit had been mobilised and shipped in great haste via Bristol to meet a crisis in Singapore. They had arrived in time to become prisoners of the Japanese. Most of them died working as slave-labourers on the Rangoon–Bangkok railway: the bridge over the Kwai. King had been one of them. As I climbed the wet concrete steps from the underground to the street, I could hear Private Edward King, scholar of Cambridge, laughing at some joke as we walked along the footpath of the canal at Devizes. I'm sure he kept a brave heart until the end.]

In the autumn of 1940, I was posted from Devizes in the West Country to the 45th Infantry Division defending Clacton-on-Sea on the south-east coast. With reinforcements from all over Britain, the division was dug in opposite the Dutch and French Channel ports.

At Clacton we lived a day-to-day existence, wondering when the enemy would come. We lay down each night not knowing what fate would bring. We had aerial photographs of the Germans massing at the other side. There would be no retreat, our Order of Battle forbade it. So we sat behind the beach and waited and waited and cleaned our rifles and watched the water rise and fall and wondered when the Germans would strike. We prayed that the foul weather would continue.

In 1588 the 45th had faced the Spaniards. Sir Francis Drake was its patron. Our emblem was *Drake's Drum*:

> Take my drum to England, hang et by the shore,
> Strike et when your powder's runnin' low;
> If the Dons sight Devon, I'll quit the port o' heaven,
> An' drum them up the Channel as we drummed
>   them long ago.*

The only Germans we saw were dead Germans washed up on the beach, and the daredevil observer pilots who daily photographed our positions at chimney-top level.

We waited for something to happen. Nothing did. The winter tides came in and went out again relentlessly. The wind howled at us from the sea. One grey, wet, cold, dreary day

---

* *Drake's Drum*, Sir Henry John Newbolt (1862–1938).

followed another. We began to feel that it might be a good thing if the Germans did come.

That Christmas, Kay and I travelled north to stay with her widowed mother in the village of Temple Sowerby in Westmorland. Kay's sister Mary joined us from a college in Wales. Their brother John was at sea. Everyone did their best to make it a happy Christmas. We took walks together through the snow-covered fields, but we never succeeded in throwing off the worries of wartime. While I was there, we heard that John's hospital ship had been bombed and sunk off the coast of France, but that he had been rescued.

After getting back to my unit I had a note from Harold Watkins, who was with Bomber Command two hundred miles away. He thought I'd like to know that Betty Weatherby had married a navy officer and had left Blackburn to live in Surrey.

Much of 1941, spent at Clacton, is a blur. The army did all the things it could think of to keep us busy – exercises, training, inspections, route marches – but morale among the men remained low. We'd been sitting staring at the sea for too long. I wrote to Kay daily; her letters sustained my spirits. Sharing a few days' leave in the spring, we decided to get married. Other than my two-shillings-a-day army pay, I had no means of supporting a wife, but it didn't seem to matter. Treasuring the gift of life, we did what we thought we should do as lovers – become one. 'You're being rash,' friends cautioned, 'wait until the war is over.' We thought rashness the most wonderful thing in the world. Besides, tomorrow might be too late.

As Kay was a Protestant and I was not much of anything, we were married in September by Father O'Hea in a brief ceremony in St Augustine Church, Oxford, before the closed altar gates. Kay and I had both kept in touch with O'Hea – he had become a father figure to us. Other than family, there were few people at our wedding. I was in uniform; I had been commissioned as a second lieutenant two days earlier. A radiant Kay wore a close-fitting blue costume, with a tiny hat perched on the front of her head. The best man, a friend in the army, had come straight from manoeuvres in camouflage battle-dress, wearing enormous boots. As her father was dead, her brother John gave her away.

It was the bare bones of a ceremony: no flowers, no candles, no incense, no singing, no bread and wine. There should have been no organ either, but the organist was a soldier too and he waived the rules. His organ thundered out to an almost empty church.

Looking at us over his spectacles as if he was seeing us for the first time, O'Hea gently led us through the ceremony. I could hardly believe my ears when he said, 'I now pronounce you man and wife.' He gave us his blessing.

Kay's mother had come to the wedding. She had arrived on the same train as my mother and my sister Brenda. They were wearing new fox furs around their necks – now that we were at war everybody had jobs, and money to burn. I thought the foxes looked sad but said nothing. Socially, the two mothers were miles apart, but they did their best for our sake.

We received lots of telegrams, including one from Harold Watkins, one from Jim Foggerty, who was back in the New Silksworth mines, and another from Miss Hesselthwaite of Bow. Hans Thiel wrote from the Isle of Man, where he was interned as an 'enemy alien', saying that to marry at this time was crazy.

The reception was at Reg's and Minnie's in Botley Road. We broke all the rationing regulations. There were lots of toasts and speeches and laughter. The fear of a German invasion was forgotten. We were wished 'A long life and much happiness.' I had to say a few words, which I found difficult. I excused myself: 'My problem is that I haven't been married before,' and that seemed to please everyone, including O'Hea. When the time came for us to leave, Kay hugged her mother; together they cried.

We said goodbye to O'Hea, who was also about to leave Oxford. He held my hands on parting, something he'd never done before. There was a touch of anxiety about him – he might have been a loving father saying goodbye to his son. He had had such hopes for me, and had acted so unselfishly on my behalf, only to lose me to war.

Kay and I had a three-day honeymoon in a country inn near Henley-on-Thames. Three days is not a long time, but it is a long time when you are living every moment. At night aircraft droned overhead. Lying in the grass on our backs the next day, we watched a dogfight. Following the thud of guns and rattle and pop, the German plane fell to earth; a parachute drifted across the sky.

On the fourth day I returned to Clacton-on-Sea. It was a grim journey in darkened trains, through the London underground, choked with people. I had left Kay behind in Oxford. I hoped she would be safe there.

Although none of us knew it at the time, it was quite purposeless for me to return to defend the shore of Essex. Germany had invaded Russia in June 1941 and by September was fully committed to war on its Eastern front.

In October, as the threat of a German invasion lessened, the 45th was moved inland; I was posted to the 24th Guards Brigade at Addington on the outskirts of London. The blessing of going to London was that Kay and I could occasionally meet. We would rent a hotel room for two or three hours. Even to spend a day together sitting on the grass in Hyde Park was bliss.

Early in 1942 my brigade was ordered to Scotland as part of the First Infantry Division. Before leaving I received a call from the adjutant of my battalion.

'You are to join the battalion in Ayr as "C-A-P-T".'

'What does that mean?'

'You don't know what that means? It's PT. It means that

you will be the chief physical training officer.'

'What on earth has physical training to do with me?' I felt hurt.

'Not ours to question why, dear boy, but to do or die. Don't take it to heart. You're not being dumped. You'll find that it will work out to your advantage. I'm only sorry to see you go.'

Two days later, I marched into the office of my new commander. 'Second Lieutenant Woodruff reporting for duty, sir.' I gave the best salute I could muster.

'Get out of here, Woodruff, and get yourself properly dressed. Don't you know you have been promoted to Captain?'

'No, sir. I don't. My friends have played a trick on me.'

Not to this day do I know who kicked me up the promotion ladder.

———<o>———

As 1942 wore on it was rumoured that we were going to North Africa. We were given a week's embarkation leave. I left for Oxford to join Kay. Her face was full of joy when I walked in on her. 'You're about to become a father,' she whispered. I reached out for her. As we held each other, I'd never felt so close to her.

We lived the week to the full: during the day we travelled in her car on her job in the countryside; at night, we were holed up together in her lodgings. The week passed as a day might pass, and we were parted once more. In tears, we agreed to use the code word 'Hope' when I had orders to sail.

When I reached Scotland again, I expected to find that some of the men, especially those who had gone home to Ireland, had not returned from leave. I was wrong. No one complained about being shipped out to Africa, nobody stopped to ask. We lived in a trance, while others arranged our lives.

To keep us busy, we were given commando training. The War Office couldn't have men standing about doing nothing. Regularly, on dark nights, we were trucked out to the inner fastnesses of the moors, where we were left without food, shelter or blankets to shift for ourselves. I'm sure it was excellent training in survival, but I'd never felt so miserable.

One night, against regulations, I took the quilted radiator cover off the truck in which I was riding. I had a cold coming on and I didn't want to lose my Christmas leave. No sooner had I bedded down in the freezing heather with the cover wrapped around me, than we were ordered to fall in and march. In addition to fifty pounds of kit, I had to carry the heavy cover, which I'd promised the driver to bring back. By dawn I was exhausted and running a fever. I left Scotland that morning to be with Kay who had gone to join her mother in Temple Sowerby.

The day-long journey was a haze and I reached Kay on the point of collapse. By the time I'd recovered from my fever, Christmas had come and gone, my leave was finished and I was on my way back to Scotland.

One morning in early January 1943, our brigade was told to parade in battle order. In endless khaki columns we marched through the streets of Ayr to the railway station. Our journey to the real battlefield had begun. Our long column hardly got a glance from passers-by. A train took us to the Clyde where our convoy waited to sail to North Africa. This was something I'd never envisaged when I joined up to defend England.

Before going on board, I phoned Kay and told her, 'Hope.' We both wept.

In June 1943 in Tunisia, I received a decoded message that read: 'Mother and son well.'

For the next three years I was tossed about in Greece, Crete, North Africa and Italy. I had so little control over my destiny that I might have been fighting anywhere. Disorder, disruption, slaughter and chaos were my lot. There were times when I felt that we'd been sent on a damn-fool mission. Witnessing the killing and dying, I wondered about the sanity of those responsible for our strategy. I fought for two-and-a-quarter years in Italy to reach what Churchill called 'the soft underbelly of Europe'.

These were the longest years of my life. To this day their pattern is indiscernible. They were years in which I had a different sense of reality, time and self. The ordeal lasted so long that its overwhelming sorrow and rage and cruelty threatened my essential humanity. Bitterly, I discovered that the essence of war is man's inhumanity to man. Life was discontinuous and fragmented; death and disease thinned our ranks. The roll call was never the same; the certainties of yesterday were not worth discussing. Eventually, I came to look upon war as a giant absurdity. It took twenty years before I was able to purge myself of the nightmare in my book *Vessel of Sadness*.

Kay and I used to say that these were the years the locusts ate. In the first five years of our married life we had five weeks together. For the rest, we waited and waited and waited while our heartache grew. Our only link were the little blue airmail forms, carried by angels we used to say, into which almost daily, year after year, we poured our love. The war ate up the marrow of our bones. How long will the war last? we kept asking each other. Love was our hope and our strength, it was a candle forever burning in the window of our life. Without hope – hope that was renewed a thousand times – we might have despaired. How many times in those dreadful days in the Mediterranean did I think of home and wife and child? I had someone to live for, someone to love. Through the hardest times they sustained me. By 1945 I no longer pleaded with God for grace to know Him; I pleaded with Him to stop the war.

Chapter XV

Afterword

In January 1945 my unit was sent from Italy to Greece to stop the Greeks from killing each other in their civil war.

However, I contracted typhoid fever and ended up lying on the floor of a bare room in a burned-out building in an Athens square. It was ironic that having escaped death in battle, a microbe should bring me down. I was left where I fell. There was an epidemic and the hospitals were full. For two weeks I saw only an army doctor who visited me each day and sat cross-legged on the floor. 'One for you, and one for me,' he'd say as he fished two bottles of cold beer out of his bag. He brought me extra blankets; I watched him through fevered eyes. No one else came. There were footsteps outside, but that was all. The long dark nights and the silence of the room oppressed me. I lay there thinking of Kay and our child and waiting for the dawn. During the day, I studied the walls and the ceiling. Sometimes the sun caught the shattered glass of the window lying on the floor. I might have been buried alive.

One morning in May 1945, I was wakened by a Greek band playing in the square below. A crowd was cheering. The war that would never end had ended. Elated, I got up and opened the door of my cell. On the other side was a skull and crossbones. Unsteadily, I made my way down the corridor, back to life.

Now that the war was over, I expected to go home. Instead, I was shuttled about from transit camps in Greece to transit camps in Italy, awaiting transport. In June I was sent with thousands of others to a camp outside Bari in southern Italy. Each day we were going home; each day only a handful got away by air. The 'first in, first out' bunkum didn't count when there were no ships and no trains. Had we known how long we would be trapped there, we would have torn the place down on arrival. The war done, the British Tommy became a piece of unfortunate baggage that needed to be repatriated. We called ourselves 'The Forgotten Army'.

To lessen the soul-destroying boredom, I began to pick up the shattered pieces of my pre-war life. Wherever I could I wrote and renewed the friendships I'd known before the war. I learned that Bow and Poplar had been devastated by bombing: half of Poplar had been levelled. From the East End I learned that the Tinker family had perished in the 'blitz'. The Hargreaves' old home in Addington Road, Bow, was a pile of rubble; all that remained of George Lansbury's house in Bow Road was a door blowing in the wind. Blessedly, he had died a few days before the German onslaught, and was spared the depths of wickedness that the war revealed.

Ma Hargreaves had died in north London. She had intended to throw herself back into social work once the war was over, but was never given the chance. They said that the war had killed her, that its brutality had undermined her strength. Clem, Emily and Chris were planning (or at least

Clem was planning) to retire to a cottage in Devon. Like so many others who had fled east London, the Hargreaves never returned to their old haunts.

Alex Hargreaves survived the war. He'd got rid of a great deal of his hostility fighting the Germans, and he'd won a Military Cross. While I was waiting to go home outside Bari, he was already back in business in London. His first wife had divorced him and he had remarried. He had switched his allegiance from the Conservative to the Labour Party and had been swept into power by the landslide Labour victory of 1945. He charmed the masses as a Member of Parliament and they loved him. Alex was going to go a long way.

Miranda, my old girlfriend, had been killed in the ambulance service during the bombing of London. The news left me sad for days. Miranda's 'I've a good 'eart, I 'ave' rang across the years. Alex had adopted the little girl she had left behind. Some said Alex had always loved Miranda; I had thought that long ago. On the surface, he'd always appeared egotistical, but at the bottom he'd been a mixture of compassion and hostility.

No one had any firm news of Milton. In an attempt to get himself killed he had joined a bomb disposal squad. Some say he survived the war. If he did, he disappeared in the postwar maze.

Carol Hargreaves was still working for Poplar Council. She hadn't remarried. While Poplar was being flattened all around her, she'd taken in the homeless and helped out with the anti-aircraft batteries in Victoria Park. She never knew again the joy she had known when caring for her dying Mike.

Harold Watkins had died in a bombing raid over the Rhine. I grieved Harold's passing, as I grieved that of Ma Hargreaves and Miranda. Harold and I had grown up together. I felt that life had not treated him fairly. By then I knew that life rarely does.

Hans Thiel – with whom I had kept up a correspondence – had become a tutor at Oxford. He had spent the war there after returning from detention on the Isle of Man. He was still a bachelor. 'When are you coming back?' he wrote. He invited me to join him.

Jim Foggerty had spent the war down the mine and in public service. He had married and was busy raising a family. He had become a miners' leader – a far more important person than either Thiel or myself. Britain was safe with men like Foggerty in charge.

Wonder of wonders, Oxford had remained untouched throughout the war. O'Hea, Rodger, Dowdell and Cole were back in their caps and gowns. O'Hea wrote to say that he was looking forward to going on where he'd left off in 1939. With the overwhelming victory of Labour, he thought he would have more support in educating working men and women.

My old landlord, Reg Tates, whom I'd expected to live to be a hundred, had died of a heart attack, and Minnie was inconsolable.

All the members of my own family had remained well and safe during the years I had been away. My sisters had gone from war work back to their homes. My brother had worked as a labourer in a factory and brought up a wonderful family. My father, having spent almost seven years helping to make fighter planes, was unemployed again.

Of my Belgian friend Jean Doeraene there was no news. [I finally ran him to earth in Nivelles in 1974. Julienne, his wife, answered my knocking. 'Je suis Guillaume,' I said, as if thirty-five years didn't matter.]

Ludwig Wolfrath survived the war. In 1939, with O'Hea's help, he had gone with a new name and yet another passport to continue his medical studies at Dublin University. Returning to his lodgings one night in 1940 he had been horrified to find a letter from the German Embassy addressed to him, by his real name: the Gestapo had caught up with him. In mortal danger, he fled to British Belfast. In 1944, with his studies completed, he became a physician at a London hospital. His parents were alive and well.

306

As a diabetic, Willi Betterman had died during the war for want of insulin.

———◇———

By August, the men in the Bari camp could stand the waiting no longer. They decided to build a train from the wrecked equipment lying on the railway sidings, and the idea was taken up with enthusiasm. It gave them a purpose and tested their ingenuity; it eased the dull ache of endless separation from home. They had all the skilled men they needed. In days, they'd set about scavenging and cannibalising every bit of railway equipment they could find, and soon, with heavy lifting gear provided by Italian wrecking crews, a skeleton of a train began to take shape.

One day, while working in the railway marshalling yard, we heard on the radio that an atom bomb (whatever that was) had destroyed Hiroshima. Some men cheered and then went back to work. After six years we'd become callous. To us, the atom bomb was just another bigger bomb. No one stood around discussing the moral implications of using it; no one was conscience-stricken. Besides, it was the Yanks' war, not ours. The fall of Hong Kong and Singapore at the beginning of the war had affected us much more. It had been mind-boggling that Britain should have been defeated by Japan.

I also learned for the first time about the holocaust of the Jews. I found it hard to believe. Until 1945, those of us who fought at the front had no inkling that the Jews were being systematically killed off in the countries under German control.

———◇———

At the beginning of December 1945, seven months after the war had ended, our train was ready to roll. Looking like a travelling circus rather than a victorious army, we pulled out of Bari station on a cold, windy day. Muffled to the ears, we peered through the wooden slats that had been nailed across the shattered windows at the cheering soldiers who were left behind. We never wanted to see Bari or Italy again.

There were ten of us to a compartment: two lying on the rebuilt racks above our heads, the rest of us sitting in the wooden troughs that had been bolted to the frame. The Italians had pillaged everything else. There was little heating. At night, our candles were put out regularly by the wind blowing through the cracks, but we were going home. Nothing else in the world mattered. Some food we took with us, most we scrounged from military depots on the way.

For two weeks our train picked its way across war-torn Italy to Brig on the Swiss frontier. The Swiss officials were reluctant to let us in, they said they'd never heard of us. We stood in the snow and eventually came to a compromise: we could cross into France, but we must use a Swiss locomotive and we must not stop at any station. That I suppose is why we stopped at Geneva for at least thirty minutes, while the populace ran up and down the station steps shouting, 'Good luck, Johnny, good luck!' Some tried to shake our hands through the wooden slats. We had hoped for chocolate.

We reached Dieppe in time to watch our troop steamer for Newhaven sail away. In a ragged line, we shouted and howled after it; we even fired our rifles into the air, but it didn't return. After some discussion, the order was given to fall in. We were to march to a transit camp on the outskirts of Dieppe to be deloused. The order was ignored; the men sat down sullenly and would not move. In six years I had never seen British troops refuse to obey, but I did then. As the sergeant-major's voice rose higher and higher, ordering the soldiers to get into line, I smelled trouble. I knew that restlessness had been growing in the ranks. These men had been too long in battle, too far from home. It had taken years to get this far and they weren't going to miss the next ship.

'What on earth are you shouting for, Sergeant-Major?' the colonel-in-charge asked as he walked towards us on the pier.

'The troops have just mutinied, sir.'

'Mutiny, Sergeant-Major? Mutiny, you say? Well for God's sake, don't stand there shouting, get some tea!'

——————◇——————

From London I took the overnight express to Scotland. As a major, I had been given a seat in a first-class compartment. I sat next to a Member of Parliament, who complained that the war had given him ulcers. He was lucky that I was too exhausted to tell him what the war had given me. Not having been deloused at Dieppe, I felt no remorse when he started scratching.

Kay met me at Carlisle station. She was wearing a dark brown winter coat and a hat edged with fur. Red-cheeked with the cold, she could not have looked more beautiful or more radiant. Yelling, I fought my way through the crowd to reach her. We fell into each other's arms. I thought my heart would burst. The pushing, shouting crowd and the steaming train did not exist. We laughed and cried and trembled with our arms around each other. Our reunion was the vision I'd seen in all the restless, terrifying moments of war. It brought a strange, almost frightening happiness. All the way home to the Eden Valley, I kept having to stop the car so that we might tell each other of our love.

On reaching Temple Sowerby, I was overcome by the stillness. The village was wrapped in snow; blue smoke curled above the roofs; the summit of Cross Fell gleamed in the distance. I stood and watched the rooks returning to the trees around the church. Nothing had changed.

The son I'd never seen was running about, shouting when my mother-in-law opened the door. He was dressed in a red woollen roll-neck pullover and grey trousers. With Kay's eyes wide with delight, I put my hand on our child's head. I felt a universe. I saw the fresh, bright face, the fair hair, the fine

309

skin, the blue eyes and the wondering innocence of his gaze. His eyes mirrored everything. For me, it was a timeless moment, a bottomless depth of bliss.

'And whose little boy are you?' I asked.

'What's in your bag?' was the reply. I pulled out a poorly made rubber ball, a cheap, unpainted, wooden Pinocchio, both of which I had obtained in Milan. 'What else?' Kay's mother looked on with moist eyes. For him and me it was a shy beginning.

My son watched as I deloused myself standing naked in a tin bath on the cobbles in the cold backyard. With him still babbling at my side, I then soaked all my cares away in the bath upstairs. Later we decorated the Christmas tree, hung the stockings and set out the candles. When darkness fell, we greeted the carol singers at the door.

I slept badly that night; I was unused to sleeping in a bed. In two-and-a-quarter years in Italy, except in hospitals, I'd slept in a proper bed only twice. But beds didn't matter; what mattered was that I no longer heard men shrieking in their sleep. For the first time in years I was at peace. It was a time of rebirth and renewal.

———◈———

In going to war, I had followed what I thought was the truth, regardless of the outcome. In support of my beliefs, I could not have offered more than my life. I came home years wiser; war had revealed the core of life to me.

I came home devoid of the political ambitions I had had when I set out. Much to other people's surprise my aspirations to become a leader in public life had died on the battlefield. Apart from voting for Labour in the transit camp in Bari, I took no part in the landslide Labour victory of 1945. The war had taught me to distrust political myths and grand panaceas. The small things in life had taken on a new intimacy; so had the heart. Before the war I had talked about building a new civilisation, at the end I knew how fragile civilisation is. All I wanted was the peaceful, private family life the war had denied me.

I came home stunned and remained stunned for some time. Finding my way back to my true self was like waking up from a six-year sleep. It took a long time for the memory of other men's deaths to fade.

Note on the author

In 1946 William Woodruff renewed his academic career in Oxford. In 1950 he was awarded a research fellowship by the Bank of England, which allowed him to write his first book. In 1952 he went as a Fulbright Scholar to Harvard University. He remained in the United States from 1953 until 1956 as a professor at the University of Illinois, after which he moved to Australia to head the Department of Economic History at the University of Melbourne. Since 1966 he has been at the University of Florida in the United States. Visiting professorships have taken him to the Institute for Advanced Study, Princeton; the Free University, Berlin; Waseda University, Tokyo; and finally, in 1978, back to Oxford to St Antony's College. He retired in 1996, a distinguished world historian.

William Woodruff has published over ten highly acclaimed books, including *Vessel of Sadness*, a novel based on his World War II experiences in the Italian Anzio campaign; *Paradise Galore*, an allegory; and *Concise History of the Modern World*, which is in its fourth edition. *The Road to Nab End*, a memoir of his childhood in Lancashire to which *Beyond Nab End* is the sequel, was a number one bestseller and was widely praised as a masterpiece.

William Woodruff has seven children: two sons by his first marriage to Kay and, following Kay's death, a daughter and four sons by his second wife Helga, to whom he was married in 1960.